# Dinner a Day Slow Cooker

## 365 Appetizing & Affordable Meals Your Family Will Love

MARGARET KAETER

**A**adamsmedia
avon, massachusetts

Published by
Adams Media, an F+W Publications Company
57 Littlefield Street, Avon, MA 02322. U.S.A.
*www.adamsmedia.com*

ISBN-10: 1-59869-616-5
ISBN-13: 978-1-59869-616-5

Printed in China.

J I H G F E D C B A

Library of Congress Cataloging-in-Publication Data
is available from the publisher.

This publication is designed to provide accurate and authoritative information
with regard to the subject matter covered. It is sold with the understanding that
the publisher is not engaged in rendering legal, accounting, or other professional advice. If legal advice or other expert assistance is required, the services
of a competent professional person should be sought.

—From a *Declaration of Principles* jointly adopted by a Committee of the
American Bar Association and a Committee of Publishers and Associations

Many of the designations used by manufacturers and sellers to distinguish their
product are claimed as trademarks. Where those designations appear in this
book and Adams Media was aware of a trademark claim, the designations have
been printed with initial capital letters.

Contains material adopted and abridged from *The Everything® Slow Cooker Cookbook* by Margaret Kaeter, Copyright © 2002 by F+W Publications, Inc. and *The
Everything® Slow Cooking for a Crowd Cookbook* by Katie Thompson, Copyright ©
2005 by F+W Publications, Inc.

*This book is available at quantity discounts for bulk purchases.*
*For information, please call 1-800-289-0963.*

# Contents

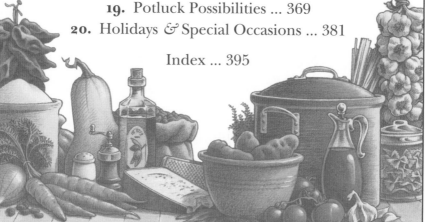

# Introduction

**Families** are busier than ever today. So it's not surprising that family dinner is the only time when the whole gang can really get together! For busy parents cooking for hungry families, this book is a must have!

The *Dinner a Day* cookbooks allow busy family cooks the opportunity to make a quick, easy, and delicious meal every night of the year. Gone are the days when women spent more than two hours preparing plain and monotonous meals. Today, with sports practices, rehearsals, appointments, etc., you need a simple and satisfying solution to the dinnertime dilemma.

With this cookbook, take some time in the morning (or even the night before) to put together some key ingredients, pop them in the slow cooker, and when you return home from a hectic day—voilà, dinner is served!

You will find everything from soups and breads to casseroles and holiday favorites (for any night of the year). With *Dinner a Day: Slow Cooker*, there's no need to stress about getting dinner done "in time," or rushing home to scrounge from the pantry.

So forget about takeout and throw away those frozen meals; now is the time to experiment with a different dinner every night—and to start enjoying your time with your family!

# Soups

# Hamburger Vegetable Soup

*This hearty yet healthy soup should fill up your family on a cold winter night.*

 **stats**

**SERVES 6**

Cooking time . . . . . . . 7–8 hours

Preparation time. . . . 15 minutes

Attention. . . . . . . . . . Minimal

Pot size . . . . . . . . . . . 3–6 quarts

½ pound lean ground beef

4 medium-sized fresh tomatoes

1 large yellow onion

½ cup celery, sliced

3 medium carrots

6 cups beef broth

½ teaspoon table salt

½ teaspoon ground black pepper

1 cup fresh peas

1 cup fresh green beans

**1.** Brown the ground beef in a medium-sized skillet on medium-high heat; drain off grease.

**2.** Cut the tomatoes into ½-inch cubes. Peel the onion and cut into ¼-inch pieces. Cut the celery into ¼-inch-thick slices. Peel the carrots and slice them into ¼-inch-thick pieces.

**3.** Place the ground beef, beef broth, tomatoes, onion, celery, carrots, salt, and pepper in slow cooker. Cover and cook on low setting for 6 hours.

**4.** Add the peas and green beans. Cover and cook on low 1 to 2 more hours.

**5.** Garnish with fresh parsley before serving.

# Minestrone Soup

*A classic family favorite—make this minestrone
for dinner, then pack it for lunch, too.*

**stats**

**SERVES 8**

Cooking time....... 9–11 hours
Preparation time.... 30 minutes
Attention.......... Medium
Pot size............ 3–6 quarts

1 pound beef stewing meat

1 (28-ounce) can tomatoes

1 medium onion

6 cups water

1 beef bouillon cube

2 tablespoons dried parsley

1½ teaspoon table salt

1½ teaspoon dried thyme

½ teaspoon ground black pepper

1 medium zucchini

2 cups cabbage, chopped

1 (16-ounce) can garbanzo
beans, drained

1 cup uncooked shell macaroni

**1.** Cut the meat into 1-inch cubes. Cut the tomatoes into ½-inch cubes; reserve liquid. Peel the onion and cut into ¼-inch pieces. Combine the beef, water, tomatoes with their liquid, bouillon cube, onion, parsley, salt, thyme, and pepper in slow cooker. Cover and cook on low for 8 to 10 hours.

**2.** Cut the zucchini into ¼-inch thick slices. Chop the cabbage into ¼-inch pieces. Add the zucchini, cabbage, beans, and macaroni to soup. Cover and cook on high for 1 hour.

**3.** Sprinkle with Parmesan cheese right before serving.

# Day-After-Thanksgiving Turkey Soup

*It doesn't have to be the day after Thanksgiving*
*for you to make this delicious soup!*

*stats*

**SERVES 6**

Cooking time . . . . . . . 6–8 hours
Preparation time . . . . 20 minutes
Attention . . . . . . . . . . Minimal
Pot size . . . . . . . . . . . . 3–8 quarts

1 large yellow onion

1 fresh green pepper

1 cup carrots, sliced

1 cup celery, diced

1 cup fresh mushrooms, sliced

1 pound leftover turkey, shredded

¼ teaspoon pepper

¼ teaspoon oregano

¼ teaspoon basil

1 tablespoon chicken bouillon

3 cups boiling water

1 cup tomato sauce

1 tablespoon soy sauce

**1.** Peel the onion and carrots, and remove the seeds and stem from the green pepper. Cut the celery, carrots, onion, and green pepper into ¼-inch pieces. Wash the mushrooms by wiping with a damp cloth; slice paper-thin with a sharp paring knife.

**2.** Add all ingredients to the slow cooker. Cover and cook on low setting 6 to 8 hours.

# Split Pea and Ham Soup

*Healthy and delicious, Split Pea and Ham Soup can be enjoyed by kids and parents alike.*

**stats**

**SERVES 6**

| | |
|---|---|
| Cooking time | 8–10 hours |
| Preparation time | 20 minutes |
| Attention | Minimal |
| Pot size | 3–8 quarts |

1 medium-sized yellow onion

3 carrots

2 stalks celery, leaves included

2 garlic cloves

1 (16-ounce) package dried green split peas, rinsed

2 cups diced ham

1 bay leaf

¼ cup fresh parsley, chopped

1 tablespoon salt

½ teaspoon ground black pepper

1½ quarts hot water

**1.** Peel and chop the onion into ¼-inch pieces. Peel the carrots and slice into ¼-inch rounds. Chop the celery ¼-inch thick. Mince the garlic with a sharp paring knife.

**2.** Add all ingredients to the slow cooker, pouring water on top; do not stir. Cover and cook on low 8 to 10 hours. Remove bay leaf before serving.

# Fancy Golden Potato Soup

*This is delicious on its own or as a complement to a grilled steak.*

*stats* **SERVES 6**

Cooking time . . . . . . . 7–9 hours
Preparation time . . . . 30 minutes
Attention . . . . . . . . . . Medium
Pot size . . . . . . . . . . . . 3–6 quarts

6 medium-sized golden potatoes

1 yellow onion

1 large celery stalk

1 large carrot

4 chicken bouillon cubes

1 tablespoon dried parsley flakes

5 cups water

1 tablespoon salt

1 teaspoon ground black pepper

⅓ cup butter

1 (13-ounce) can evaporated milk

**1.** Peel the potatoes and cut into 1-inch squares. Peel the onion and chop into ¼-inch pieces. Chop the celery into ¼-inch pieces. Peel the carrot and chop into ¼-inch pieces.

**2.** Place all the ingredients except the milk into slow cooker. Cover and cook on low setting for 7 to 8 hours.

**3.** Add the milk and cook an additional half-hour, covered, on low setting.

# Cauliflower and Ham Chowder

*Serve with an array of pickled vegetables to
offset the creamy sweet flavor of this soup.*

**stats**

**SERVES 6**

Cooking time . . . . . . . 8–9 hours
Preparation time . . . . 20 minutes
Attention . . . . . . . . . . Minimal
Pot size . . . . . . . . . . . . 3–6 quarts

2 cups ham, diced

3 cups fresh cauliflower, chopped

1 small white onion

1 cup canned evaporated milk

2 tablespoons flour

1 cup Swiss cheese, grated

2 cups water

1 cup light cream

**1.** Cut the ham into ½-inch pieces. Cut the cauliflower into ½-inch pieces. Peel the onion and chop finely.

**2.** Mix the evaporated milk and flour in the slow cooker.

**3.** Add the ham, cauliflower, onion, Swiss cheese, and water. Cover and cook on low setting for 8 to 9 hours.

**4.** Ten minutes before serving, stir in the cream.

# A Bit of Everything Soup

*Serve with an assortment of crackers and cheeses.*

 **stats**

**SERVES 8**

| | |
|---|---|
| Cooking time | 8–10 hours |
| Preparation time | 30 minutes |
| Attention | Minimal |
| Pot size | 4–8 quarts |

6 slices bacon

1 pound ham

1 pound beef

2 skinless chicken breasts

6 medium carrots

3 celery ribs

1 large yellow onion

1 cup fresh green beans

1 cup fresh peas

1 cup fresh corn

1 pound crabmeat, chunks or shredded

1 teaspoon table salt

¼ teaspoon ground black pepper

6 cups water

**1.** Brown the bacon in a medium-sized skillet on medium-high heat; place on paper towels to cool, then break into crumbles. Cut ham, beef, and chicken into 1-inch cubes. Peel the carrots and slice into ¼-inch thick discs. Slice the celery ¼-inch thick. Peel the onion and slice into ¼-inch pieces. Remove the stems from the green beans.

**2.** Add all ingredients except peas and crabmeat to the slow cooker. Cover and cook on low setting for 7 to 9 hours. Add peas and crabmeat, and cook for 1 to 2 hours.

# Pork, Pea, and Spinach Curry Soup

*Serve with some plain bread for dipping.*
*This soup is sure to be a tangy treat for everyone.*

 **SERVES 8**

Cooking time . . . . . . . 10–12 hours
Preparation time . . . . 20 minutes
Attention . . . . . . . . . . Minimal
Pot size . . . . . . . . . . . . 3–6 quarts

1½-pound pork roast

1 cup baby carrots

1 celery rib

1 medium-sized white onion

1 cup yellow split peas, rinsed

6 cups chicken broth

2 teaspoons curry powder

½ teaspoon paprika

¼ teaspoon ground cumin

¼ teaspoon ground black pepper

2 cups fresh spinach, torn

**1.** Trim the fat from the pork roast and cut into ½-inch cubes. Cut the baby carrots in half. Chop the celery into ¼-inch pieces. Peel and chop the onion into ¼-inch pieces.

**2.** Add all the ingredients except the spinach to slow cooker. Stir well. Cover and cook on low setting for 10 to 12 hours.

**3.** Tear the spinach into 1-inch pieces; stir into soup right before serving.

# Cousin Jimmy's Favorite Lima Bean Soup

*You don't have to have your own cousin Jimmy!*
*Serve with bread and an assortment of cheeses.*

 **stats**

**SERVES 8**

| | |
|---|---|
| Cooking time | 8–10 hours |
| Preparation time | 20 minutes |
| Attention | Minimal |
| Pot size | 3–6 quarts |

1 large yellow onion

2 ribs celery

3 large potatoes

3 medium carrots

2 cups kielbasa, sliced

1-pound bag large dry lima beans

1 tablespoon table salt

1 teaspoon pepper

1 teaspoon dried oregano

2 bay leaves

6 cups beef broth

4 cups water

**1.** Peel the onion and chop into ¼-inch pieces. Chop the celery into ¼-inch pieces. Peel the potatoes and cut into ½-inch cubes. Peel the carrots and cut into ¼-inch pieces. Slice the kielbasa into ¼-inch rounds. Rinse the lima beans.

**2.** Add all ingredients to the slow cooker; stir well. Cover and cook on low setting for 8 to 10 hours. Remove the bay leaves before serving.

# Cheesy Broccoli Noodle Soup

*Perfect for a cold winter night; this is a classic family favorite.*

 *stats*

**SERVES 6**

Cooking time ....... 4–5 hours
Preparation time. ... 30 minutes
Attention.......... Minimal
Pot size............ 3–6 quarts

2 cups noodles

2 cups fresh broccoli, chopped

1 medium-sized white onion

2 cups processed cheese, cubed

2 tablespoons butter

1 tablespoon flour

½ teaspoon table salt

5½ cups skim milk

**1.** Cook the noodles in boiling water in a saucepan until they are limp but still crunchy in the middle. Chop the broccoli into 1-inch pieces. Peel and chop the onion into ¼-inch pieces. Cut the cheese into ½-inch cubes.

**2.** Combine all ingredients in the slow cooker. Cover and cook on low setting for 4 to 5 hours.

# Ham and Chicken Gumbo

*Serve with bread and an assortment of cheeses for a full, delicious meal.*

**stats**

**SERVES 8**

Cooking time . . . . . . . 7–9 hours
Preparation time. . . . 30 minutes
Attention . . . . . . . . . . Minimal
Pot size . . . . . . . . . . . . 3–8 quarts

1½ pounds chicken breasts

½ pound smoked ham

1 tablespoon oil

1 cup fresh okra, sliced

2 medium-sized white onions

1 medium-sized green bell
pepper

4 large red tomatoes

¼ cup canned or fresh green
chilies, diced

2 tablespoons fresh cilantro,
chopped

6 cups chicken broth

3 (16-ounce) cans navy beans
or 3½–4 cups dry navy beans,
cooked

½ cup dry white rice

¾ teaspoon table salt

½ teaspoon ground black pepper

**1.** Remove the bones and skin from the chicken and discard. Cut the chicken and ham into 1-inch pieces. Place the oil, ham, and chicken in medium-sized skillet and cook on medium heat until chicken is no longer pink inside. Cut the okra into ¼-inch pieces. Peel the onions and cut into ¼-inch pieces. Remove the stem and seeds from the green pepper and chop into ¼-inch pieces. Cut the tomatoes into ½-inch pieces. Dice the green chilies with a sharp paring knife. Chop the cilantro into ¼-inch pieces.

**2.** Combine all the ingredients except the cilantro in the slow cooker. Cover and cook on low setting for 7 to 9 hours. Stir in cilantro right before serving.

# Clam, Chicken, and Ham Chowder

*Serve with an assortment of pickled vegetables
and cheeses—and no one will go hungry!*

 *stats*

**SERVES 8**

Cooking time . . . . . . . 8–10 hours
Preparation time . . . . 30 minutes
Attention . . . . . . . . . . Minimal
Pot size . . . . . . . . . . . . 3–8 quarts

4 chicken breasts

1 pound bacon

½ pound ham

2 large yellow onions

4 medium carrots

4 celery ribs

4 medium potatoes

1 cup clams, with juice

2 cups whole kernel corn, with liquid

4 cups chicken broth

½ teaspoon table salt

½ teaspoon ground black pepper

1 bunch green onions

¾ cup flour

4 cups milk

4 cups Cheddar cheese, shredded

½ cup whipping cream

**1.** Remove the skin and bones from the chicken breasts and cut meat into 1-inch pieces. Cut the bacon into 1-inch pieces. Cut the ham into ½-inch cubes. Peel the yellow onions and chop into ¼-inch pieces. Peel the carrots and chop into ¼-inch rounds. Chop the celery into ¼-inch pieces. Peel the potatoes and cut into ½-inch cubes.

**2.** Put the bacon, ham, and chicken meat in a large skillet with the celery and yellow onions; sauté on medium heat until the bacon is crisp. Drain grease off and put the mixture in the slow cooker. Add the carrots, potatoes, clams, corn, salt, pepper, and chicken broth. Cover and cook on low setting for 7 to 9 hours.

**3.** Remove the roots and first layer of peel from the green onions and chop the onions, including the green stems, into ¼-inch pieces. In a medium mixing bowl combine the flour, milk, cheese, and cream. Whisk quickly until slightly frothy; stir into soup. Cover and cook on low setting for 1 hour. Stir in the green onions right before serving.

# Beer Soup

*This is a fun soup to bring to a friend's party
or to enjoy as a game-day early supper!*

**SERVES 6**

Cooking time . . . . . . . 4 hours
Preparation time . . . . 15 minutes
Attention . . . . . . . . . . Minimal
Pot size . . . . . . . . . . . . 3–8 quarts

2½ tablespoons butter

1½ tablespoons flour

2 cups pilsner beer

½ cinnamon stick

½ teaspoon sugar

2 egg yolks

½ cup milk

**1.** Melt the butter in a medium-sized skillet on medium heat. Add the flour and cook until the flour browns; transfer the flour mixture to the slow cooker. Add the beer, cinnamon, and sugar. Cover and cook on high setting for 4 hours.

**2.** Turn slow cooker down to low setting. Whisk together the egg yolks and milk; stir into the soup. Cook 15 minutes uncovered on high setting. Strain before serving.

# Italian Vegetable Soup

*Serve with a side of garlic buttered linguine—yum!*

 **stats**

**SERVES 6**

Cooking time . . . . . . . 6–8 hours
Preparation time . . . . 20 minutes
Attention . . . . . . . . . . Minimal
Pot size . . . . . . . . . . . . 3–6 quarts

2 pounds hamburger

1 small zucchini

3 medium potatoes

1 can corn

1 (16-ounce) can tomato sauce

2 tablespoons ground oregano

⅛ teaspoon basil

½ teaspoon garlic salt

3 bay leaves

1. Brown the hamburger in a medium-sized skillet on medium-high heat on the stove; drain off the grease.

2. Cut the zucchini into ½-inch pieces. Peel and cut the potatoes into ½-inch squares.

3. Add all ingredients to the slow cooker. Cook covered on low setting for 6 to 8 hours.

# Barley Lamb Soup

*Serve with a fresh green salad and hardboiled eggs.*

 *stats*

**SERVES 8**

| | |
|---|---|
| Cooking time | 7–9 hours |
| Preparation time | 20 minutes |
| Attention | Minimal |
| Pot size | 3–8 quarts |

2½ pounds lamb

2 medium-sized white onions

3 celery ribs

3 cups parsley, chopped

3 tablespoons butter

1 cup medium-sized barley

½ teaspoon table salt

½ teaspoon ground black pepper

1 bay leaf

6 cups water

**1.** Cut the lamb into 1-inch cubes, trimming off the fat as you cut. Peel and chop the onions into ¼-inch pieces. Chop the celery, including leaves, into ¼-inch pieces. Chop the parsley into ½-inch pieces.

**2.** Heat the butter in a large skillet on medium heat until brown; add the lamb and sauté for about 10 minutes. Using a slotted spoon, remove the meat from the skillet and put it into the slow cooker. Add the onion to the skillet and sauté until translucent. Drain off the grease and add the onion to the slow cooker. Add the celery, parsley, barley, salt, pepper, bay leaf, and water to the slow cooker. Cover and cook on low setting for 7 to 9 hours.

# Curried Tomato Soup

*Add a bit of kick to your traditional tomato soup and surprise the whole family.*

 **SERVES 8**

Cooking time . . . . . . . 8–10 hours

Preparation time. . . . 30 minutes

Attention . . . . . . . . . . Minimal

Pot size . . . . . . . . . . . . 3–8 quarts

*1 medium-sized white onion*

*2 garlic cloves*

*12 plum tomatoes*

*4 cups chicken broth*

*1 tablespoon curry powder*

*¼ teaspoon cinnamon*

*½ teaspoon table salt*

*4 cups dry egg noodles*

**1.** Peel the onion and chop into ¼-inch pieces. Peel the garlic and mince with a sharp kitchen knife. Chop the tomatoes into ¼-inch pieces.

**2.** Combine all the ingredients except the egg noodles in the slow cooker. Cover and cook on low setting for 7 to 9 hours.

**3.** Add the egg noodles. Cover and cook on low setting 1 additional hour.

# Golden Potato, Ham, and Vidalia Onion Soup

*Serve with gourmet crackers and fresh vegetables
such as red pepper, carrot, and celery sticks.*

 **SERVES 8**

Cooking time . . . . . . . 8–10 hours
Preparation time . . . . 15 minutes
Attention . . . . . . . . . . Minimal
Pot size . . . . . . . . . . . . 3–8 quarts

1 cup ham

2 large Vidalia onions

½ small red bell pepper

4 large golden potatoes

2 cups chicken broth

½ teaspoon ground black pepper

1 cup skim milk

1 cup ricotta cheese

**1.** Cut the ham into ½-inch pieces. Peel and cut the onions into ¼-inch pieces. Remove the stem and seeds from the red pepper and cut into ¼-inch pieces. Peel the potatoes and cut into ½-inch pieces.

**2.** Add the ham, onions, bell pepper, potatoes, chicken broth, and black pepper to the slow cooker. Cover and cook on low setting for 8 to 10 hours. A half-hour before serving, add skim milk and ricotta cheese; mix in. Cover and continue to cook on low setting.

# Wisconsin Cheesy Beer Soup

*Serve sprinkled with freshly made white popcorn—what a fun treat!*

**SERVES 8**

| | |
|---|---|
| Cooking time | 1–2 hours |
| Preparation time | 10 minutes |
| Attention | Frequent |
| Pot size | 3–8 quarts |

1 large onion

1 cup sharp Cheddar cheese

½ cup vegetable broth

1 cup pilsner beer

2 cups 1 percent milk

½ teaspoon garlic powder

½ teaspoon ground black pepper

Peel the onion and chop into ¼-inch pieces. Shred the cheese with a vegetable grater. Combine all ingredients in the slow cooker. Cover and cook on low setting for 1 to 2 hours, stirring every 10 minutes. Do not overcook, as the cheese will begin to separate.

# Easy Corn and Cheese Chowder

*The name says it all. For a simple and tasty dinner solution, give this a shot.*

**SERVES 6**

Cooking time ....... 8–9 hours
Preparation time.... 15 minutes
Attention.......... Minimal
Pot size ............ 3–6 quarts

1 medium-sized yellow onion

4 medium carrots

4 celery ribs

1½ cups shredded Cheddar cheese

¾ cup water

1 teaspoon table salt

1 teaspoon ground black pepper

2 cups whole kernel corn, canned or fresh

2 cups canned creamed corn

3 cups milk

**1.** Remove peel and chop the onion into ¼-inch pieces. Peel the carrots and chop into ¼-inch slices. Chop the celery into ¼-inch slices.

**2.** Combine the water, onions, carrots, celery, salt, and pepper in slow cooker. Cover and cook on low setting for 8 to 9 hours. One hour before serving, add the corn, milk, and cheese. Cover and cook on low setting for 1 more hour.

# Creamy Asparagus and Leek Soup

*Serve with simple bread and assorted cheeses for a complete meal.*

*stats*  **SERVES 6**

Cooking time . . . . . . . 8–10 hours
Preparation time . . . . 20 minutes
Attention . . . . . . . . . . Medium
Pot size . . . . . . . . . . . . 3–8 quarts

2 medium potatoes

2 large leeks

3 medium carrots

2 celery ribs

2 pounds asparagus

2 teaspoons thyme

4 cups chicken broth

2 cups 1 percent milk

**1.** Peel and chop the potatoes and leeks into ¼-inch pieces. Chop the carrots and celery into ¼-inch pieces. Remove the tips from the asparagus and set aside. Chop the green part of the stalks into ¼-inch pieces.

**2.** Put the carrots, celery, potatoes, leek, thyme, asparagus stalks, and chicken broth in slow cooker. Cover and cook on low setting for 7 to 9 hours.

**3.** Put the mixture into a blender and purée until creamy. Stir in the milk and add the asparagus tips. Cover and cook on low setting for 1 additional hour.

# Swedish Fruit Soup

*This is excellent served warm over a traditional*
*white cake with vanilla ice cream—what a treat!*

**stats**

**SERVES 8**

Cooking time . . . . . . . 8–10 hours
Preparation time . . . . 30 minutes
Attention . . . . . . . . . . Minimal
Pot size . . . . . . . . . . . . 3–8 quarts

1 cup dried apricots

1 cup dried apples

1 cup dried prunes

1 cup dried pears

1 cup dried peaches

1 cup canned dark, sweet
cherries, pitted

½ cup sweet red wine

1 cup orange juice

¼ cup lemon juice

½ cup brown sugar

½ cup quick-cooking tapioca

**1.** Cut dried fruit into 1-inch pieces.

**2.** Add all the ingredients to the slow cooker; stir well. Cover and cook on low setting for 8 to 10 hours.

**3.** Check after 5 hours to determine if water needs to be added (it should have the consistency of a light syrup—if it is thicker than that, add ½ cup water).

# Danish Pork and Pea Soup

*Serve with open-faced cucumber and cream cheese sandwiches on rye toast.*

**SERVES 8**

Cooking time....... 8–10 hours
Preparation time.... 30 minutes
Attention........... Minimal
Pot size............. 3–8 quarts

*1 pound yellow split peas*

*2 pounds lean bacon*

*1 pound pork sausage links*

*4 medium leeks*

*3 medium carrots*

*2 celery ribs*

*1 teaspoon salt*

*1 teaspoon ground black pepper*

*6 cups vegetable stock*

**1.** Rinse the split peas. Chop the bacon and sausage into 1-inch pieces. Peel the leeks and chop into ¼-inch pieces. Cut the celery and carrots into ¼-inch pieces.

**2.** Put the bacon and sausage into a large skillet and cook on medium-high heat until meat is brown on all sides; drain off the grease. Spread out the meat on paper towels to absorb more grease.

**3.** Add all ingredients to the slow cooker. Cover and cook on low setting for 8 to 10 hours.

# Stews

# Tomato and Bean Stew

*A bit more hearty than plain tomato soup,*
*this stew will satisfy your troop easily.*

**SERVES 6**

| | |
|---|---|
| Cooking time | 8–10 hours |
| Preparation time | 20 minutes |
| Attention | Minimal |
| Pot size | 4–8 quarts |

2 medium potatoes

1 large white onion

1 medium-sized red bell pepper

1 medium-sized green bell pepper

2 medium carrots

1 (15-ounce) can garbanzo beans

1 (15-ounce) can kidney beans

1 cup dry lentils

1 (10-ounce) package chopped frozen spinach

1 (14½-ounce) can Italian stewed tomatoes

4 cups tomato juice

2 cups water

2 tablespoons dried parsley

2 tablespoons chili powder

2 teaspoons dried basil

2 teaspoons garlic powder

1 teaspoon ground cumin

**1.** Wash the potatoes but do not peel them; cut into 1-inch cubes. Peel the onion and cut into ¼-inch pieces. Remove the stem and seeds from the red and green peppers and cut into ¼-inch pieces. Wash the carrots and chop them into ¼-inch rounds. Drain and rinse the beans. Rinse the lentils.

**2.** Add all ingredients to the slow cooker; mix lightly. Cover and cook on low setting for 8 to 10 hours.

# Cuban Black Bean Stew

*Serve with pan-fried plantain slices for an authentic Cuban meal.*

**SERVES 8**

Cooking time . . . . . . . 8–10 hours
Preparation time. . . . 15 minutes
Attention. . . . . . . . . . Minimal
Pot size . . . . . . . . . . . . 6 quarts

*1 large yellow onion*

*1 green bell pepper*

*4 garlic cloves*

*8 ounces (1 cup) peeled baby carrots*

*2 celery stalks*

*4 fresh tomatoes*

*2 tablespoons olive oil*

*1 teaspoon ground black pepper*

*1 teaspoon cayenne pepper*

*1 teaspoon dried thyme*

*1 bay leaf*

*2 cups dried black beans, rinsed*

*2 chicken bouillon cubes*

*4 cups water*

*4 tablespoons balsamic vinegar*

**1.** Peel and chop the onion into ½-inch pieces. Remove the stem and seeds from the green pepper; chop the pepper into ½-inch pieces. Peel the garlic cloves and mince with a sharp kitchen knife. Cut the baby carrots in half. Chop the celery into ¼-inch pieces. Chop the tomatoes into ½-inch pieces.

**2.** Heat the olive oil in a large skillet on medium-high heat on the stove. Add the onion, green pepper, garlic, and ground spices. Sauté, stirring constantly, until the onions are soft, about 5 minutes. Drain off the oil and place the mixture in the slow cooker.

**3.** Add the carrots, celery, black beans, bay leaf, tomatoes, and crumbled bouillon cubes to the slow cooker. Add the water; stir until all ingredients are mixed. Cook covered on low setting for 8 to 10 hours.

**4.** 10 minutes before serving, stir in the balsamic vinegar.

# Moravian Ham, Tomato, and Green Bean Stew

*Serve over mashed potatoes with a side of squash for a fall harvest treat.*

**stats**

**SERVES 6**

Cooking time . . . . . . . 5–6 hours
Preparation time . . . . 10 minutes
Attention . . . . . . . . . . Minimal
Pot size . . . . . . . . . . . . 3–6 quarts

2 cups precooked ham, chopped
4 medium-sized yellow onions
4 cups diced fresh tomatoes
6 cups fresh green beans
¾ teaspoon table salt
½ teaspoon ground black pepper

**1.** Chop the ham into 1-inch cubes. Peel and chop the onions into ½-inch pieces. Peel the tomatoes with a sharp paring knife, gently lifting the peel from the flesh. and dice the tomatoes in ¼-inch pieces. Snap the ends off the green beans and discard the ends.

**2.** Add all ingredients to the slow cooker. Stir 2 or 3 times with a wooden spoon. Cook covered on low setting 5 to 6 hours.

# Polish Stew

*Full of different ingredients, this stew is great for kids
who like hot dogs and could use a couple more veggies!*

 **stats**

**SERVES 4**

Cooking time....... 8–9 hours
Preparation time.... 20 minutes
Attention.......... Minimal
Pot size............ 3–6 quarts

1½ pounds Polish sausage

2 medium-sized onions

4 medium potatoes

1 cup shredded Monterey jack cheese

4 cups sauerkraut

1 (10¾-ounce) can cream of celery condensed soup

⅓ cup brown sugar

**1.** Cut the Polish sausage into ½-inch-thick slices. Peel the onions and chop into ¼-inch pieces. Peel the potatoes and cut into 1-inch cubes. Shred the cheese using a vegetable grater. Drain the sauerkraut.

**2.** Combine the soup, brown sugar, sauerkraut, sausage, potatoes, and onions in the slow cooker. Cover and cook on low for 8 to 9 hours. Stir in the cheese 10 minutes before serving.

# Fruity Beef Stew

*Serve with wild rice for a nice mix of flavors.*

**SERVES 8**

Cooking time . . . . . . . 10 hours
Preparation time . . . . 30 minutes
Attention . . . . . . . . . . Medium
Pot size . . . . . . . . . . . . 6–8 quarts

2 *pounds beef round roast*

2 *cups chopped yellow onions*

6 *cloves garlic*

2 *teaspoons crushed, dried
red peppers*

¾ *teaspoon turmeric*

¾ *teaspoon ground cinnamon*

¾ *teaspoon ground ginger*

½ *teaspoon salt*

2 *tablespoons extra-virgin olive oil*

2 *cups beef broth*

1 *cup dried pitted dates*

1 *cup dried apricots*

1 *tablespoon cornstarch*

2 *tablespoons water*

**1.** Cut the meat into 1¼-inch pieces. Peel the onion and chop into ¼-inch pieces. Peel and mince the garlic. In a small mixing bowl, combine the red peppers, turmeric, ginger, cinnamon, and salt; coat the meat with this seasoning mixture. In a large skillet heat the olive oil over medium heat until hot, then brown the meat; drain off grease.

**2.** Place the meat in the slow cooker the with onions, beef broth, dates, and apricots. Cover and cook on low setting for 9 hours. Remove the meat, onions, and fruit. Make a paste out of the cornstarch and water and stir into the juice in the slow cooker. Cook on high setting, stirring periodically, until mixture thickens into a gravy.

**3.** Add the meat, vegetables, and fruit back into slow cooker. Cover and cook on low setting for 1 more hour.

# Savory Garlic Chicken Stew

*Although it is excellent served alone, to create a complete meal, ladle the stew over some bread. Add color to the plate with a garnish of fresh orange slices and purple grapes.*

**stats**

**SERVES 4**

Cooking time . . . . . . . 6–8 hours
Preparation time. . . . 30 minutes
Attention. . . . . . . . . . Minimal
Pot size . . . . . . . . . . . . 3–6 quarts

5 cups canned or frozen chicken broth

2 cups water

¼ cup all-purpose flour

8 garlic cloves

½ teaspoon low-fat oil

2 cups fresh carrots, sliced

6 medium golden potatoes

1 medium-sized yellow onion

1 cup fresh celery, sliced

2 pounds fresh or frozen boneless, skinless chicken breasts

1 teaspoon salt

¼ teaspoon white pepper

**1.** Put the chicken broth, water, and flour in a mixing bowl and whisk quickly until smooth.

**2.** Peel the garlic cloves and mash individually by placing the side of a large knife over each clove and pressing until the clove "pops," allowing the juice to come out. The cloves do not need to be cut into pieces. Sauté the mashed garlic in oil on medium heat until lightly golden.

**3.** Peel and cut the carrots and potatoes into 1-inch chunks. Dice the onion with a paring knife until pieces are smaller than ⅛-inch square. Cut the celery into ¼-inch slices. Cut the chicken into 1-inch cubes.

**4.** Combine all ingredients except the pepper in the slow cooker Stir until ingredients are well mixed and covered with liquid. Cook 6 to 8 hours covered on low heat. Remove cover 15 minutes before serving. Stir well and add pepper.

# Traditional Beef Stew

*Filling and delicious, this great stew will last for packed lunches too.*

**stats**

**SERVES 6**

Cooking time . . . . . . . 8–9 hours
Preparation time . . . . 30 minutes
Attention . . . . . . . . . . Minimal
Pot size . . . . . . . . . . . . 3–6 quarts

2 pounds beef chuck

6 medium carrots

6 medium-sized yellow onions

6 medium potatoes

6 celery ribs

1 (10¾-ounce) can condensed tomato soup

1 cup water

¼ cup flour

2 beef bouillon cubes

½ teaspoon salt

½ teaspoon pepper

**1.** Cut the beef into 1-inch cubes, trimming off all fat. Peel the carrots, onions, and potatoes. Slice the celery and carrots into 1-inch pieces. Quarter the onions and potatoes.

**2.** Mix the soup, bouillon cubes, water, and flour together in a medium-sized bowl with a fork until the mixture is smooth and the bouillon cubes have dissolved. Place the beef in the bottom of the slow cooker. Cover with the liquid mixture. Add the carrots, onions, celery, and potatoes. Sprinkle with salt and pepper. Cook on low setting for 8 to 9 hours.

# New Brunswick Chicken Stew

*The flavor of this stew improves when it is*
*refrigerated overnight and reheated the following day.*

**stats**

**SERVES 6**

Cooking time . . . . . . . 6–8 hours
Preparation time . . . . 20 minutes
Attention . . . . . . . . . . Minimal
Pot size . . . . . . . . . . . . 3–6 quarts

1 *stewing chicken*

2 *quarts (8 cups) water*

2 *large yellow onions*

4 *cups fresh tomatoes, chopped*

3 *medium potatoes*

2 *cups okra, chopped*

2 *cups lima beans*

4 *cups fresh sweet corn*
*(about 8 ears)*

3 *tablespoons table salt*

1 *teaspoon pepper*

1 *tablespoon sugar*

**1.** Cut the chicken into pieces and put them in the slow cooker with two quarts of water. Cook covered on high setting for 2 hours. Remove the chicken and set aside to cool.

**2.** Peel and slice the onions into ¼-inch-thick rings. Cut the tomatoes into ½-inch cubes. Peel and cut the potatoes into ½-inch cubes. Cut the sweet corn from the cob. Chop the okra into ½-inch pieces. Remove the meat from the chicken bones.

**3.** Add the meat, onions, tomatoes, potatoes, sweet corn, okra, lima beans, salt, pepper, and sugar to slow cooker. Cook covered on low setting for 6 to 8 hours.

# Apple Cider Beef Stew

*Perfect for fall, enjoy this stew after a day outside
and it will warm you up in no time.*

*stats*

**SERVES 6**

Cooking time . . . . . . . 10–12 hours

Preparation time . . . . 15 minutes

Attention . . . . . . . . . . Minimal

Pot size . . . . . . . . . . . . 3–6 quarts

2 pounds stewing beef

8 carrots

6 medium potatoes

2 Granny Smith apples

1 small white onion

2 teaspoons salt

½ teaspoon thyme

2 cups apple cider

¼ cup flour

**1.** Cut the beef into ½-inch cubes. Peel and slice the carrots ⅛ inch thick. Peel the potatoes and cut into ½-inch cubes. Peel the apples and cut into ½-inch pieces. Peel the onion and finely chop.

**2.** Place the carrots, potatoes, and apples in the slow cooker. Add the meat and sprinkle with salt, thyme, and onion. Pour the cider over the top. Cover and cook on low setting for 10 to 12 hours. Before serving, mix the flour with enough water to make a paste and add mixture to the stew; stir in. Cover and cook on high setting until thickened, about 15 minutes.

# Layered Beef Stew

*Thick and delicious, this stew is perfect with a light salad or plain bread.*

**SERVES 6**

Cooking time . . . . . . . 9–10 hours
Preparation time. . . . 20 minutes
Attention. . . . . . . . . . Minimal
Pot size . . . . . . . . . . . . 3–6 quarts

*2½ pounds beef stewing meat*

*1 large yellow onion*

*6 medium carrots*

*4 celery ribs*

*4 large ripe tomatoes*

*10 small new potatoes*

*2 tablespoons Worcestershire sauce*

*¼ cup red wine*

*3 tablespoons brown sugar*

*1 teaspoon table salt*

*½ teaspoon ground black pepper*

*¼ teaspoon allspice*

*¼ teaspoon dried marjoram*

*¼ teaspoon dried thyme*

*2 bay leaves*

*6 tablespoons quick-cooking tapioca*

**1.** Cut the beef into 1-inch cubes. Peel the onion and cut into ¼-inch-thick slices. Peel the carrots and cut in half lengthwise. Remove the leaves from the celery and cut ribs in half. Chop the tomatoes into ¼-inch pieces.

**2.** Layer all ingredients in the slow cooker in the following order: beef, onions, potatoes, carrots, celery, Worcestershire sauce, red wine, brown sugar, salt, pepper, allspice, marjoram, thyme, bay leaves, tapioca, tomatoes. Cover and cook on low setting for 9 to 10 hours.

# French Countryside Chicken and Pork Stew

*The name alone is so enchanting!*
*Enjoy this stew in your own home and dream about France!*

 **stats**

**SERVES 4**

Cooking time . . . . . . . 8–9 hours
Preparation time . . . . 20 minutes
Attention . . . . . . . . . . Minimal
Pot size . . . . . . . . . . . . 3–6 quarts

3 pounds pork chops

4 chicken breasts

10 pearl onions

8 ounces (1 cup) fresh mushrooms, quartered

4 garlic cloves

1 tablespoon olive oil

2 cups beef broth

¼ cup dry white wine

2 tablespoons Dijon mustard

1 teaspoon flour

1 teaspoon warm water

**1.** Remove the bones from the pork and cut the meat into ½-inch cubes. Remove the bones and skin from the chicken and discard; cut the chicken into ½-inch cubes. Peel the pearl onions. Clean the mushrooms by wiping with a damp cloth; cut into quarters. Peel the garlic and mince.

**2.** Sauté the pork, chicken, onions, and garlic in olive oil over medium heat in a large skillet until the meat is browned. Drain off grease and add mixture to the slow cooker. Combine beef broth, wine, and mustard in a medium-sized bowl and pour mixture into the slow cooker. Add mushrooms on top. Cover and cook on low setting for 8 to 9 hours.

**3.** About 30 minutes before serving, make a paste of the warm water and flour; add to the slow cooker, stirring well. Cook uncovered, stirring occasionally, until a gravy develops.

**4.** Top with chopped parsley right before serving.

# Chicken Peanut Stew

*Sprinkle with chopped peanuts and flaked coconut*
*before serving over freshly cooked rice.*

**SERVES 4**

Cooking time....... 4–6 hours
Preparation time.... 15 minutes
Attention.......... Minimal
Pot size............ 3–6 quarts

4 chicken breasts

1 green bell pepper

1 red bell pepper

2 medium-sized yellow onions

1 (6-ounce) can tomato paste

¾ cup crunchy peanut butter

3 cups chicken broth

1 teaspoon table salt

1 teaspoon chili powder

1 teaspoon sugar

½ teaspoon ground nutmeg

**1.** Remove the skin and bones from the chicken breasts and discard; cut the meat into 1-inch cubes. Remove the stems and seeds from the peppers and cut into ¼-inch rings. Peel the onions and cut into ¼-inch rings.

**2.** Combine all the ingredients in the slow cooker; stir until all the ingredients are well mingled. Cover and cook on low setting for 4 to 6 hours.

# Stewed Mushrooms, Peppers, and Tomatoes

*For a large meal, serve this to complement Lean, Mean Meatloaf (page 79).*

**SERVES 8**

Cooking time . . . . . . . 8–9 hours
Preparation time . . . . 20 minutes
Attention . . . . . . . . . . Minimal
Pot size . . . . . . . . . . . . 3–6 quarts

12 plum tomatoes

2 red bell peppers

2 yellow bell peppers

2 green bell peppers

2 large yellow onions

12 ounces (1½ cups) oyster
mushrooms, quartered

6 garlic cloves

2 tablespoons olive oil

3 bay leaves

2 teaspoons dried basil

1 teaspoon salt

1 teaspoon ground black pepper

**1.** Chop the tomatoes into ½-inch pieces. Remove the stems and seeds from the peppers and cut into ¼-inch-thick strips. Peel the onions and cut into ¼-inch rings. Clean the mushrooms by wiping with a damp cloth; cut into fourths. Peel the garlic and cut into eighths.

**2.** Heat the olive oil in medium-sized skillet on medium heat. Add the peppers, onions, garlic, and mushrooms and sauté for 5 minutes. Drain off grease. Transfer the vegetables to the slow cooker. Add the spices and tomatoes; stir well. Cover and cook on low setting for 8 to 9 hours.

# Shrimp and Clam Stew with Tomatoes

*Chop one bunch of green onions into ¼-inch pieces, including the green stems, and sprinkle on top of the soup before serving with French bread.*

**stats**

**SERVES 6**

Cooking time . . . . . . . 6–9 hours
Preparation time . . . . 20 minutes
Attention . . . . . . . . . . Minimal
Pot size . . . . . . . . . . . . 4–8 quarts

½ pound small to medium shrimp

3 cups canned or shelled fresh clams

2 medium-sized yellow onions, chopped

4 medium-sized ripe tomatoes

2 medium-sized white potatoes

1 medium-sized green bell pepper

2 celery ribs

2 medium carrots

4 garlic cloves

1 tablespoon olive oil

1 cup tomato sauce

1 teaspoon dried thyme

½ teaspoon ground black pepper

1 tablespoon hot pepper sauce

**1.** Boil the shrimp for 10 minutes. Drain and rinse in cool water. Remove the shells and tails. Remove the black veins by running the tine of a fork along the back of each shrimp. If using fresh clams, remove the shells. Peel the onions and chop into ¼-inch pieces. Chop the tomatoes into ½-inch pieces. Peel the potatoes and chop into ½-inch pieces. Remove the seeds and stem from the green pepper and chop the pepper into ¼-inch pieces. Chop the celery into ¼-inch pieces. Peel and chop the carrot into ¼-inch rounds. Peel and mince the garlic.

**2.** Sauté the onion and garlic in olive oil in a large skillet on medium heat until the onion is translucent and limp. Add the tomatoes, potatoes, green pepper, celery, carrots, tomato sauce, thyme, pepper, and hot sauce; sauté for 5 minutes.

**3.** Transfer mixture to the slow cooker. Cover and cook on low setting for 6 to 8 hours. Add the shrimp and clams. Cover and cook on high setting for 30 additional minutes.

# Pickelsteiner Three-Meat Stew

*The original recipe calls for veal, but the slow cooker
will tenderize tougher cuts of beef just as well.*

 *stats*

**SERVES 18**

Cooking time . . . . . . . 6–8 hours
Preparation time . . . . 30 minutes
Attention . . . . . . . . . . Minimal
Pot size . . . . . . . . . . . . 5 quarts

1 onion
2 pounds beef
2 pounds lamb
2 pounds pork
2 tablespoons butter
½ cup flour
2 pounds potatoes
2 cups tomato sauce
2 cups beef stock
¼ teaspoon salt
¼ teaspoon black pepper
1 bouquet garni

**1.** Mince the onion. Cut the meat into 1-inch cubes.

**2.** Sauté the meat and onion in butter in a pan over medium heat until browned. Stir in the flour until well mixed. Transfer to the slow cooker.

**3.** Cube the potatoes. Combine with the tomato sauce, stock, salt, pepper, and bouquet garni in the slow cooker.

**4.** Cover and heat on a low setting for 6 to 8 hours.

**5.** Before serving, remove the bouquet garni.

# Busy Day Beef Stew

*This dish is great to include in a party menu. It's very simple,
and you can set it to cook and leave it alone until it's done.*

**SERVES 6**

| | |
|---|---|
| Cooking time....... | 4–5 hours |
| Preparation time.... | 30 minutes |
| Attention.......... | Minimal |
| Pot size............ | 3–5 quarts |

2 pounds stew meat

1 tablespoon vegetable oil

1 green pepper

12 pearl onions

12 baby carrots

12 small red potatoes

30 cherry tomatoes

4 tablespoons tapioca

2 tablespoons sugar

½ teaspoon salt

¼ teaspoon pepper

**1.** Sauté the meat in oil in a pan over medium heat until browned, then drain and transfer meat to the slow cooker.

**2.** Coarsely chop the green pepper. Peel the onions and scrub the carrots and potatoes.

**3.** Put the green pepper, onions, carrots, potatoes, tomatoes, tapioca, sugar, salt, and pepper in the slow cooker.

**4.** Cover and heat on a low setting for 4 to 5 hours.

# Meat and Potato Stew

*Use your meat of choice to personalize this stew,*
*and serve with crusty bread for dipping.*

**stats**

**SERVES 6**

| | |
|---|---|
| Cooking time | 4–5 hours |
| Preparation time | 30 minutes |
| Attention | Minimal |
| Pot size | 3–5 quarts |

2 *pounds stew meat*

1 *tablespoon oil*

4 *carrots*

6 *potatoes*

1 *onion*

4 *stalks celery*

1 *teaspoon salt*

¼ *teaspoon pepper*

1 *tablespoon parsley*

½ *teaspoon basil*

¼ *teaspoon marjoram*

¼ *teaspoon tarragon*

2 *tablespoons tapioca*

1 *teaspoon sugar*

2 *cups beef broth*

1 *small can V8 juice*

**1.** Cube the meat. Sauté the meat in oil in a pan over high heat until browned. Drain the meat and transfer it to the slow cooker.

**2.** Scrub and halve the carrots and potatoes. Quarter the onion and slice the celery.

**3.** Combine the vegetables, salt, spices, tapioca, sugar, broth, and juice in the slow cooker.

**4.** Cover and heat on a low setting for 4 to 5 hours. Do not lift cover while cooking.

# Pork Stew with Dumplings

*You can use a biscuit mix to make dumplings (as shown in this recipe),
or make Delightful Dumplings (page 45) from scratch.*

(page 45)

*stats*

**SERVES 6**

| | |
|---|---|
| Cooking time | 7–9 hours |
| Preparation time | 45 minutes |
| Attention | Moderate |
| Pot size | 3–5 quarts |

6 small red potatoes

6 carrots

2 stalks celery

2 pounds pork stew meat

¼ cup flour

1½ teaspoons salt

½ teaspoon pepper

3 tablespoons vegetable oil

1 clove garlic

4 onions

4 cups water

2 teaspoons sugar

1 teaspoon Worcestershire sauce

1 bay leaf

1 small bunch fresh parsley

1 egg

1 cup buttermilk baking mix

3 tablespoons milk

**1.** Halve the potatoes and diagonally slice the carrots and celery. Arrange the vegetables in the slow cooker.

**2.** Cube the pork. Combine the flour, salt, and pepper and use to coat the meat cubes. Sauté the cubes in oil in a pan over medium heat until the meat is lightly browned. Mince the garlic and quarter the onions. Mix the garlic and onions with the meat cubes and arrange over the vegetables.

**3.** Mix the water, sugar, and Worcestershire sauce in a bowl. Pour into the slow cooker; add the bay leaf.

**4.** Cover and heat on a low setting for 6 to 8 hours.

**5.** To make the dumplings: Chop the parsley and beat the egg. Half an hour before serving, mix the parsley, egg, baking mix, and milk in a separate bowl, stirring only briefly. Drop by spoonfuls into the slow cooker. Cook with cover removed for 10 minutes. Replace cover and continue cooking for another 15 minutes.

# Beefy Pepper Stew

*Try this stew with chicken or pork instead of beef.*
*If you have a hunter in the family, substitute moose or elk!*

**SERVES 6**

Cooking time . . . . . . . 4–5 hours
Preparation time . . . . 30 minutes
Attention . . . . . . . . . . Minimal
Pot size . . . . . . . . . . . . 3–5 quarts

2 pounds stew beef

1 onion

3 cloves garlic

2 green bell peppers

1 teaspoon chili powder

2 tablespoons vegetable oil

1 pound tomatoes

2 dried corn tortillas or 15 tortilla chips

2 cups water

½ teaspoon salt

2 bay leaves

1 teaspoon ground cloves

1 teaspoon ground oregano

¼ teaspoon pepper

1. Cube the beef. Coarsely chop the onion, garlic, and green peppers.

2. Sauté the beef, onion, garlic, green peppers, and chili powder in oil in a pan over medium heat until the beef is browned. Transfer to the slow cooker.

3. Coarsely chop the tomatoes. Crumble the corn tortillas. Add the tomatoes, tortillas, water, salt, and spices to the slow cooker.

4. Cover and heat on a low setting for 4 to 5 hours.

5. Before serving, remove the bay leaves.

# Delightful Dumplings

*These dumplings are a great addition to*
*any soup or can be enjoyed on their own.*

*stats*

**SERVES 6–8**

| | |
| --- | --- |
| Cooking time | 7–9 hours |
| Preparation time | 45 minutes |
| Attention | Moderate |
| Pot size | 3–5 quarts |

6 small red potatoes

6 carrots

2 stalks celery

2 pounds pork stew meat

¼ cup flour

1½ teaspoons salt

½ teaspoon pepper

3 tablespoons vegetable oil

1 clove garlic

4 onions

4 cups water

2 teaspoons sugar

1 teaspoon Worcestershire sauce

1 bay leaf

1 small bunch fresh parsley

1 egg

1 cup buttermilk baking mix

3 tablespoons milk

**1.** Halve the potatoes and diagonally slice the carrots and celery. Arrange the vegetables in the slow cooker.

**2.** Cube the pork. Combine the flour, salt, and pepper and use to coat the meat cubes. Sauté the cubes in oil in a pan over medium heat until the meat is lightly browned. Mince the garlic and quarter the onions. Mix the garlic and onions with the meat cubes and arrange over the vegetables.

**3.** Mix the water, sugar, and Worcestershire sauce in a bowl. Pour into the slow cooker; add the bay leaf.

**4.** Cover and heat on a low setting for 6 to 8 hours.

**5.** To make the dumplings: Chop the parsley and beat the egg. Half an hour before serving, mix the parsley, egg, baking mix, and milk in a separate bowl, stirring only briefly. Drop by spoonfuls into the slow cooker. Cook with cover removed for 10 minutes. Replace cover and continue cooking for another 15 minutes.

# Chef Jeff's Chili

*Try substituting other types of beans, like pinto,
black, or butter beans, for a different flavor.*

**stats**

**SERVES 8**

Cooking time....... 4–5 hours
Preparation time.... 30 minutes
Attention.......... Minimal
Pot size............ 3–5 quarts

2 *pounds ground beef*

1 *onion*

2 *cloves garlic*

3 *stalks celery*

2 *pounds tomatoes*

1 *bell pepper*

2 *pounds cooked kidney beans*

1 *cup tomato paste*

2 *tablespoons chili powder*

1 *teaspoon basil*

1 *teaspoon pepper*

2 *bay leaves*

1 *teaspoon salt*

**1.** Sauté the beef in a pan over medium heat until brown, then drain, reserving ½ cup of the fat and juices. Transfer the meat to the slow cooker.

**2.** Coarsely chop the onion, garlic, and celery. Sauté in the pan with the meat fat and juices over medium heat until soft. Transfer the onion mixture to the slow cooker.

**3.** Dice the tomatoes and bell pepper. Add the tomatoes, bell pepper, beans, tomato paste, spices, and salt to the slow cooker.

**4.** Cover and heat on a low setting for 4 to 5 hours. Before serving, remove the bay leaves.

CHAPTER

3

# Small Meals & Breads

# Hot Western BBQ Ribs

*Be sure to provide plenty of napkins for your guests,*
*and don't serve this in a room with white carpet!*

**SERVES 6**

Cooking time....... 4–6 hours
Preparation time.... 15 minutes
Attention.......... Minimal
Pot size............ 3–5 quarts

3 pounds beef short ribs

1 onion

1 clove garlic

1 cup catsup

½ cup water

¼ cup brown sugar

3 tablespoons Worcestershire sauce

1 teaspoon salt

2 teaspoons mustard

**1.** Cut the ribs into serving-size portions.

**2.** Arrange the ribs in the slow cooker.

**3.** Mince the onion and garlic. Combine with the other ingredients and pour the mixture over the ribs.

**4.** Cover and heat on a low setting for 4 to 6 hours.

# Meatballs with Mushrooms

*Serve these meatballs with skewers or, for a more substantial dish, provide rolls and let your guests make little meatball sandwiches.*

*stats*

**SERVES 4–6**

Cooking time . . . . . . . 3–4 hours
Preparation time . . . . 60 minutes
Attention . . . . . . . . . . Minimal
Pot size . . . . . . . . . . . . 3–5 quarts

1 clove garlic

1 pound ground beef

¼ cup chopped celery

½ cup uncooked rice

½ cup bread crumbs

½ teaspoon sage

½ teaspoon white pepper

½ teaspoon salt

2 tablespoons vegetable oil

½ pound mushrooms

1 onion

2 tablespoons vegetable oil

1 tablespoon flour

1 cup water

1 cup tomato sauce

**1.** Crush and mince the garlic. Combine the meat, garlic, and celery with the rice, crumbs, spices, and salt.

**2.** Form into ¾-inch balls. Brown in 2 tablespoons vegetable oil in a pan over medium heat and drain. Arrange in the slow cooker.

**3.** Mince the mushrooms and onion. Sauté the mushrooms and onion in 2 tablespoons vegetable oil. Add the flour to the mushroom mixture and stir to thicken. Add the water and tomato sauce to this slowly and mix until smooth.

**4.** Pour the tomato and mushroom mixture over balls.

**5.** Cover and heat on a low setting for 3 to 4 hours.

# Royal Meatballs

*These flavorful meatballs are prepared with Regal Caper Sauce (see facing page).*
*Serve them either skewered or with slices of mini pumpernickel.*

*stats*

**SERVES 6**

Cooking time . . . . . . . 3–4 hours
Preparation time . . . . 60 minutes
Attention . . . . . . . . . . Minimal
Pot size . . . . . . . . . . . . 3–5 quarts

1 onion

6 shallots

3 tablespoons butter

½ pound lamb

½ pound veal

½ pound bacon

1 small bunch parsley

12 anchovies

¼ cup chives

1 clove garlic

½ teaspoon salt

¼ teaspoon pepper

¼ teaspoon nutmeg

⅛ teaspoon cayenne pepper

½ cup water

2 eggs

3 cups Regal Caper Sauce
(see facing page)

**1.** Mince the onion and shallots, then sauté in the butter in a pan over medium heat until soft. Transfer the onion and shallots to a mixing bowl and set aside the pan with remaining butter.

**2.** Coarsely grind or mince the meat. Finely chop the parsley, anchovies, and chives. Crush the garlic and then mince it.

**3.** Combine all ingredients except Regal Caper Sauce with the onion mixture in the mixing bowl and mix well. Form into ¾-inch balls; heat the meatballs in the pan over medium heat until browned, then drain.

**4.** Arrange the meatballs in the slow cooker and cover with Regal Caper Sauce.

**5.** Cover and heat on a low setting for 3 to 4 hours.

# Regal Caper Sauce (for Royal Meatballs)

*You will have to make this sauce prior to cooking
the meatballs (on the facing page).*

2 tablespoons butter, plus
1 tablespoon

2 tablespoons flour

1 cup stock

½ teaspoon salt

½ teaspoon peppercorns

1 egg yolk

6 tablespoons capers

**1.** Melt 2 tablespoons of butter in a saucepan over medium heat and mix in the flour,
stirring until the flour is well mixed and
slightly browned. Add the stock and mix well,
then transfer to the slow cooker. Add the salt
and the peppercorns.

**2.** Cover and heat on a low setting for 1 to
2 hours. Then, half an hour before serving,
skim with a strainer. Stir in the egg yolk and
1 tablespoon of butter, then add the capers.

# Grandpa Riley's Tamales

*If you aren't able to get small heads of baby cabbage for the tamale wrappers, use large leaves cut in half. You can also try this with red cabbage, or a mixture of both.*

*stats*

**YIELDS 48**

Cooking time . . . . . . . 4–5 hours
Preparation time . . . . 90 minutes
Attention . . . . . . . . . . Minimal
Pot size . . . . . . . . . . . 3–5 quarts

1½ pounds pork

1½ cups cooked rice

1 tablespoon salt

1 tablespoon pepper

48 small cabbage leaves

2 cloves garlic

3 tablespoons chili powder

2½ cups cubed tomatoes

1 cup water

**1.** Coarsely grind pork. Mix with rice, salt, and pepper.

**2.** Place 2 tablespoons of the meat mixture in each cabbage leaf and roll, tucking under the ends.

**3.** Arrange the rolls tightly in the slow cooker.

**4.** Mince the garlic. Mix chili powder, tomatoes, garlic, and water; pour over cabbage rolls. Place an inverted glass plate or baking dish on top of the rolls to hold them in place.

**5.** Cover and cook on medium setting for 4 to 5 hours.

# Paprika Meatballs

*These can be served with skewers as a finger food or over pasta as a main dish. They are excellent with fresh angel hair pasta.*

**stats**

**SERVES 8**

Cooking time . . . . . . . 3–4 hours
Preparation time. . . . 60 minutes
Attention. . . . . . . . . . Minimal
Pot size . . . . . . . . . . . . 3–5 quarts

1 pound veal
1 pound pork
1 clove garlic
¼ pound Mozzarella cheese
3 eggs
1 tablespoon paprika
1 teaspoon salt
1 cup bread crumbs
½ cup milk
2 tablespoons vegetable oil
2 tomatoes
1 cup tomato sauce

**1.** Coarsely grind the meat. Crush and mince the garlic; grate or finely dice the cheese.

**2.** Combine the meat, garlic, and cheese in a mixing bowl with the eggs, paprika, salt, crumbs, and milk; mix well.

**3.** Form into ¾-inch balls and sauté in oil in a pan over medium heat until browned. Drain and arrange the meatballs in the slow cooker.

**4.** Dice the tomatoes. Pour the tomatoes and tomato sauce over the meatballs.

**5.** Cover and heat on a low setting for 3 to 4 hours.

# Sweet Ham Balls

*You don't need to add salt in this recipe; the ham should provide just enough.*
*As a variation, try substituting ¼ cup molasses for the brown sugar.*

*stats*

**SERVES 12**

Cooking time . . . . . . . 3–4 hours
Preparation time . . . . 45 minutes
Attention . . . . . . . . . . Minimal
Pot size . . . . . . . . . . . 3–5 quarts

1 pound ground beef

1 pound ground ham

2 eggs

1 cup graham cracker crumbs

1 cup milk

¼ cup canola or corn oil

½ teaspoon pepper

2 cups tomato sauce

½ cup brown sugar

1 cup vinegar

2 teaspoons dry mustard

**1.** Mix the beef, ham, eggs, crumbs, milk, and pepper. Form into ¾-inch balls and sauté in oil in a pan over medium heat until browned.

**2.** Drain the meatballs and arrange in the slow cooker.

**3.** Mix the tomato sauce, brown sugar, vinegar, and mustard; pour over the balls.

**4.** Cover and heat on a low setting for 3 to 4 hours.

# Bob's Beer Sausages

*Sometimes the simple things in life are the best! Keep some browned,*
*cut sausages in the freezer, ready to slow cook for a quick halftime treat.*

 *stats*

**SERVES 12**

Cooking time . . . . . . . 2–3 hours
Preparation time . . . . 15 minutes
Attention . . . . . . . . . . Minimal
Pot size . . . . . . . . . . . 3–5 quarts

3 pounds spicy Italian pork
sausages

2 bottles beer

**1.** Heat the sausages in a pan over medium heat until browned. Drain and cut them into bite-size pieces.

**2.** Combine the browned sausage with the beer in the slow cooker.

**3.** Cover and heat on a low setting for 2 to 3 hours.

# Sweet Buttermilk Meatballs

*Serve this with a sprinkle of diced sweet red pepper for a garnish.*
*It will add color, as well as a nice dash of flavor!*

**SERVES 8**

Cooking time ....... 2–3 hours
Preparation time.... 60 minutes
Attention........... Minimal
Pot size ............ 3–5 quarts

1 onion

2 pounds ground beef

1 cup bread crumbs

½ cup milk

1 teaspoon salt

¼ teaspoon pepper

3 tablespoons butter

¼ cup butter

¼ cup flour

2¼ cups buttermilk

2 tablespoons sugar

¼ teaspoon salt

⅛ teaspoon pepper

1½ teaspoons dry mustard

1 egg

**1.** Mince the onion. Mix the onion, ground beef, bread crumbs, milk, salt, and pepper. Form into ¾-inch balls.

**2.** Sauté the balls in 3 tablespoons butter in a pan over medium heat until browned; drain, discarding the grease. Transfer the meatballs to the slow cooker.

**3.** Add the remaining butter to the pan and melt it over low heat. Stir in the flour until well blended.

**4.** Slowly add the buttermilk to the flour mixture; blend well. Add the sugar, salt, spices, and egg; stir over low heat to thicken. Pour the sauce over the meatballs in the slow cooker.

**5.** Cover and heat on a low setting for 2 to 3 hours.

# Sherry Meatballs

*When serving these as finger foods, be sure to include small slices of French bread to soak up the rich sauce.*

**stats**

**SERVES 8**

Cooking time . . . . . . . 3–4 hours
Preparation time. . . . 60 minutes
Attention. . . . . . . . . . Minimal
Pot size . . . . . . . . . . . . 3–5 quarts

6 slices bacon

2 onions

2 cloves garlic

1 cup dry bread crumbs

2 pounds ground beef

2 eggs

1 teaspoon salt

½ teaspoon pepper

½ teaspoon oregano

1 pound mushrooms

3 tablespoons butter

2 tablespoons flour

½ cup milk

½ cup water

½ cup sherry

**1.** Heat the bacon in a pan over medium heat until browned. Remove the browned slices from the pan to drain; set aside most of the bacon fat to use later.

**2.** Dice the onion and garlic. Sauté the onion and garlic in the remaining bacon fat, then remove the onion mixture from the pan and add it to the bread crumbs, beef, eggs, salt, and spices in a mixing bowl. Form the meat mixture into ¾-inch balls. Sauté the balls in the bacon fat you set aside over medium heat; drain. Crumble the bacon; arrange the meatballs in the slow cooker with the crumbled bacon.

**3.** Slice the mushrooms. Sauté in butter in a pan over medium heat until browned; stir in the flour and allow the juices to thicken. Slowly stir in the milk and water. Pour the thickened mushroom sauce over the meatballs in the slow cooker.

**4.** Cover and heat on a low setting for 2 to 3 hours.

**5.** Half an hour before serving, add the sherry.

# Tangy Burgundy Ribs

*You can serve this as a finger food, or with rice as a more substantial dish. Don't forget to include plenty of napkins!*

 **stats**

**SERVES 8**

Cooking time . . . . . . . 5–6 hours
Preparation time . . . . 30 minutes
Attention . . . . . . . . . . Minimal
Pot size . . . . . . . . . . . . 3–5 quarts

4 pounds lean short ribs

½ cup flour

¼ teaspoon coarsely ground black pepper

2 tablespoons oil

4 stalks celery

2 onions

3 teaspoons prepared mustard

2 tablespoons Worcestershire sauce

1 teaspoon salt

1 cup catsup

½ cup wine vinegar

1 cup Burgundy wine

**1.** Cut the ribs into serving-size pieces. Mix the flour and pepper and use to lightly coat the ribs.

**2.** Heat the ribs in oil in a pan over medium heat until browned, and then drain.

**3.** Slice the celery and onions. Combine with the meat, mustard, Worcestershire sauce, salt, catsup, and vinegar in the slow cooker.

**4.** Cover and heat on a medium setting for 4 to 5 hours. Half an hour before serving, add the wine to the slow cooker.

# Burgundy Pepper Beef

*You can serve this with small forks, or provide your guests with small bowls of warm egg noodles to enjoy with the sauce.*

*stats*

**SERVES 8**

Cooking time . . . . . . . 4–5 hours
Preparation time . . . . 45 minutes
Attention . . . . . . . . . . Moderate
Pot size . . . . . . . . . . . . 3–5 quarts

2 pounds stew beef, such as blade roast or chuck steak

½ cup flour

½ teaspoon black pepper

2 tablespoons oil

2 onions

½ pound mushrooms

1 tablespoon Worcestershire sauce

½ teaspoon salt

1 tablespoon sugar

1 cup water

½ cup vinegar

2 tablespoons flour

1 cup Burgundy wine

**1.** Cube the beef. Mix the flour and pepper. Use the flour mixture to coat the beef cubes. Heat the meat in oil in a pan over medium heat until browned. Transfer the beef to the slow cooker, but keep the oil in the pan.

**2.** Quarter the onions and halve the mushrooms. Sauté the onions and mushrooms over medium heat in the pan in the oil used for the beef, until the onion mixture is soft.

**3.** Put the beef, onions, mushrooms, Worcestershire sauce, salt, sugar, water, and vinegar in the slow cooker.

**4.** Cover and heat on a low setting for 3 to 4 hours.

**5.** An hour before serving, take 2 tablespoons of sauce from the slow cooker and let it cool briefly before mixing it well with the remaining flour. Stir this into the sauce in the slow cooker, mixing well. Add the Burgundy.

# Imperial Meatballs

*Serve with chopsticks. To be kind, provide pointed ones so your guests can use them to skewer their food, in case they're not chopstick pros.*

**stats**

**SERVES 8**

Cooking time . . . . . . . 3–4 hours
Preparation time . . . . 45 minutes
Attention . . . . . . . . . . Minimal
Pot size . . . . . . . . . . . . 3–5 quarts

1 onion

¼ cup water chestnuts

2 pounds ground beef

4 eggs

1 cup bread crumbs

1 teaspoon pepper

2 tablespoons sesame oil

4 cloves garlic

2 cups soy sauce

4 teaspoons ground ginger

½ cup sugar

**1.** Finely chop the onion. Peel and cut the chestnuts into fine strips. Combine with the ground beef, eggs, crumbs, and pepper and form into ¾-inch balls.

**2.** Sauté the balls in oil in a pan over high heat until browned, then drain and arrange them in the slow cooker.

**3.** Crush and slice the garlic and distribute over the meatballs. Combine the soy sauce, ginger, and sugar in a mixing bowl, and then pour over the meatballs and garlic in the slow cooker.

**4.** Cover and heat on a low setting for 3 to 4 hours.

# Hawaiian Sausage

*This sweet and savory dish works well using smoked sausages.*
*If using canned pineapple, delete the ¼ cup of brown sugar.*

 **stats** · **SERVES 12**

Cooking time . . . . . . . 3–4 hours
Preparation time. . . . 30 minutes
Attention. . . . . . . . . . Minimal
Pot size . . . . . . . . . . . . 3–5 quarts

3 pounds link sausages

2 pounds fresh pineapple, peeled, cored, and cubed

¼ cup brown sugar

¼ cup cornstarch

1 cup water

½ cup brown sugar

1 tablespoon prepared mustard

1 tablespoon soy sauce

1. Sauté the sausage in a pan over medium heat until browned. Drain and cut into bite-size pieces; if using cocktail-size link sausages, leave whole.

2. Arrange the pineapple in the slow cooker with the sausages. Sprinkle with ¼ cup brown sugar while arranging in the slow cooker.

3. Blend the cornstarch with water.

4. Add ½ cup brown sugar, mustard, and soy sauce to the cornstarch mixture and blend well. Pour the brown sugar mixture over the sausage and pineapple in the slow cooker.

5. Cover and heat on a low setting for 3 to 4 hours.

# Homemade Tamales

*For a more authentic feel, you can use shredded beef or pork*
*instead of the ground beef in this recipe.*

**stats**

**YIELDS ABOUT 20**

Cooking time . . . . . . . 3–4 hours
Preparation time . . . . 2 hours
Attention . . . . . . . . . . Minimal
Pot size . . . . . . . . . . . . 3–5 quarts

½ pound corn husks
½ pound spicy pork sausage
½ pound ground beef
1 teaspoon cumin
2½ cups water
½ cup lard (or shortening)
2 cups cornmeal
2 teaspoons baking powder
½ teaspoon salt
String
1 cup water

**1.** If using dried husks, soak them in warm water for 2 hours to soften before using. Alternatively, fresh husks should be laid out on trays and lightly dried overnight, uncovered, or heated for several hours in a 150°F oven.

**2.** Simmer the meat with the cumin in 2½ cups water until cooked. Drain and set aside meat; save 1½ cups of the liquid. After the liquid cools, use a large spoon to skim off any solidified fat; discard the fat.

**3.** Cut the lard into the cornmeal, baking powder, and salt. Slowly add the set-aside meat broth and mix well into the cornmeal mixture.

**4.** Lay out the husks on a flat surface. On the smooth side of each husk, spread about 1½ tablespoons of the cornmeal dough. Top with about ¾ tablespoon of meat. Fold the dough around the meat. Roll the husk around the dough and tie it with a string around the middle of the bundle. Arrange the bundles on a trivet or rack in the slow cooker, and pour water around the base.

**5.** Cover and heat on a high setting for 3 to 4 hours.

# Spicy Plum Chicken

*Fresh plums can add a nice twist to this recipe. Throw in six (without the pits), with ¼ cup sugar. Leave off the lid for the last half hour to condense the sauce.*

*stats*

**SERVES 6**

Cooking time . . . . . . . 3–4 hours
Preparation time . . . . 30 minutes
Attention . . . . . . . . . . Minimal
Pot size . . . . . . . . . . . . 3–5 quarts

2 pounds boneless chicken
½ teaspoon white pepper
½ teaspoon ground ginger
½ teaspoon cinnamon
¼ teaspoon ground cloves
1 tablespoon soy sauce
3 tablespoons soy sauce
2 tablespoons honey
½ cup plum jelly
2 teaspoons sugar
2 teaspoons vinegar
¼ cup chutney

1. Cut the chicken into serving-size pieces. Mix the spices and divide the spice mixture in half. Sprinkle the chicken with half of this mixture.

2. To the other half of the spice mixture, add 1 tablespoon soy sauce. Sprinkle this over the chicken, as well. Refrigerate the chicken for 4 hours or overnight.

3. Arrange the chicken pieces in the slow cooker.

4. Mix the remaining 3 tablespoons of soy sauce with the honey, jelly, sugar, vinegar, and chutney. Dribble this mixture over the chicken pieces in the slow cooker.

5. Cover and heat on a low setting for 3 to 4 hours.

# Classic Brown Bread

*This old-fashioned bread is dense and sweet. Slow cooking is the only way to bring out the rich, caramelized flavors of the grains.*

**YIELDS 3 LOAVES**

Cooking time . . . . . . . 3–4 hours
Preparation time . . . . 45 minutes
Attention . . . . . . . . . . Minimal
Pot size . . . . . . . . . . . . 3–5 quarts

1 pound rye flour

1 pound graham flour

2 pounds cornmeal

1 pound wheat flour

3 teaspoons baking powder

1 quart molasses

1½ quarts milk

2 teaspoons salt

2 cups water

**1.** Sift the flour and baking powder together in a mixing bowl.

**2.** Mix the molasses, milk, and salt in a second mixing bowl. Add the milk mixture to the flour mixture to form a soft dough.

**3.** Grease and flour 3 loaf pans. Fill the pans one-half to three-quarters full; loosely cover each pan with foil or a glass or ceramic lid. Arrange the pans on a trivet or rack in the slow cooker, and pour 2 cups water around the base of the trivet.

**4.** Cover and heat on a high setting for 3 to 4 hours.

# Family Date Bread

*Try this toasted with butter or honey. Or try with cream butter*
*with honey and serve the mixture as a spread for the bread.*

**stats**

**YIELDS 3 LOAVES**

Cooking time . . . . . . . 2–3 hours
Preparation time . . . . 45 minutes
Attention . . . . . . . . . . Minimal
Pot size . . . . . . . . . . . . 3–5 quarts

*8 ounces dried dates*

*1½ cups water*

*4 tablespoons butter*

*2 cups sugar*

*½ teaspoon vanilla*

*1 egg*

*½ teaspoon salt*

*1 cup raisins*

*1 cup nuts*

*4 cups flour*

*2 teaspoons baking soda*

*4 teaspoons baking powder*

**1.** Chop the dates. Boil the water and pour it over the dates; let stand.

**2.** Cream the butter and sugar. Add the vanilla, egg, and salt to the butter mixture. Add the cooled dates, and the water they're sitting in, to the egg mixture. Fold in the raisins and nuts.

**3.** Sift the flour, baking soda, and baking powder together in a bowl. Add the egg mixture to the flour mixture.

**4.** Grease and flour 3 loaf pans, or the equivalent. Fill the pans one-half to three-quarters full; loosely cover each pan with foil or a glass or ceramic lid. Arrange the pans on a trivet or rack in the slow cooker, and pour water around the base of the trivet.

**5.** Cover and heat on a high setting for 2 to 3 hours.

# Fresh Apple Bread

*You'll be amazed at the range of tastes different apple varieties take on after baking. Try this recipe with different types of apples for a change of flavor.*

**YIELDS 1 LOAF**

Cooking time . . . . . . . 2–3 hours
Preparation time . . . . 45 minutes
Attention . . . . . . . . . . Minimal
Pot size . . . . . . . . . . . . 3–5 quarts

1 cup sugar

½ cup shortening

2 eggs

1½ teaspoons vanilla

1½ tablespoons buttermilk

½ teaspoon salt

1½ cups peeled and minced apples

1 cup pecans

2 cups flour

1 teaspoon baking soda

1 teaspoon cinnamon

3 tablespoons sugar

**1.** Cream the first cup of sugar with the shortening.

**2.** Beat the eggs. Add the eggs, vanilla, buttermilk, and salt to the creamed ingredients. Fold the minced apples and pecans into the liquid mixture.

**3.** Sift the flour and baking soda together. Add the liquid mixture to the sifted mixture.

**4.** Grease and flour 1 loaf pan, or the equivalent. Fill the baking dish one-half to three-quarters full. Sprinkle the batter with the cinnamon and sugar. Loosely cover with foil or a glass or ceramic lid to prevent condensation from falling in. Arrange the dish on a trivet or rack in the slow cooker, and pour water around the base of the trivet.

**5.** Cover and heat on a high setting for 2 to 3 hours.

# Pineapple Banana Bread

*This is nice to serve at parties in the winter, when everyone wants to be on a tropical island instead of shoveling snow.*

**YIELDS 2 LOAVES**

| | |
|---|---|
| Cooking time....... | 2–3 hours |
| Preparation time.... | 30 minutes |
| Attention.......... | Minimal |
| Pot size........... | 3–5 quarts |

3 cups flour

2 cups sugar

½ teaspoon baking soda

1½ teaspoons baking powder

3 eggs

½ pound pineapple

1½ cups oil

½ teaspoon salt

2 cups bananas

**1.** Combine and mix the flour, sugar, baking soda, and baking powder well.

**2.** Beat the eggs in a separate bowl. Crush or dice the pineapple. If the pineapple is canned, include the juice; otherwise, supplement with ¼ cup water or fruit juice.

**3.** Mix the eggs, pineapple, oil, salt, and bananas, and then add to the dry ingredients.

**4.** Grease and flour 2 loaf pans. Fill the pans one-half to three-quarters full; loosely cover each pan with foil or a glass or ceramic lid. Arrange the pans on a trivet or rack in the slow cooker, and pour water around the base of the trivet.

**5.** Cover and heat on a high setting for 2 to 3 hours.

# Orange Raisin Bread

*This bread goes well with wild game. The citrus flavor is an especially nice complement to duck and goose, lightening the richness of the meat.*

*stats*

**YIELDS 1 LOAF**

Cooking time . . . . . . . 2–3 hours
Preparation time . . . . 45 minutes
Attention . . . . . . . . . . Minimal
Pot size . . . . . . . . . . . . 3–5 quarts

1 orange

¾ cup raisins

½ cup water

2 tablespoons butter

1 cup sugar

1 teaspoon baking soda

1 teaspoon vanilla

2 cups flour

1 teaspoon baking powder

⅛ teaspoon salt

1 egg

**1.** Grate the orange peel. Extract the juice from the orange, reserve; discard the remaining flesh. Mix the grated peel with the raisins and grind or finely mince together.

**2.** Boil the water and add it to the juice; add this to the peel-and-raisin mixture. Add the butter, sugar, baking soda, and vanilla to this; then let this orange mixture cool.

**3.** Sift the flour, baking powder, and salt together. Beat the egg and add it to the cooled orange mixture; then add the flour mixture to the orange-and-egg mixture.

**4.** Grease and flour 1 loaf pan or the equivalent. Fill the baking dish one-half to three-quarters full; loosely cover the dish with foil or a glass or ceramic lid. Arrange the dish on a trivet or rack in the slow cooker, and pour water around the base of the trivet.

**5.** Cover and heat on a high setting for 2 to 3 hours.

# Pecan Rhubarb Bread

*To make sour milk, add 1 tablespoon white vinegar or lemon juice to enough fresh milk to make a total of 1 cup. Let it stand for 15 minutes before using.*

*stats*

**YIELDS 2 LOAVES**

Cooking time....... 2–3 hours
Preparation time.... 45 minutes
Attention.......... Minimal
Pot size............ 3–5 quarts

1½ cups diced rhubarb

½ cup chopped pecans

1½ cups brown sugar

⅔ cup salad oil

1 egg

1 cup sour milk

1 teaspoon salt

1 teaspoon baking soda

1 teaspoon vanilla

2½ cups flour

½ cup sugar mixed with
1 tablespoon butter

**1.** Mix all the ingredients (except sugar–butter mixture) in the order listed.

**2.** Grease and flour 2 loaf pans or the equivalent. Fill the baking dishes one-half to three-quarters full.

**3.** Sprinkle the batter with the sugar–butter blend.

**4.** Loosely cover each dish with foil or a glass or ceramic lid. Arrange the dishes on a trivet or rack in the slow cooker, and pour water around the base of the trivet.

**5.** Cover and heat on a high setting for 2 to 3 hours.

# Pumpkin Pie Bread

*Pumpkin is a wonderful flavor year-round, not just during the holidays. This bread goes well with poultry, and it freezes well.*

**stats**

**YIELDS 2 LOAVES**

| | |
|---|---|
| Cooking time | 2–3 hours |
| Preparation time | 30 minutes |
| Attention | Minimal |
| Pot size | 3–5 quarts |

3½ cups flour

2 teaspoons baking soda

1½ teaspoons salt

1 teaspoon nutmeg

1 teaspoon cinnamon

⅛ teaspoon mace

4 eggs

2 cups cooked pumpkin

3 cups sugar

1 cup oil

1 teaspoon vanilla

**1.** Sift the flour and baking soda, then add the salt and spices.

**2.** Beat the eggs and blend with the pumpkin, sugar, oil, and vanilla. Add the liquid mix to the dry ingredients and mix well.

**3.** Grease and flour 2 loaf pans or the equivalent. Fill the baking dishes one-half to three-quarters full; loosely cover each dish with foil or a glass or ceramic lid. Arrange the dishes on a trivet or rack in the slow cooker, and pour water around the base of the trivet.

**4.** Cover and heat on a high setting for 2 to 3 hours.

# Cinnamon Orange Oat Bread

*You can also make this with lemonade instead of orange juice.*
*Just be sure it's lemonade; straight lemon juice would be too tart.*

*stats*

**YIELDS 1 LOAF**

| | |
|---|---|
| Cooking time | 2–3 hours |
| Preparation time | 45 minutes |
| Attention | Minimal |
| Pot size | 3–5 quarts |

1½ cups flour

2 teaspoons baking powder

½ teaspoon baking soda

½ cup sugar

½ teaspoon salt

1 teaspoon cinnamon

¾ cup raisins

1 cup uncooked oats

1 egg

2 tablespoons shortening

½ cup orange juice

½ cup water

¼ cup raisins

**1.** Sift the flour, baking powder, and baking soda together. Stir in the sugar, salt, cinnamon, raisins, and oats.

**2.** Beat the egg; mix it with the shortening, orange juice, and water. Add to the dry mixture and mix well.

**3.** Grease and flour 1 loaf pan or the equivalent. Fill the baking dish one-half to three-quarters full and sprinkle with ¼ cup raisins.

**4.** Loosely cover the dish with foil or a glass or ceramic lid. Arrange the dish on a trivet or rack in the slow cooker, and pour water around the base of the trivet.

**5.** Cover and heat on a high setting for 2 to 3 hours.

# Tropical Bread

*This pineapple-and-coconut-flavored bread goes well with
curry dishes like Chicken Mulligatawny Soup (page 287).*

 **stats**

**YIELDS 3 LOAVES**

Cooking time . . . . . . . 2–3 hours
Preparation time. . . . 30 minutes
Attention. . . . . . . . . . Minimal
Pot size . . . . . . . . . . . . 3–5 quarts

3½ cups pineapple

1½ cups sugar

2 teaspoons salt

2 teaspoons baking soda

4 eggs

10 ounces flaked coconut

4 cups flour

**1.** Crush or shred the pineapple. If using canned pineapple, include the juice. If fresh, add water or fruit juice to cover the fruit.

**2.** Add the sugar, salt, and baking soda to the fruit. Beat the eggs well and stir into the fruit mixture, then fold in the coconut.

**3.** Add the liquid mixture to the flour.

**4.** Grease and flour 3 loaf pans or the equivalent. Fill the baking dishes one-half to three-quarters full; loosely cover each dish with foil or a glass or ceramic lid. Arrange the dishes on a trivet or rack in the slow cooker, and pour water around the base of the trivet.

# Beef Entrées

# Beef Roast with Dried Fruit

*This hearty dish will satisfy your family's hunger and sweet tooth!*

**stats**

**SERVES 8**

| | |
|---|---|
| Cooking time | 6–8 hours |
| Preparation time | 15 minutes |
| Attention | Minimal |
| Pot size | 3–6 quarts |

2 medium-sized yellow onions

1 clove garlic

3–4 pound boneless pot roast

1½ cups mixed dried fruit

1½ cups dried apple rings

¾ cup pale ale

1 cup water

¼ cup packed brown sugar

1 bay leaf

¼ teaspoon ground cinnamon

2½ teaspoons salt

¼ teaspoon ground black pepper

**1.** Peel and slice the onions about ¼-inch thick. Peel and mince the garlic using a sharp kitchen knife.

**2.** Place the onions in bottom of the slow cooker. Place the roast on top. Cover with the mixed dried fruit. Mix together the beer, water, garlic, brown sugar, bay leaf, cinnamon, salt, and pepper; pour over the roast. Cover and cook on low setting 6–8 hours.

**3.** Remove the bay leaf and top with the apple rings before serving.

# Cajun Vegetable Beef Soup

*With a bit of spice, this beef soup is really something special!*

**stats**

**SERVES 8**

Cooking time . . . . . . . 8–10
Preparation time. . . . 30 minutes
Attention. . . . . . . . . . Minimal
Pot size . . . . . . . . . . . . 4–6 quarts

1½ pounds beef brisket

1½ cups chopped green onions

1 cup chopped celery

½ cup chopped fresh parsley

1 teaspoon fresh, chopped mint

1½ cups fresh green beans

3½ cups potatoes, chopped

1½ cups fresh tomatoes, chopped

2 cups green bell pepper, chopped

3 cups turnips, chopped

3 garlic cloves

2 cups Brussels sprouts

1½ cups fresh corn

3½ cups dry white wine

16 cups water

2 tablespoons hot pepper sauce

1 tablespoon soy sauce

1 tablespoon salt

**1.** Cut the brisket into 1-inch cubes. Remove the roots and the first layer of peel from the onions. Chop the onions, celery, parsley, and mint into ½-inch pieces. Cut the stems off of green beans. Peel and cut the potatoes into ¼-inch-thick slices. Peel the tomatoes and cut into ½-inch pieces. Remove the seeds and stem from the green pepper and cut the green pepper into ¼-inch pieces. Peel the turnips and cut into ¼-inch pieces. Peel the garlic and mince with a sharp paring knife.

**2.** Combine all ingredients in the slow cooker. Cover and cook on low setting for 8 to 10 hours.

# Grandma Opal's Vegetable Oxtail Soup

*Take a cue from Grandma Opal, she always knows best!*

**SERVES 6**

Cooking time . . . . . . . 6–8 hours
Preparation time . . . . 20 minutes
Attention . . . . . . . . . . Minimal
Pot size . . . . . . . . . . . . 3–6 quarts

*1 small yellow onion*

*1 cup carrots, diced*

*½ cup celery, diced*

*2 cups white potatoes, cubed*

*1 pound (16 ounces) canned tomatoes, liquid retained*

*2 turnips*

*2 pounds oxtail*

*2 quarts (8 cups) water*

*1 teaspoon salt*

*1 teaspoon celery salt*

*1 pound (16 ounces) canned whole kernel corn, liquid retained*

**1.** Peel and chop the onion into ¼-inch pieces. Peel the carrots with a potato peeler and cut into ¼-inch pieces. Cut the celery into ¼-inch pieces. Peel the potatoes and cut into ½-inch pieces. Cut the tomatoes into ½-inch pieces, reserving the liquid. Peel and chop the turnips into ¼-inch pieces.

**2.** Place the meat bones, water, salts, onions, carrots, turnips, and celery in the slow cooker. Cover and cook on low setting for 5 to 6 hours. Take the oxtail out of the slow cooker and remove the meat from the bones; discard the bones and return the meat to the slow cooker. Add the potatoes, tomatoes, and corn, including the liquid from the corn and tomatoes. Cover and cook on low setting for 1 to 2 additional hours.

# Porcupine Meatballs

*Don't worry, you don't have to go out to the yard for ingredients!*
*Enjoy this funny-named feast with your family on a winter night.*

**SERVES 6**

Cooking time . . . . . . . 7–8 hours
Preparation time . . . . 20 minutes
Attention . . . . . . . . . . Minimal
Pot size . . . . . . . . . . . . 3–6 quarts

½ cup chopped yellow onion

½ cup chopped green bell pepper

1½ cups lean ground beef

½ cup uncooked white rice

1 egg

1 teaspoon table salt

½ teaspoon ground black pepper

1 (10¾-ounce) can condensed
tomato soup

**1.** Peel and chop the onion into ⅛-inch pieces. Remove the stem and seeds from the green pepper and chop into ⅛-inch pieces. In a mixing bowl, combine the ground beef, rice, onion, green pepper, egg, salt, and pepper; mix well with your hands until well blended.

**2.** Shape the mixture into about 24 golf ball–sized balls. Place in the slow cooker. Pour the soup over the meatballs. Cover and cook on low setting for 7 to 8 hours.

# Spicy Pot Roast

*Mix the liquid from the slow cooker with*
*2 tablespoons flour to create a luscious gravy.*

*stats* **SERVES 8**

Cooking time . . . . . . . 8–10 hours
Preparation time. . . . 15 minutes
Attention. . . . . . . . . . Minimal
Pot size . . . . . . . . . . . . 3–6 quarts

1 yellow onion

4 large white potatoes

4-pound pot roast

1 cup water

¼ cup dry white wine

¼ cup ketchup

2 teaspoons Dijon mustard

1 teaspoon Worcestershire sauce

1 package brown gravy mix

⅛ teaspoon garlic powder

¼ teaspoon ground black pepper

½ teaspoon table salt

**1.** Peel and chop the onion into ¼-inch pieces. Peel the potatoes and cut in half lengthwise.

**2.** Place all ingredients except the pot roast in the slow cooker; stir well. Add the pot roast. Cover and cook on low setting 8 to 10 hours.

# Lean, Mean Meatloaf

*Drizzle Heinz 57 Sauce over the top of the meatloaf*
*before serving for a spicy, tangy flavor.*

 **stats**

**SERVES 6**

Cooking time . . . . . . . 4–6 hours
Preparation time . . . . 15 minutes
Attention . . . . . . . . . . Minimal
Pot size . . . . . . . . . . . . 3–6 quarts

*2 cups cabbage, shredded*

*1 medium-sized white onion*

*1 green bell pepper*

*1 pound lean ground beef*

*½ teaspoon caraway seed*

*1 teaspoon table salt*

**1.** Shred the cabbage into ¼-inch strips with a large kitchen knife. Peel and chop the onion into ¼-inch pieces. Remove the stem and seeds from the green pepper and chop the pepper into ¼-inch pieces.

**2.** Combine all ingredients in a mixing bowl. Shape into a round loaf. Place loaf on a meat rack or vegetable steamer in the slow cooker. Cook covered on high setting for 4 to 6 hours.

# Slow-Cooked Sauerbraten

*This method will produce a tender and delicious treat.*

**SERVES 8**

Cooking time . . . . . . . 5 hours
Preparation time . . . . 15 minutes
Attention . . . . . . . . . . Minimal
Pot size . . . . . . . . . . . . 4–6 quarts

2 yellow onions
4-pound beef roast
½ teaspoon table salt
½ teaspoon ground black pepper
2 cups beef broth
⅓ cup brown sugar
⅓ cup cider vinegar
8 gingersnap cookies

**1.** Peel and chop the onions into 1-inch pieces. Sprinkle the beef roast with salt and pepper. Place the roast in the slow cooker. Add the onion, broth, brown sugar, and vinegar. Cover and cook on high setting for 5 hours.

**2.** Remove the roast from the slow cooker. Crumble gingersnap cookies and add to the sauce in the slow cooker. Stir slowly for about 10 minutes, or until the sauce thickens. Slice the meat and ladle the sauce over slices.

# A Dilly of a Pot Roast

*This is excellent served with a sauce made of 1 cup sour cream and 2 teaspoons dill weed.*

### stats
**SERVES 6**

Cooking time . . . . . . . 8–10 hours
Preparation time . . . . 20 minutes
Attention . . . . . . . . . . Minimal
Pot size . . . . . . . . . . . . 4–6 quarts

3-pound chuck roast

1 teaspoon table salt

½ teaspoon ground black pepper

2 teaspoons dried dill weed

¼ cup water

1 tablespoon vinegar

Sprinkle both sides of the meat with salt, pepper, and dill weed. Place the roast in the slow cooker. Pour water and vinegar over the top. Cover and cook on low setting for 8 to 10 hours.

# Sparkling Beef Tips

*Easy to make and yummy to eat, this simple meal will satisfy all.*

**SERVES 4**

| | |
|---|---|
| Cooking time | 8–10 hours |
| Preparation time | 10 minutes |
| Attention | Minimal |
| Pot size | 4–6 quarts |

*2-pound chuck roast*

*2 cups fresh mushrooms, sliced*

*1 (10¾-ounce) can cream of mushroom condensed soup*

*1 envelope dry onion soup mix*

*1 cup lemon-lime carbonated drink.*

Cut the meat into 1-inch cubes, trimming off the fat as you go. Clean the mushrooms by wiping with a damp cloth; slice ⅛-inch thick. Add all ingredients to the slow cooker; mix well. Cook covered on low setting for 8 to 10 hours.

# Beef Bourguignon

*Serve over wide egg noodles and a vegetable for a complete meal.*

**stats**

**SERVES 4**

| | |
|---|---|
| Cooking time | 8–10 hours |
| Preparation time | 20 minutes |
| Attention | Minimal |
| Slow cooker size | 4–6 quarts |

*2-pound chuck roast*

*1½ tablespoons flour*

*4 large yellow onions*

*1 cup fresh mushrooms, sliced*

*1 teaspoon table salt*

*¼ teaspoon dried marjoram*

*¼ teaspoon dried thyme*

*¼ teaspoon ground black pepper*

*1 cup beef broth*

*1 cup burgundy wine*

**1.** Cut the meat into 1-inch cubes, trimming off the fat as you go. Dredge the meat in flour by pressing the chunks firmly into a bowl containing the flour. Peel and slice the onions into ¼-inch rings. Wash the mushrooms by wiping with a damp cloth; slice ⅛-inch thick.

**2.** Add all ingredients to the slow cooker. Cover and cook on low setting for 8 to 10 hours.

# Hungarian Goulash #1

*Serve over cooked elbow macaroni for an authentic look.*

**SERVES 8**

Cooking time ....... 8–10 hours
Preparation time.... 20 minutes
Attention.......... Minimal
Pot size ............ 4–8 quarts

2 pounds round steak

½ teaspoon onion powder

½ teaspoon garlic powder

½ teaspoon table salt

½ teaspoon ground black pepper

1½ teaspoon paprika

2 tablespoons flour

1 (10¾-ounce) can condensed tomato soup

½ cup water

1 cup sour cream

**1.** Cut the steak into 1-inch cubes. Mix the meat, onion powder, garlic powder, salt, pepper, paprika, and flour together until meat is well coated. Place in the slow cooker. Pour soup and water over the top. Cover and cook on low setting for 8 to 10 hours.

**2.** About a half-hour before serving, stir in the sour cream. Cover and cook on low setting.

# Beefy Spanish Rice

*Serve as a complement to Wisconsin Cheesy Beer Soup (page 19)*
*for a hearty, flavorful meal.*

 **stats**

**SERVES 8**

| | |
|---|---|
| Cooking time | 8–10 hours |
| Preparation time | 20 minutes |
| Attention | Minimal |
| Pot size | 3–6 quarts |

1 pound lean ground beef

1 medium-sized yellow onion

1 red bell pepper

1 cup tomato sauce

1 cup water

1 teaspoon chili powder

2 teaspoons Worcestershire sauce

1 cup raw white rice

**1.** Brown the ground beef in a medium-sized skillet on medium-high heat. Drain off fat and spread the meat on paper towels to soak up more fat. Peel the onion and chop into ¼-inch pieces. Remove the stem and seeds from the red pepper and chop into ¼-inch pieces.

**2.** Combine all ingredients in the slow cooker. Cover and cook on low setting for 8 to 10 hours.

# Japanese Pepper Steak

*Serve over cellophane noodles for an authentic taste.*

*stats*

**SERVES 4**

| | |
|---|---|
| Cooking time | 6–8 hours |
| Preparation time | 15 minutes |
| Attention | Minimal |
| Pot size | 3–6 quarts |

*1 pound steak*

*2 garlic cloves*

*1 green bell pepper*

*1 cup fresh mushrooms, sliced*

*1 medium-sized white onion*

*3 tablespoons soy sauce*

*1 teaspoon ground ginger or
2 teaspoons fresh, minced ginger*

*½ teaspoon crushed, dried red
pepper*

**1.** Slice the steak about ½-inch thick. Peel the garlic and mince with a sharp kitchen knife. Remove the stem and seeds from the green pepper and slice lengthwise into ¼-inch strips. Wash the mushrooms by wiping with a damp cloth; slice paper-thin. Peel the onion and slice into ¼-inch-thick rings.

**2.** Combine all the ingredients in the slow cooker; stir well. Cover and cook on low setting for 6 to 8 hours.

# Beef Chop Suey

*Serve over white rice and sprinkle with sesame seeds.*

**stats**

**SERVES 6**

| | |
|---|---|
| Cooking time | 4–5 hours |
| Preparation time | 30 minutes |
| Attention | Minimal |
| Pot size | 6 quarts |

3 pounds flank steak

½ cup chopped celery

1 cup chopped bok choy

1 small chopped onion

½ cup water

2 tablespoons dark soy sauce

1½ tablespoon dark molasses

1 teaspoon hot sauce

1 tablespoon flour

2 tablespoons water

Combine all the ingredients except the flour and 2 tablespoons water in the slow cooker; mix well. Cook on high for 4 to 5 hours. Combine the flour and water, and add mixture to the contents of the slow cooker; stir until thick.

# Vietnamese Sweet-and-Sour Beef

*Serve with sliced cabbage in a vinegar and oil dressing.*

**SERVES 4**

Cooking time . . . . . . . 8–9 hours
Preparation time. . . . 20 minutes
Attention. . . . . . . . . . Minimal
Pot size . . . . . . . . . . . . 3–6 quarts

2 pounds round steak

2 cups carrots, sliced

2 cups pearl onions

1 medium-sized green bell pepper

2 large ripe tomatoes

2 tablespoons oil

2 (8-ounce) cans tomato sauce

⅓ cup vinegar

½ cup light molasses

1 teaspoon paprika

¼ cup sugar

1 teaspoon table salt

**1.** Cut the beef into 1-inch pieces. Peel the carrots and cut into ¼-inch-thick rounds. Remove the peels from the onions. Remove the stem and seeds from the green pepper and cut lengthwise into ¼-inch strips. Cut the tomatoes into 1-inch pieces.

**2.** Place the oil and steak in a skillet. Cook on medium-high heat until the meat is brown, stirring occasionally. Place this and all other ingredients in the slow cooker; stir so ingredients are mingled. Cover and cook on low setting 8 to 9 hours.

# Corned Beef Dinner

*Use slices of leftover corned beef from this recipe*
*to make a Classic Reuben (page 329).*

 **stats**

**SERVES 8**

| | |
|---|---|
| Cooking time | 6–8 hours |
| Preparation time | 30 minutes |
| Attention | Minimal |
| Pot size | 3–5 quarts |

6 carrots

6 potatoes

1 head cabbage

2 onions

2 cloves garlic

6 whole cloves

2 bay leaves

4 pounds corned beef brisket

1 cup water

**1.** Peel and halve the carrots and potatoes. Cut the cabbage into 8 wedges. Arrange the cut vegetables in the bottom of the slow cooker.

**2.** Slice the onions and mince the garlic. Mix with the cloves. Put half the onion mixture and one bay leaf on the vegetables in the slow cooker.

**3.** Cut the beef into serving-size slices. Arrange on the onion mixture, then cover with the remaining onion mixture and last bay leaf. Add the water.

**4.** Cover and heat on a low setting for 6 to 8 hours.

# Simple Beef with Vegetables

*Turnips become sweet and tender when cooked. For efficient cooking, try putting the harder root vegetables, like turnips, at the bottom of your slow cooker.*

*stats*

**SERVES 6**

Cooking time . . . . . . . 6–8 hours
Preparation time . . . . 30 minutes
Attention . . . . . . . . . . Minimal
Pot size . . . . . . . . . . . . 3–5 quarts

2 onions

2 leeks

½ head cabbage

2 stalks celery

4 pounds stew beef

4 carrots

2 turnips

½ teaspoon salt

12 peppercorns

1 cup water

**1.** Coarsely chop the onions. Slice the leeks and quarter the cabbage. Diagonally slice the celery. Cut the beef, carrots, and turnips into 1-inch sections.

**2.** Combine the cut vegetables and meat in the slow cooker. Add the salt, peppercorns, and water.

**3.** Cover and heat on a low setting for 6 to 8 hours.

# Beef in Red

*Wine, like vinegar, helps tenderize meats by breaking down the meat tissue.*
*Use your red wine of choice for this recipe.*

**stats**

**SERVES 6**

Cooking time . . . . . . . 6–8 hours
Preparation time. . . . 30 minutes
Attention. . . . . . . . . . Minimal
Pot size . . . . . . . . . . . 3–5 quarts

5 pounds beef

2 onions

2 carrots

1 cup red wine

1 cup water

1 bouquet garni

2 tablespoons butter

2 tablespoons flour

12 small red potatoes

**1.** Cube the beef. Slice the onions and carrots. Combine the beef, onions, carrots, wine, water, and bouquet garni. Cover and marinate for 24 hours in the refrigerator.

**2.** After marinating, transfer the beef to a pan; set aside the liquids and vegetables.

**3.** Sauté the beef in the butter in a pan over medium heat until the meat is browned. Stir in the flour and mix while heating until the flour browns.

**4.** Halve the potatoes. Combine the beef, marinade with vegetables, and potatoes in the slow cooker, arranging the potatoes on the bottom.

**5.** Cover and heat on a low setting for 6 to 8 hours.

# Slow Beef Roast

*This dish cooks all day, letting you relax for a while before you entertain in the evening. For a variation, try substituting goose for the roast.*

 **stats**

**SERVES 8**

| | |
|---|---|
| Cooking time | 6–8 hours |
| Preparation time | 30 minutes |
| Attention | Minimal |
| Pot size | 3–5 quarts |

*1 8-ounce can tomato sauce*

*2 tablespoons Worcestershire sauce*

*½ cup catsup*

*2 tablespoons brown sugar*

*2 tablespoons cider vinegar*

*½ teaspoon coarsely ground pepper*

*1 onion*

*1 clove garlic*

*3 slices raw bacon*

*4 pounds beef rump roast*

**1.** Mix the sauces, catsup, sugar, vinegar, and pepper in a small bowl.

**2.** Chop the onion and mince the garlic. Mix the onion and garlic. Cut the bacon into 1-inch pieces, and cut the roast into serving-size pieces.

**3.** Put half of the onion mixture in the bottom of the slow cooker, and sprinkle it with one-fourth of the sauce mixture.

**4.** Arrange the beef and bacon on top of this, and cover it with half of the remaining sauce mixture. Put the remaining onion mixture on the top, and cover with the rest of the sauce mixture.

**5.** Cover and heat on a low setting for 6 to 8 hours.

# Simple Beef and Potatoes

*Consider this a basic recipe, and add your own personality to it.*
*Use wild game instead of beef, or add your favorite herbs.*

**SERVES 6**

| | |
|---|---|
| Cooking time | 6–8 hours |
| Preparation time | 15 minutes |
| Attention | Minimal |
| Pot size | 3–5 quarts |

*2 pounds baby carrots*

*1 onion*

*6 potatoes*

*3 stalks celery*

*3 pounds beef roast*

*3 cubes beef bouillon*

*½ cup water*

**1.** Thinly slice the carrots, onion, potatoes, and celery. Transfer to the slow cooker in that order. Cube the beef, and arrange on top of the vegetables.

**2.** Dissolve the bouillon cubes in the water and pour over the beef.

**3.** Cover and heat on a low setting for 6 to 8 hours.

# Peppery Southwestern Beef

*Hot, sweet, spicy, smoky, and tart; this beef has it all. With slow cooking,*
*flavors blend and mature over time to create something unique.*

**stats**

**SERVES 8**

Cooking time . . . . . . . 6–8 hours
Preparation time . . . . 30 minutes
Attention . . . . . . . . . . Minimal
Pot size . . . . . . . . . . . . 3–5 quarts

½ cup catsup

1 tablespoon soy sauce

2 teaspoons Worcestershire sauce

1 tablespoon liquid smoke

¼ teaspoon red pepper flakes

¼ teaspoon ground nutmeg

2 teaspoons coarsely ground
pepper

2 teaspoons celery salt

¼ cup brown sugar

1 tablespoon fresh lemon juice

1 tablespoon prepared mustard

1 onion

1 clove garlic

½ cup water

4 pounds beef rump roast

**1.** Mix the catsup, sauces, liquid smoke, spices, celery salt, sugar, juice, and mustard in a small bowl.

**2.** Chop the onion and mince the garlic; mix the onion and garlic. Put half of the onion mixture in the bottom of the slow cooker. Add the water. Sprinkle the onions with one-fourth of the sauce mixture.

**3.** Cut the meat into serving-size pieces. Arrange it in the slow cooker, on top of the onion and sauce layers. Sprinkle the meat with half of the remaining sauce mixture.

**4.** Put the remaining onion mixture and sauce mixture on top of the meat.

**5.** Cover and heat on a low setting for 6 to 8 hours.

# Beef Brisket with Beer

*If you have time, you can brown the coated beef slices
and onion in a tablespoon of olive oil before cooking.*

**SERVES 6**

Cooking time . . . . . . . 6–8 hours

Preparation time. . . . 30 minutes

Attention. . . . . . . . . . Minimal

Pot size . . . . . . . . . . . 3–5 quarts

3 pounds beef brisket

½ teaspoon seasoning salt

¾ cup brown sugar

1 onion

1 can beer

**1.** Cut the beef into serving-size pieces and rub with seasoning salt and brown sugar. Thinly slice the onion. Arrange the beef and onion in the slow cooker and add the beer.

**2.** Cover and heat on a low setting for 6 to 8 hours.

# Flamed Beef

*Be sure to use caution when flaming the meat!*
*You can serve this dish with hot and buttery wide egg noodles.*

**stats**

**SERVES 6**

Cooking time . . . . . . . 5–7 hours
Preparation time . . . . 30 minutes
Attention . . . . . . . . . . Minimal
Pot size . . . . . . . . . . . 3–5 quarts

4 slices bacon

2½ pounds beef chuck

¼ cup flour

1 teaspoon salt

½ teaspoon pepper

¼ cup brandy

2 cloves garlic

1 onion

1 teaspoon thyme

¼ teaspoon marjoram

¼ teaspoon sage

½ cup water

1¾ cups burgundy

½ pound mushrooms

**1.** Sauté the bacon in a pan over medium heat until crisp. Set aside the bacon slices, leaving the bacon drippings in the pan.

**2.** Cube the beef. Combine the flour, salt, and pepper. Roll the beef cubes in the flour mixture. Sauté in the bacon drippings in the pan over medium heat until lightly browned. Drain the meat; transfer the browned beef cubes to the slow cooker.

**3.** Warm the brandy in a saucepan over medium heat until it steams, then pour the brandy over the meat in the slow cooker and light it.

**4.** Mince the garlic and dice the onion. Add the garlic, onion, herbs, water, and half of the burgundy to the slow cooker after the flame is extinguished. Cover and heat on a low setting for 4 to 6 hours.

**5.** Slice the mushrooms. An hour before serving add the mushrooms and the remaining burgundy.

# Peking Gin Roast

*Don't be alarmed by the coffee and gin in this recipe.*
*They add a nice rich flavor to the meat.*

 **SERVES 10**

Cooking time . . . . . . . 6–8 hours
Preparation time . . . . 30 minutes
Attention . . . . . . . . . . Minimal
Pot size . . . . . . . . . . . . 3–5 quarts

1 onion

5 pounds beef roast

1 cup vinegar

2 tablespoons oil

2 cups black coffee

1 cup water

½ teaspoon salt

¼ teaspoon pepper

½ cup gin

**1.** Slice the onion. Cut the meat into serving-size pieces and mix with the onion slices. Put the meat mixture in a glass dish and cover with the vinegar. Refrigerate for 24 to 48 hours, then discard the vinegar.

**2.** Sauté the meat and onions in oil in a pan over high heat until the meat is browned. Transfer the mixture to the slow cooker.

**3.** Pour the coffee and water over the meat and onions.

**4.** Cover and heat on a low setting for 6 to 8 hours.

**5.** Half an hour before serving, add the salt, pepper, and gin.

# Savory Beef Stroganoff

*This dish is best prepared the day before, and left overnight in the refrigerator.*
*Then reheat and serve over egg noodles with poppy seeds.*

**stats**

**SERVES 6**

Cooking time ....... 6–8 hours
Preparation time .... 30 minutes
Attention .......... Moderate
Pot size ............ 3–5 quarts

1 clove garlic

2 stalks celery

1 onion

1 pound mushrooms

2 tablespoons butter

2 pounds beef steak

3 tablespoons flour

2 tablespoons butter

2 tablespoons catsup

2 tablespoons sherry

1 cup beef broth

1 tablespoon Worcestershire
sauce

1 small bunch parsley

½ cup sour cream

**1.** Mince the garlic and slice the celery. Transfer to the slow cooker. Slice the onion and mushrooms. Sauté in butter in a pan over medium heat until the onions are soft. Set aside the mushroom mixture but keep the juices in the pan.

**2.** Slice the meat into ¼-inch strips. Coat with the flour, and sauté in the pan with the mushroom juices, plus an additional 2 tablespoons butter, until lightly browned. Mix the onion and meat mixtures together as they are transferred to the slow cooker.

**3.** Mix the catsup, sherry, broth, and Worcestershire sauce in a small bowl. Pour the mixture into the slow cooker. Cover and heat on a low setting for 6 to 8 hours.

**4.** Let stand overnight in the refrigerator.

**5.** Reheat the mixture. Mince the parsley. Half an hour before serving, stir in the sour cream and parsley.

# Poultry

# Peachy Georgia Chicken Legs

*Serve with a green salad for a fresh and delicious meal.*

**SERVES 4**

Cooking time . . . . . . . 5 hours
Preparation time. . . . 30 minutes
Attention. . . . . . . . . . Minimal
Pot size . . . . . . . . . . . . 4–6 quarts

4 ripe peaches

8 chicken drum sticks

1 cup dried prunes

3 tablespoons water

1 tablespoon sugar

Salt and pepper to taste

Peel the peaches; cut into 1-inch pieces, removing and discarding the pits. Place chicken drum sticks in the slow cooker. Stir together the peaches, prunes, water, sugar, salt, and pepper in a small bowl; pour mixture over the chicken. Cover and cook for 5 hours on the high setting.

# Barbecued Chicken and Beans Casserole

*Perfect for summertime—enjoy the day outdoors,*
*then come home to this yummy meal.*

**SERVES 4**

Cooking time . . . . . . . 8–10 hours
Preparation time . . . . 10 minutes
Attention . . . . . . . . . . Minimal
Pot size . . . . . . . . . . . . 3–6 quarts

2 cups (16 ounces) canned pork
and beans

3-pound chicken, cut into serving
pieces

¼ cup ketchup

2 tablespoons peach marmalade

2 teaspoons dried minced onion

¼ teaspoon soy sauce

¼ cup brown sugar

Place the beans in the slow cooker. Add the chicken pieces on top of the beans; do not stir. Mix the ketchup, marmalade, onion, soy sauce, and brown sugar in a small mixing bowl; pour mixture over the top of the chicken. Cover and cook on low setting for 8 to 10 hours.

# Heroic Chicken Livers

*This delicate-tasting dish is best served over thick egg noodles.*

 *stats*

**SERVES 4**

Cooking time . . . . . . . 6 hours
Preparation time. . . . 45 minutes
Attention. . . . . . . . . . Medium
Pot size . . . . . . . . . . . . 4–6 quarts

1 pound chicken livers

¼ pound lean, thick-cut bacon

1 teaspoon whole black peppercorns

1 large leek

½ pound (1 cup) mushrooms, sliced

½ cup flour

1 teaspoon table salt

1 cup chicken broth

1 (10¾-ounce) can golden mushroom condensed soup

¼ cup dry white wine

**1.** Cut the chicken livers into ½- inch pieces. Cut the bacon into 1-inch pieces. Wrap the whole peppercorns in paper towels; smash the peppercorns with a hammer. Cut the top and roots off the leek, discard them, and thoroughly wash the leek; Chop coarsely. Clean the mushrooms by wiping individually with a moistened paper towel; slice the mushrooms paper-thin.

**2.** Fry the bacon in a large skillet on medium heat Remove the bacon from the skillet when the bacon is crispy; set the bacon aside and retain the grease in the skillet. Mix together the flour, salt, and pepper. Coat the chicken livers in the flour mixture. Cook the livers in the bacon drippings until golden brown. Remove the chicken livers from the skillet with a slotted spoon and place them in the slow cooker. Place the bacon on top of the chicken livers. Pour the chicken broth into the skillet, mixing to combine with the grease; pour mixture over the chicken livers and bacon. Add the golden mushroom soup, leeks, mushrooms, and wine. Cover and cook on low for 6 hours.

# Dilled Turkey Breast

*Slice the turkey breast and drizzle with the sauce before serving.*
*Sprinkle with additional dill weed.*

**stats**

**SERVES 8**

Cooking time . . . . . . . 7–9 hours
Preparation time . . . . 30 minutes
Attention . . . . . . . . . . Minimal
Pot size . . . . . . . . . . . . 8 quart

1 boneless turkey breast

1 teaspoon table salt

½ teaspoon ground pepper

2 teaspoons dill weed, plus extra
for garnish

¼ cup water

1 tablespoon red wine vinegar

3 tablespoons flour

1 cup sour cream

**1.** Sprinkle the turkey breast with salt, pepper, and half of the dill; place in the slow cooker. Add water and vinegar. Cover and cook on low for 7 to 9 hours or until tender.

**2.** Remove the turkey breast. Turn the slow cooker to high. Dissolve the flour in a small amount of water and stir into the meat drippings in the cooker. Add the remaining dill. Cook on high until the sauce thickens. Turn off heat. Stir in the sour cream.

# Chicken Breast with Mushrooms and Peas

*Serve with fresh orange and apple slices.*

*stats*

**SERVES 2**

Cooking time . . . . . . . 6–8 hours
Preparation time . . . . 20 minutes
Attention . . . . . . . . . . Medium
Pot size . . . . . . . . . . . . 2–6 quarts

1 small white onion

12 ounces fresh sliced mushrooms

2 tablespoons minced green onion

2 boneless, skinless chicken breasts

3 tablespoons flour

¼ teaspoon ground tarragon

¼ teaspoon salt

½ teaspoon pepper

1 cup milk

½ cup fresh or frozen peas

**1.** Peel the onion and slice ¼-inch thick. Clean the mushrooms by wiping with a damp cloth; slice paper-thin. Remove the roots and the first layer of peel from the green onions and mince the onions, including the green stems. Place the chicken breasts on the bottom of the slow cooker, then layer the onions, green onions, and mushrooms on top of the chicken breasts. Cook covered on low heat for 4 hours.

**2.** After the 4 hours are up, blend the flour, tarragon, salt, pepper, and milk by stirring slowly. Pour mixture over the chicken. Add the peas.

**3.** Cook covered on low setting 2 to 4 hours, until thick, stirring occasionally.

# Orange Chicken

*Serve over white rice for a light-tasting meal.*

**stats**

**SERVES 6**

Cooking time . . . . . . . 8–9 hours
Preparation time . . . . 30 minutes
Attention . . . . . . . . . . Minimal
Pot size . . . . . . . . . . . 4–6 quarts

3 pounds chicken breasts

2 garlic cloves

2 tablespoons diced green pepper

3 medium oranges

1 cup orange juice

⅓ cup chili sauce

2 tablespoons soy sauce

1 tablespoon molasses

1 teaspoon dry mustard

½ teaspoon table salt

**1.** Remove the skin from the chicken breasts. Peel the garlic and mince with a sharp kitchen knife. Remove the stem and seeds from the green pepper and chop into ¼-inch pieces. Remove the peels from the oranges and separate oranges into slices.

**2.** Place the chicken breasts in the bottom of the slow cooker. Combine the orange juice, chili sauce, soy sauce, molasses, dry mustard, garlic, and salt in a medium-sized bowl; mix well. Cover and cook on low setting for 8 to 9 hours.

**3.** Thirty minutes before serving, add the oranges and green pepper to the slow cooker; stir well. Cover and cook on low for the remaining 30 minutes.

# Cranberry Barbecued Chicken

*Serve with cauliflower for a nice mix of flavors.*

**SERVES 4**

Cooking time . . . . . . . 6–8 hours

Preparation time. . . . 10 minutes

Attention. . . . . . . . . . Minimal

Pot size . . . . . . . . . . . . 3–6 quarts

3 pounds chicken breasts

½ teaspoon table salt

½ teaspoon ground black pepper

2 celery ribs, chopped

1 cup barbecue sauce

1 medium-sized yellow onion, chopped

2 cups whole berry cranberry sauce

Remove the skin from the chicken breasts and place the meat in the bottom of the slow cooker. Cover with remaining ingredients. Cover slow cooker and cook on low setting for 6 to 8 hours.

# Easy Italian Chicken Legs

*Remove the meat from the bones and serve on hard rolls.*

**SERVES 4**

| | |
|---|---|
| Cooking time | 8–10 hours |
| Preparation time | 10 minutes |
| Attention | Minimal |
| Pot size | 3–6 quarts |

*3 pounds chicken legs*

*1 package dry Italian dressing mix*

*1 (12-ounce) can or bottle beer, a lager or pilsner is best*

Remove the skin from the chicken legs and place the chicken in the slow cooker. Mix the beer with the Italian dressing mix in a medium-sized bowl; pour over the chicken legs. Cook covered on low setting 8 to 10 hours.

# Mandarin Chicken Breasts

*Get a taste of Asia with these sweet and savory chicken breasts.*

*stats*

**SERVES 4**

Cooking time . . . . . . . 6–8 hours
Preparation time . . . . 20 minutes
Attention . . . . . . . . . . Minimal
Pot size . . . . . . . . . . . . 3–6 quarts

3 pounds chicken breasts

1 medium-sized red bell pepper

1 yellow onion

½ cup chicken broth

½ cup orange juice

½ cup ketchup

2 tablespoons soy sauce

1 tablespoon light molasses

1 tablespoon prepared mustard

½ teaspoon garlic salt

1 cup fresh or frozen peas

1 (11-ounce) can mandarin oranges

2 teaspoons flour

**1.** Remove the skin from the chicken and discard. Remove the stem and seeds from red pepper and cut into ¼-inch strips. Peel the onion and cut into ¼-inch pieces.

**2.** Place the chicken in the slow cooker. Combine the broth, juice, ketchup, soy sauce molasses, mustard, and garlic salt in a mixing bowl; stir until well combined and pour over chicken. Add the onions, peas, and green peppers. Cover and cook on low setting for 6 to 8 hours.

**3.** Thirty minutes before serving, remove the chicken and vegetables from the slow cooker. Measure one cup of liquid from the slow cooker and place it in a saucepan. Discard the remaining liquid. Bring the liquid in the saucepan to a boil. Drain the oranges, retaining 1 tablespoon of the drained juice; mix this juice with the flour. Add mixture to the boiling liquid. Stir in the oranges.

**4.** Put the chicken and vegetables back into the slow cooker. Pour the orange sauce over the chicken. Cover and cook on low setting for the remaining 30 minutes.

**5.** Sprinkle with sesame seeds before serving.

# Tropical Chicken

*Serve with a medley of fresh tropical fruits:*
*kiwi, papaya, banana, and guava, for example.*

**SERVES 6**

| | |
|---|---|
| Cooking time | 7–9 hours |
| Preparation time | 10 minutes |
| Attention | Minimal |
| Pot size | 3–6 quarts |

3 *pounds chicken breasts*

¼ *cup molasses*

2 *tablespoons Worcestershire sauce*

2 *teaspoons Dijon mustard*

¼ *teaspoon hot pepper sauce*

2 *tablespoons pineapple juice*

¼ *cup dried coconut*

**1.** Remove the skin and bones from the chicken breasts and discard.

**2.** Combine the molasses, Worcestershire sauce, mustard, hot pepper sauce, and pineapple juice in a small mixing bowl.

**3.** Brush mixture on both sides of the chicken breasts using a pastry brush. Cover and cook on low setting for 7 to 9 hours.

**4.** Sprinkle with coconut before serving.

# Chicken Fajitas

*Spoon onto warm flour tortillas and top with chopped*
*tomato, sour cream, grated Colby cheese, and guacamole.*

*stats*

**SERVES 4**

Cooking time . . . . . . . 6–8 hours
Preparation time . . . . 20 minutes
Attention . . . . . . . . . . Minimal
Pot size . . . . . . . . . . . . 3–6 quarts

1 pound chicken breasts

1 medium-sized yellow onion

2 garlic cloves

1 green bell pepper

1 red bell pepper

2 tablespoons lime juice

½ teaspoon oregano

½ teaspoon ground cumin

½ teaspoon chili powder

½ teaspoon ground black pepper

**1.** Remove the bones and skin from the chicken breasts and cut into ½-inch-wide strips. Peel the onion and cut into ¼-inch-thick rings; put the onion in the slow cooker. Peel the garlic and mince with a sharp kitchen knife. Remove the stems and seeds from the green and red peppers and cut into ¼-inch-wide strips.

**2.** Combine the garlic, lime juice, oregano, cumin, chili powder, and black pepper in a medium-sized mixing bowl. Add the chicken and toss well to coat. Pour the chicken and juice mixture over the onion. Cover and cook on low setting for 6 to 8 hours. About 30 minutes before serving, stir in the green and red pepper strips; continue cooking, covered, on low for the remaining 30 minutes.

# Chicken with Black Olives and Artichokes

*A Mediterranean combination, olives and artichokes
add a great tang to this chicken!*

**SERVES 6**

Cooking time . . . . . . . 5–6 hours
Preparation time . . . . 20 minutes
Attention . . . . . . . . . . Minimal
Pot size . . . . . . . . . . . . 3–6 quarts

*6 chicken breasts*

*1 medium-sized white onion*

*6 garlic cloves*

*1 cup dry white wine*

*2 cups chicken broth*

*2 cups water*

*1 cup canned, sliced black olives,
including juice*

*1 cup canned artichoke hearts,
including juice, cut up*

*1 cup dry shell macaroni*

*1 envelop dry onion soup mix*

**1.** Remove the bones and skin from the chicken breasts and discard. Peel the onion and slice into ¼-inch-thick rings. Peel the garlic and mince with a sharp kitchen knife.

**2.** Put the chicken in the slow cooker; top with onion. Combine the wine, broth, water, black olives, artichoke hearts, garlic, and macaroni in a medium-sized mixing bowl; pour mixture over the chicken and onions. Sprinkle the onion soup mix on top. Cover and cook on low setting for 5 to 6 hours.

# Chicken Cacciatore #1

*Serve over hot spaghetti noodles for an authentic Italian meal.*

**SERVES 4**

| | |
|---|---|
| Cooking time | 8–10 hours |
| Preparation time | 25 minutes |
| Attention | Minimal |
| Pot size | 3–8 quarts |

*3 pounds chicken*

*3 garlic cloves*

*1 cup fresh mushrooms, quartered*

*1 medium-sized yellow onion*

*1 cup sliced black olives*

*¼ cup flour*

*2 tablespoons olive oil*

*6 cups tomato juice*

*1 (12-ounce) can tomato paste*

*2 tablespoons dried parsley*

*2 tablespoons sugar*

*2 teaspoons table salt*

*1 tablespoon dried oregano*

*½ teaspoon dried thyme*

*1 bay leaf*

**1.** Cut the chicken into serving-sized pieces. Peel the garlic and mince using a sharp kitchen knife. Clean the mushrooms by wiping with a damp cloth and slice into quarters. Peel the onion and slice into ¼-inch-thick rings. Drain the black olives.

**2.** Place the flour and chicken in a plastic bag and shake to coat. Heat the olive oil in a medium-sized skillet on medium-high heat and brown the chicken. Transfer the chicken to the slow cooker. Combine the remaining ingredients in a medium-sized mixing bowl and pour over the chicken. Cover and cook on low setting for 8 to 10 hours.

# Chicken à la King

*This simple and delicious meal will make mouths water.*

 **SERVES 4**

Cooking time . . . . . . . 6–7 hours
Preparation time. . . . 15 minutes
Attention. . . . . . . . . . Minimal
Pot size . . . . . . . . . . . . 3–6 quarts

4 chicken breasts

1 medium-sized white onion

1 (10¾-ounce) can cream of chicken condensed soup

3 tablespoons flour

½ teaspoon ground black pepper

1 cup fresh or canned peas

2 tablespoons chopped pimientos

½ teaspoon paprika

**1.** Remove the bones and skin from the chicken breasts and discard. Cut the chicken into 1-inch cubes; place in the slow cooker. Peel the onion and chop into ¼-inch pieces

**2.** Combine the soup, flour, and pepper in a medium-sized mixing bowl; pour mixture over chicken. Cover and cook on low setting for 5 to 6 hours. Stir in the peas, onions, pimientos, and paprika. Cover and cook on low setting for 1 additional hour.

# Nebraskan Creamed Chicken Soup

*Serve with fresh fruit for a completely balanced meal.*

**stats**

**SERVES 4**

Cooking time ....... 8–10 hours
Preparation time.... 10 minutes
Attention.......... Medium
Pot size ............ 3–6 quarts

1 cup chicken, cubed

2 celery ribs

4 medium carrots

1 medium-sized white onion

1 small zucchini

½ cup (4 ounces) canned pimientos, diced

1 cup fresh peas

1 cup fresh sweet corn

½ cup uncooked rice

3 cups chicken broth

2 cups prepared Alfredo sauce

**1.** Chop the chicken into ½-inch pieces. Slice the celery ribs into ¼-inch pieces. Peel and slice the carrots into ¼-inch rounds. Peel and slice the onion into ¼-inch pieces. Chop the zucchini into ½-inch pieces. Dice the pimientos into ¼-inch pieces.

**2.** Add all ingredients except the Alfredo sauce to the slow cooker; stir gently. Cover and cook on low setting for 8 to 10 hours. A half-hour before serving, stir in the Alfredo sauce. Cover and continue cooking on low.

# Easy BBQ Chicken Dinner

*You can dress up this simple dish by making your own barbecue sauce.*

**SERVES 4–6**

Cooking time . . . . . . . 3–4 hours

Preparation time . . . . 15 minutes

Attention . . . . . . . . . . Minimal

Pot size . . . . . . . . . . . . 3–5 quarts

1 onion

1 pound baby red potatoes

1 pound mushrooms

2 pounds chicken breasts

1½ cups barbecue sauce

**1.** Thinly slice the onion and potatoes; halve the mushrooms. Arrange in the slow cooker in that order; lay the chicken on top. Cover with barbecue sauce.

**2.** Cover and heat on a low setting for 3 to 4 hours.

# Chili Beer Chicken

*This is definitely a safe bet for a Super Bowl party,
but it is also a tasty addition to a holiday buffet.*

**stats**

**SERVES 6**

Cooking time . . . . . . . 3–4 hours
Preparation time . . . . 45 minutes
Attention . . . . . . . . . . Minimal
Pot size . . . . . . . . . . . . 3–5 quarts

*3 pounds chicken*

*½ cup flour*

*½ teaspoon salt*

*½ teaspoon pepper*

*2 onions*

*6 tablespoons butter*

*1 bottle beer*

*1 cup tomato sauce*

*½ teaspoon chili powder*

*½ teaspoon salt*

**1.** Cut the chicken into serving-size pieces. Coat the chicken pieces in a mixture of the flour, ½ teaspoon salt, and pepper.

**2.** Slice the onions. Sauté the chicken pieces and half of the sliced onions in butter in a pan over medium heat until the chicken is browned.

**3.** Arrange the chicken mixture and the remaining uncooked onion in the slow cooker.

**4.** Mix the beer, tomato sauce, chili powder, and remaining salt in a bowl; pour the mixture over the chicken and onions.

**5.** Cover and heat on a low setting for 3 to 4 hours.

# Chicken Cacciatore #2

*Serve this classic dish with wild rice, egg noodles,*
*or small pumpernickel rolls to soak up the sauce.*

*stats* **SERVES 6**

Cooking time....... 4–5 hours
Preparation time.... 45 minutes
Attention.......... Minimal
Pot size............ 3–5 quarts

3 pounds chicken

1 onion

½ cup olive oil

1 clove garlic

5 tomatoes

½ teaspoon salt

¼ teaspoon pepper

1 cup chicken broth

½ cup white wine

**1.** Cut the chicken into serving-size pieces. Slice the onion. Sauté the chicken pieces and onion in olive oil in a pan over medium heat until the chicken is browned.

**2.** Crush the garlic. Coarsely chop the garlic and tomatoes.

**3.** Combine the chicken mixture, garlic, and tomatoes in the slow cooker. Sprinkle with the salt and pepper; add the broth.

**4.** Cover and heat on low setting for 3 to 4 hours.

**5.** Half an hour before serving, add the wine.

# Tamales with Chicken and Olives

*You can buy tamales fresh, frozen, or bottled, but they're much better made from scratch. Try the recipe for Homemade Tamales (page 62).*

**stats**

**SERVES 6**

Cooking time . . . . . . . 3–4 hours
Preparation time. . . . 45 minutes
Attention. . . . . . . . . . Minimal
Pot size . . . . . . . . . . . . 3–5 quarts

1 tablespoon butter

1 tablespoon flour

1 cup chicken broth

1 cup olives, pitted

1 pound boneless chicken meat

1 cup tomato puree

1 cup corn

¼ cup raisins

½ teaspoon salt

2 teaspoons chili powder

8 large tamales (or 16 small)

½ cup shredded Monterey Jack cheese

**1.** Melt the butter in a saucepan over low heat; add the flour and stir to blend and thicken. Blend in the chicken broth and mix until smooth over low heat.

**2.** Mince the olives and cube the chicken meat. Add the olives, chicken, tomato puree, corn, raisins, salt, and chili powder to the thickened chicken sauce.

**3.** Remove the husks from the tamales and arrange the tamales in the slow cooker. Top each layer of tamales with sauce and cheese.

**4.** Cover and heat on a low setting for 3 to 4 hours.

# Cinnamon Chicken Pasta

*Cinnamon and chicken aren't commonly combined,*
*but they work together perfectly in this recipe.*

**stats**

### SERVES 6

Cooking time . . . . . . . 4–5 hours

Preparation time . . . . 45 minutes

Attention . . . . . . . . . . Minimal

Pot size . . . . . . . . . . . . 3–5 quarts

3 pounds chicken

½ teaspoon salt

½ teaspoon pepper

½ lemon

½ cup olive oil

6 ounces tomato paste

1 cup water

1 stick cinnamon bark

4 cups cooked pasta, firm

**1.** Cut the chicken into serving-size pieces. Roll the chicken pieces in salt and pepper, then drizzle with the juice from the ½ lemon. Sauté the chicken pieces in olive oil in a pan over medium heat until lightly browned. Transfer the chicken to a slow cooker, but retain the juices in the pan.

**2.** Add the tomato paste, water, and cinnamon stick to the same pan and stir over low heat until well mixed with the chicken juices.

**3.** Pour the tomato mixture over the chicken in the slow cooker.

**4.** Cover and heat on a low setting for 3 to 4 hours.

**5.** Half an hour before serving, stir the pasta into the sauce. Remove cinnamon stick before serving, if not completely dissolved.

# White Pasta Sauce with Chicken

*Use fresh Parmesan or Romano cheese, grated from a block,*
*instead of the packaged kind. Serve with fresh pasta.*

*stats*

**SERVES 5**

Cooking time . . . . . . . 3–4 hours
Preparation time. . . . 60 minutes
Attention. . . . . . . . . . Minimal
Pot size . . . . . . . . . . . . 3–5 quarts

3 pounds boneless, skinless chicken

2 tablespoons olive oil

2 cloves garlic

1 green pepper

½ pound mushrooms

4 ounces pimento

2 tablespoons flour

1½ cups chicken broth

½ teaspoon salt

¼ teaspoon pepper

2 tablespoons Worcestershire sauce

6 stalks celery

¼ pound Parmesan cheese

**1.** Cube the chicken; sauté in olive oil in a pan over medium heat until the chicken is browned. Set aside the chicken pieces. Retain the chicken juices in the pan.

**2.** Crush the garlic. Coarsely chop the garlic, green pepper, and mushrooms. Slice the pimento into thin strips. Sauté the garlic, green pepper, mushrooms, and pimento in the juices and oil remaining from the chicken. Add the flour and stir over low heat to blend and thicken. Add the chicken broth and stir over low heat until smooth. Remove from heat and add the salt, pepper, and Worcestershire sauce.

**3.** Thinly slice the celery. Put half of the celery in the slow cooker, then the chicken, half of the mushroom mixture, the remainder of the celery, and the remainder of the mushroom mixture.

**4.** Cover and heat on a low setting for 3 to 4 hours.

**5.** Grate the cheese and provide as a garnish.

# Pork

# Salt Pork in Mustard Greens

*This may be an acquired taste, but give this salt pork a shot.*
*It could be a new family favorite.*

 **stats**

**SERVES 4**

| | |
|---|---|
| Cooking time | 6–8 hours |
| Preparation time | 20 minutes |
| Attention | Minimal |
| Pot size | 3–6 quarts |

1 pound salt pork

2 large white onions

4 garlic cloves

4 large bunches mustard greens

6 cups water

1 cup dry white wine

1 tablespoon jalapeño pepper sauce

2 tablespoons soy sauce

1 teaspoon table salt

**1.** Cut the salt pork into 1-inch pieces. Remove the peel and cut the onions into ¼-inch-thick slices. Peel the garlic and mince with a sharp paring knife. Wash the mustard greens and tear into 2-inch pieces.

**2.** Mix the water and wine in a separate bowl. Sauté the meat, onions, and garlic in ½ cup of the water and wine mixture in a large skillet on medium-high heat until the onions are limp and transparent. Put all the ingredients in the slow cooker. Cover and cook on low setting for 6 to 8 hours.

# Prosciutto, Walnut, and Olive Pasta Sauce

*Serve over spinach linguine noodles with a side of garlic toast.*

**stats**

**SERVES 4**

| | |
|---|---|
| Cooking time | 6–8 hours |
| Preparation time | 25 minutes |
| Attention | Minimal |
| Pot size | 3–6 quarts |

½ pound thin-sliced prosciutto

1 red bell pepper

3 garlic cloves

¼ cup olive oil, divided in half

1 cup chopped walnuts

½ cup chopped fresh parsley

¼ cup chopped fresh basil

½ cup chopped black olives, drained

**1.** Cut the prosciutto into ½-inch pieces. Remove the stem and seeds from the red pepper; cut into ¼-inch strips. Brush the pepper strips with half of the olive oil and bake in a 350°F oven for 1 hour. Peel and mince the garlic with a sharp kitchen knife. Chop the walnuts, parsley, basil, and olives into ¼-inch pieces.

**2.** Put the remaining olive oil in a medium-sized skillet and sauté the garlic on medium-high heat until the garlic is brown. Remove and set aside the garlic so it doesn't burn. Add the prosciutto and sauté until crisp. Add the walnuts and sauté until they are brown. Add the cooked garlic

**3.** Put all ingredients in the slow cooker; stir until well mixed. Cover and cook on low setting for 6 to 8 hours.

# Ham and Asparagus Roll-ups

*Garlic bread and pickled vegetables are the perfect complement to this dish.*

**SERVES 6**

Cooking time . . . . . . . 6–8 hours
Preparation time . . . . 10 minutes
Attention . . . . . . . . . . Minimal
Pot size . . . . . . . . . . . . 2–6 quarts

12 thin slices ham
24 fresh asparagus spears
12 slices Swiss cheese
1 teaspoon garlic salt
½ cup chicken broth

**1.** Lay the ham slices flat on a cutting board. Top each with two asparagus spears. Sprinkle with garlic salt. Top each with a slice of Swiss cheese. Roll up so that the asparagus spears stick out of both ends.

**2.** Put the chicken broth in the slow cooker. Add the ham roll-ups. Cover and cook on low setting for 6 to 8 hours, or until asparagus is soft but not mushy.

# Ham Sandwiches

*Sound so simple, bit add a couple of extra ingredients
and this will be the best Ham Sandwich you've ever had!*

 **SERVES 8**

Cooking time . . . . . . . 8–10 hours
Preparation time. . . . 10 minutes
Attention. . . . . . . . . . Minimal
Pot size . . . . . . . . . . . . 2–4 quarts

*2 pounds ham, cut into slices*

*2 cups apple juice*

*1 cup brown sugar*

*2 teaspoons Dijon mustard*

**1.** Combine the apple juice, brown sugar, and mustard. Put the ham in the bottom of the slow cooker and pour the liquid mixture over the top. Cover and cook on low setting for 8 to 10 hours. Remove the ham and discard the juice.

**2.** Put ham on your choice of bread and enjoy.

# Cherry Pork Chops

*Heat the remaining half of the cherry pie filling
and ladle it onto the pork chops before serving.*

 **SERVES 6**

Cooking time . . . . . . . 4–5 hours
Preparation time. . . . 15 minutes
Attention. . . . . . . . . . Minimal
Pot size . . . . . . . . . . . . 4–6 quarts

6 pork chops
½ teaspoon table salt
½ teaspoon ground black pepper
1 (21-ounce) can cherry pie filling
1 chicken bouillon cube
2 teaspoons lemon juice

**1.** Place the pork chops in a large skillet on the stove. Brown on medium-high heat for 5 minutes. Sprinkle with salt and pepper.

**2.** Mix half of the can of cherry pie filling, the crushed bouillon cube, and the lemon juice in the slow cooker. Place the pork chops on top of mixture. Cover and cook on low setting for 4 to 5 hours.

# Roast Pork with Ginger and Cashew Stuffing

*This is a wonderful winter meal when served with a hearty vegetable—try squash!*

**SERVES 8**

Cooking time....... 8–10 hours
Preparation time.... 30 minutes
Attention.......... Minimal
Pot size............ 3–6 quarts

¾ cup yellow onion, diced

1½ teaspoons fresh ginger, grated

1 cup cashews, chopped

1 teaspoon orange rind, grated

3 tablespoons parsley, chopped

2 eggs

2 tablespoons butter

4 cups corn bread crumbs

1 teaspoon table salt

1 teaspoon ground black pepper

6-pound pork roast

**1.** Peel and chop the onion into ¼-inch pieces. Grate the ginger finely with a vegetable grater. Chop the cashews into ¼-inch pieces. Grate the orange rind without peeling the orange. Chop the parsley into ⅛-inch pieces. Lightly beat the eggs with a fork until yolk and whites are well integrated.

**2.** Melt the butter in a large frying pan on the stove at medium heat. Add the onions, cashews, and ginger and cook for five minutes, stirring. Transfer to the slow cooker and add orange rind, parsley, bread crumbs, salt, pepper, and eggs. Stir well so that all the ingredients are well mixed.

**3.** Push the stuffing to the sides of the slow cooker and place the pork roast in the pocket. Cook covered on low setting for 8 to 10 hours.

# Pork Pisole

*To complement the flavors in this dish, serve it with*
*a salad of field greens with a red wine vinegar dressing.*

**SERVES 4**

Cooking time . . . . . . . 5–6 hours
Preparation time . . . . 20 minutes
Attention . . . . . . . . . . Minimal
Pot size . . . . . . . . . . . . 3–6 quarts

*2 pounds pork chops*

*1 large white onion*

*1 garlic clove*

*4 ripe, fresh tomatoes*

*1 15-ounce can white hominy*

*1 15-ounce can yellow hominy*

*2 teaspoons chili powder*

*1 teaspoon table salt*

*½ teaspoon thyme*

**1.** Debone the pork chops and cut the meat into 1-inch cubes. Peel and chop the onion into ¼-inch pieces. Peel and mince the garlic using a sharp paring knife. Place the pork in a large skillet on medium-high heat and cook until brown, about 5 minutes (you may need to add a bit of oil if using very lean pork). Add the onion and garlic; turn the heat down to medium and sauté for 5 more minutes.

**2.** Chop the tomatoes into 1-inch pieces. Combine the pork, onion, garlic, tomatoes, hominy, and spices in the slow cooker. Cook covered on low setting for 5 to 6 hours.

# Fall Is in the Air Pork Roast

*Serve with fresh green beans and mashed potatoes.*

**SERVES 8**

Cooking time ....... 8–10 hours
Preparation time.... 15 minutes
Attention.......... Minimal
Pot size ........... 4–6 quarts

*1 cup diced fresh cranberries*

*1 teaspoon grated orange peel*

*4-pound pork roast*

*1 teaspoon table salt*

*1 teaspoon ground black pepper*

*¼ cup honey*

*⅛ teaspoon ground cloves*

*⅛ teaspoon ground nutmeg*

**1.** Chop the cranberries into ¼-inch pieces. Grate the orange peel while still on the orange by rubbing it over a vegetable grater.

**2.** Place the pork roast in the slow cooker. Sprinkle with salt and pepper. Combine the cranberries, orange peel, honey, cloves, and nutmeg; mix well. Pour mixture over the pork roast. Cover and cook on low setting for 8 to 10 hours.

# Bavarian Pork Chops

*This Old World, hearty meal will excite and surprise your group!*

**SERVES 6**

Cooking time . . . . . . . 7–8 hours

Preparation time . . . . 15 minutes

Attention . . . . . . . . . . Minimal

Pot size . . . . . . . . . . . . 3–6 quarts

6 pork chops

2 cups sauerkraut

¼ cup brown sugar

1 envelope dry onion soup mix

1 teaspoon caraway seeds

½ cup water

Place the pork chops in the slow cooker. Drain sauerkraut. Combine the sauerkraut, brown sugar, onion soup mix, caraway seeds, and water in a medium-sized bowl; pour mixture over the pork chops. Cover and cook on low setting for 7 to 8 hours.

# Peachy Keen Pork Chops

*Offset the sweet taste of this meal by serving it with pickled cauliflower and beets.*

**SERVES 6**

Cooking time . . . . . . . 4–6 hours

Preparation time. . . . 15 minutes

Attention. . . . . . . . . . Minimal

Pot size . . . . . . . . . . . 3–6 quarts

*6 pork chops*

*1 teaspoon table salt*

*½ teaspoon ground black pepper*

*1 (29-ounce) can peach halves in syrup*

*¼ cup syrup from peaches*

*¼ cup brown sugar*

*¼ teaspoon ground cinnamon*

*¼ teaspoon ground cloves*

*1 (8-ounce) can tomato sauce*

*¼ cup vinegar*

**1.** Place the pork chops in a large skillet on the stove; sprinkle with salt and pepper. Brown for 5 minutes at medium-high heat. Drain off the fat and place the pork chops in the slow cooker. Place the drained peach halves on top of the pork chops.

**2.** Combine the ¼ cup of syrup from the peaches, the brown sugar, cinnamon, cloves, tomato sauce, and vinegar; pour mixture over the peaches and pork chops. Cover and cook on low setting for 4 to 6 hours.

# German-Style Ham Hocks

*A traditional German meal calls for baked beans and brown beer with this dish.*

 **stats**

**SERVES 4**

| | |
|---|---|
| Cooking time | 8–10 hours |
| Preparation time | 15 minutes |
| Attention | Minimal |
| Pot size | 3–6 quarts |

*4 smoked ham hocks*

*2 cans (15-ounce) sauerkraut, liquid retained*

*4 large white potatoes, peeled and quartered*

*½ teaspoon ground black pepper*

Place all the ingredients in the slow cooker including the liquid from the canned sauerkraut. Cover and cook on low setting for 8 to 10 hours. Remove the ham hocks and take the meat off the bones. Discard the bones and return the meat to the slow cooker.

# Blueberry Pork Roast

*Complement the sweet flavor of this dish by serving
it with spinach or another bitter vegetable.*

**SERVES 6**

Cooking time . . . . . . . 7–8 hours
Preparation time . . . . 20 minutes
Attention . . . . . . . . . . Minimal
Pot size . . . . . . . . . . . . 3–6 quarts

*3-pound pork loin*

*1 teaspoon grated orange peel*

*2 cups fresh blueberries*

*½ cup white grape juice*

*½ cup sugar*

*1 teaspoon table salt*

Place the pork loin in the slow cooker. Grate the orange peel using a vegetable grater. Wash the blueberries and remove the stems. Combine the grape juice, sugar, orange peel, blueberries, and salt; pour mixture over the pork loin. Cover and cook on low setting for 7 to 8 hours.

# Teriyaki Pork Tips

*Soy sauce adds a tangy taste to these pork tips—truly delicious!*

**stats**

**SERVES 6**

| | |
|---|---|
| Cooking time | 7–8 hours |
| Preparation time | 15 minutes |
| Attention | Minimal |
| Pot size | 3–6 quarts |

3-pound boneless pork loin roast

¾ cup unsweetened apple juice

2 tablespoons sugar

2 tablespoons soy sauce

1 tablespoon vinegar

1 teaspoon ground ginger

½ teaspoon garlic powder

½ teaspoon ground black pepper

2 tablespoons flour

2 tablespoons water

**1.** Cut the pork roast into 1-inch cubes and place in the slow cooker. Combine the apple juice, sugar, soy sauce, vinegar, ginger, garlic powder, and pepper in a medium-sized mixing bowl; pour mixture over the meat and stir well. Cover and cook on low setting for 7 to 8 hours.

**2.** A half-hour before serving, make a paste of the flour and water and add the mixture to the slow cooker. Stir well so that there are no lumps of flour. Cook uncovered on high setting for 20 to 30 minutes, stirring frequently.

# Pop Chops

*If you don't like lemon-lime soda pop, try your favorite in this recipe.*
*Soda is acidic, like vinegar, and helps tenderize the meat.*

*stats*

**SERVES 6**

Cooking time . . . . . . . 6–8 hours
Preparation time . . . . 30 minutes
Attention . . . . . . . . . . Minimal
Pot size . . . . . . . . . . . . 3–5 quarts

6 pork chops

3 tablespoons flour

2 tablespoons oil

1 can lemon-lime soda pop

¼ cup catsup

1 teaspoon brown sugar

1 teaspoon Worcestershire sauce

1 teaspoon vinegar

1 teaspoon salt

¼ teaspoon dry mustard powder

¼ teaspoon celery seed

⅛ teaspoon pepper

¼ cup coarsely chopped onion

**1.** Coat the pork chops in the flour. Sauté in oil in a pan over medium heat until browned, then drain.

**2.** Mix the soda pop, catsup, sugar, Worcestershire sauce, vinegar, salt, and spices in a small bowl.

**3.** Arrange the pork chops in the slow cooker, sprinkling each with chopped onion and the soda pop mixture.

**4.** Cover and heat on a low setting for 6 to 8 hours.

# Peppery Pork Pot

*This goes well with chewy wheat dinner rolls. Serve them warm in a basket, wrapped in a soft cotton cloth to contain the heat.*

 **stats**

**SERVES 6**

| | |
|---|---|
| Cooking time....... | 6–8 hours |
| Preparation time.... | 30 minutes |
| Attention.......... | Minimal |
| Pot size............ | 3–5 quarts |

4 onions

1 stalk celery

2 leeks

1 green bell pepper

¼ pound butter

2 tablespoons flour

2 pounds pork

1 pound potatoes

1 tablespoon black peppercorns

8 cups chicken stock

1 bouquet garni

½ teaspoon salt

¼ cup parsley

**1.** Chop the onions, slice the celery and leeks, and dice the green pepper. Sauté the onions, celery, leeks, and green pepper in butter in a pan over medium heat until soft. Stir in the flour until it is well mixed in.

**2.** Cube the pork and potatoes. Arrange the ingredients in the slow cooker: potatoes first, then pork, and then the onion mixture. Freshly grind some peppercorns and sprinkle them over the ingredients as they are added.

**3.** Add the stock, bouquet garni, and salt.

**4.** Cover and heat on a low setting for 6 to 8 hours.

**5.** Chop the parsley. Half an hour before serving, stir in the parsley.

# Pull-Apart Pork

*This is excellent on sandwiches, or by itself. It also freezes well and can be stored in single-serving containers for quick meals.*

**stats**

**SERVES 6**

| | |
|---|---|
| Cooking time | 6–8 hours |
| Preparation time | 30 minutes |
| Attention | Minimal |
| Pot size | 3–5 quarts |

*2 pounds pork stew meat*

*2 yellow onions*

*1 tablespoon oil*

*4 cloves garlic*

*4 pounds tomatoes*

*4 teaspoons hot chili powder*

*¼ teaspoon ground cinnamon*

*¼ teaspoon cayenne pepper*

*1 tablespoon dried oregano*

*1 tablespoon ground cumin*

*½ teaspoon salt*

*¼ cup cider vinegar*

*½ cup golden raisins*

**1.** Cube the pork and coarsely chop the onions. Sauté the meat and onions in the oil in a pan over medium heat until the meat is lightly browned.

**2.** Mince the garlic and chop the tomatoes; mix the tomatoes and garlic.

**3.** Mix the spices, salt, vinegar, and raisins in a small bowl.

**4.** Put half of the tomato mixture in the bottom of the slow cooker. Sprinkle with one-quarter of the spice mixture. Put the meat mixture over this, and sprinkle with half of the spice mixture. Put the remaining tomato mixture on top of the meat, and sprinkle with the remaining spice mixture.

**5.** Cover and heat on a low setting for 6 to 8 hours.

# Fennel Chops

*These chops are very flavorful; all you need is a*
*simple side of white rice or fresh homemade bread.*

 **SERVES 6**

Cooking time ....... 3–4 hours
Preparation time.... 30 minutes
Attention........... Minimal
Pot size ............. 3–5 quarts

2 cloves garlic

½ teaspoon salt

6 pork chops

2 tablespoons olive oil

1 tablespoon fennel seed

1 cup white wine

**1.** Crush the garlic and salt into a paste; rub the paste over the chops.

**2.** Sauté the chops in olive oil in a pan over medium heat until lightly browned. Put the chops, pan drippings, fennel seed, and white wine in the slow cooker.

**3.** Cover and heat on a low setting for 3 to 4 hours.

# Pepper Chops

*This is a really simple recipe for a great dish.*
*Try this with a chilled side like coleslaw or fruit salad.*

*stats*

**SERVES 6**

Cooking time . . . . . . . 3–4 hours

Preparation time . . . . 30 minutes

Attention . . . . . . . . . . Minimal

Pot size . . . . . . . . . . . 3–5 quarts

1 onion

6 pork chops

3 teaspoons seasoning salt

2 teaspoons cracked black peppercorns

2 tablespoons olive oil

½ cup water

**1.** Slice the onion and rub the chops with the salt and peppercorns. Sauté the chops and onion in oil in a pan over medium heat until lightly browned. Put chops, onions, and water in the slow cooker.

**2.** Cover and heat on a low setting for 3 to 4 hours.

# Caper Pork

*Here is your opportunity to use capers in your cooking.*
*The capers in this recipe give the pork a refreshing zing.*

*stats*

**SERVES 4**

Cooking time . . . . . . . 7–9 hours
Preparation time . . . . 30 minutes
Attention . . . . . . . . . . Minimal
Pot size . . . . . . . . . . . . 3–5 quarts

2 *pounds pork*

2 *tablespoons olive oil*

1 *onion*

4 *stalks celery*

2 *carrots*

3 *cloves garlic*

1 *cup tomato sauce*

6 *black olives*

¼ *cup dry white wine*

1 *tablespoon capers*

**1.** Cut the meat into serving-size pieces. Sauté in the olive oil in a pan over medium heat until the meat is lightly browned. Set the meat aside, leaving the meat juices in the pan.

**2.** Cut the onion, celery, and carrots into ½-inch slices. Mince the garlic. Use the same pan to heat the vegetables and garlic over high heat for 5 minutes.

**3.** Transfer the vegetable mix, then the meat, to the slow cooker. Pour the tomato sauce over the meat.

**4.** Cover and heat on a low setting for 6 to 8 hours.

**5.** Quarter the olives. Half an hour before serving, add the olives, wine, and capers (with caper juice) to the slow cooker.

# Sweet and Sour Pork

*Serve this dish with rice, preferably stir-fried with*
*some eggs, sliced green onion, and a dash of soy sauce.*

*stats* **SERVES 6**

| | |
|---|---|
| Cooking time | 6–8 hours |
| Preparation time | 30 minutes |
| Attention | Minimal |
| Pot size | 3–5 quarts |

3 *pounds pork*

1 *tablespoon oil*

1 *pound fresh pineapple*

4 *tablespoons cornstarch*

1 *cup water*

⅔ *cup vinegar*

½ *cup brown sugar*

1 *teaspoon salt*

2 *tablespoons soy sauce*

2 *cups pineapple juice*

1 *green pepper*

1 *onion*

**1.** Cube the pork. Sauté the pork in oil in a pan over medium heat until lightly browned.

**2.** Cube the pineapple. Transfer the pork and pineapple to the slow cooker, mixing them well.

**3.** Dissolve the cornstarch in the water in a mixing bowl. Add the vinegar, sugar, salt, soy sauce, and pineapple juice. Pour over the meat mixture.

**4.** Cover and heat on a low setting for 6 to 8 hours.

**5.** Thinly slice the green pepper and onion. Half an hour before serving, stir in the green pepper and onion.

# Seafood

# Cream of Shrimp Soup

*Lighter than a chowder, this shrimp soup*
*will fill you up without slowing you down.*

**SERVES 8**

Cooking time . . . . . . . 5½–7 hours
Preparation time . . . . 30 minutes
Attention . . . . . . . . . . Medium
Pot size . . . . . . . . . . . . 4–6 quarts

1 pound potatoes

1 white onion

1 celery rib

2 carrots

2 cups water

½ cup vegetable broth

2 tablespoons white wine

¼ teaspoon dried thyme

½ pound baby shrimp (or large precooked shrimp cut into ½-inch pieces)

2 cups shredded Swiss cheese

1 cup whole milk

½ teaspoon ground black pepper

**1.** Peel the potatoes and cut into ½-inch cubes. Peel the onions and chop into ¼-inch pieces. Chop the celery into ¼-inch pieces. Peel the carrots and shred using a vegetable grater. Place the potatoes, onions, celery, carrots, water, vegetable broth, white wine, and thyme into the slow cooker. Cook covered on high heat 4 to 6 hours.

**2.** Use a hand-held mixer to purée the vegetables in the slow cooker; the resulting mixture should be the consistency of baby food. Add the shrimp and cook covered for 30 minutes on low setting. Shred the cheese using a vegetable grater. Add the cheese, milk, and pepper to the soup. Cook covered on low setting for about 1 hour, stirring every 15 minutes, until the cheese is melted.

**3.** Garnish with fresh sprigs of cilantro.

# Salmon in White Wine with Dried Peaches

*Serve with fresh steamed broccoli drizzled with fresh-squeezed lime juice.*

 **stats**

**SERVES 4**

Cooking time . . . . . . . 2–3 hours
Preparation time. . . . 20 minutes
Attention. . . . . . . . . . High
Pot size . . . . . . . . . . . . 4–6 quarts

*1½ pounds salmon fillets*

*¼ cup all-purpose flour*

*2 tablespoons extra-virgin olive oil*

*1 cup dry white wine*

*½ cup vegetable stock*

*1 cup dried peaches, quartered*

*½ teaspoon freshly ground black pepper*

**1.** Pat the salmon dry with paper towels. Coat with a light layer of flour. Heat the olive oil in a frying pan at medium heat. Add the salmon and brown on all sides. Discard the oil and place the salmon fillets on paper towels to soak up additional oil.

**2.** Add the wine and vegetable stock to the slow cooker and cook on high setting until it bubbles. Turn the slow cooker to the low setting. Place the salmon fillets in the bottom of the slow cooker. Place the quartered dried peaches on top. Sprinkle with pepper. Cook covered on low setting for 2 to 3 hours.

# Minnesota Mock Lobster

*Cheaper and perhaps easier to find, try this mock lobster for a change.*

**SERVES 6**

Cooking time . . . . . . . 2–4 hours

Preparation time. . . . 15 minutes

Attention. . . . . . . . . . Minimal

Pot size . . . . . . . . . . . . 4–6 quarts

3 stalks celery

1 medium onion

½ cup water

½ cup lemon juice

2 tablespoons butter or margarine

3 pounds frozen torsk fillets

1 teaspoon salt

1 teaspoon paprika

6 lemon wedges

½ cup melted butter

**1.** Chop the celery into 1-inch pieces. Peel and quarter the onion.

**2.** Add the celery, onion, water, lemon juice, and butter to the slow cooker. Cook uncovered on high setting until the butter is melted. Stir mixture and turn the slow cooker to low setting. Lay the torsk fillets on the bottom of the slow cooker. Sprinkle salt and paprika over the fillets. Cook covered on low setting for 2 to 4 hours. Serve with melted butter and lemon wedges.

# Rice Curry with Vegetables and Scallops

*Serve with a dry white wine for a real treat!*

**SERVES 6**

Cooking time . . . . . . . 7–9 hours
Preparation time . . . . 30 minutes
Attention . . . . . . . . . . Medium
Pot size . . . . . . . . . . . . 4–6 quarts

1 large yellow onion

3 cloves garlic

1 tablespoon olive oil

1 pound baby scallops

1½ cups water

1 tablespoon curry powder

½ teaspoon cinnamon

½ teaspoon table salt

2 large potatoes

1 large zucchini

2 large carrots

1 (16-ounce) can tomatoes,
liquid retained

**1.** Peel and chop the onions into ¼-inch pieces. Peel and slice the garlic paper-thin with a sharp kitchen knife. Heat the olive oil in medium-sized skillet; sauté the scallops, onions, and garlic on medium-high heat until the onions are translucent and limp. The scallops should be slightly brown. Drain off the oil and place the scallops, onions, and garlic in the slow cooker.

**2.** Add the water, curry powder, cinnamon, and salt to the slow cooker; stir well. Cook covered on high setting for 1 hour.

**3.** Peel and cut the potatoes into 1-inch cubes. Slice the zucchini into ¼-inch-thick pieces. Peel and slice the carrots into ¼-inch pieces. Slice the tomatoes into 1-inch pieces, retaining the juice. Add the potatoes, zucchini, and tomatoes to the slow cooker. Cook covered on low setting for 6 to 8 hours.

# Shrimp Marinara

*Serve over linguine noodles. Top with Parmesan cheese and dried parsley flakes.*

**SERVES 4**

Cooking time . . . . . . . 6–9 hours
Preparation time . . . . 20 minutes
Attention . . . . . . . . . . Minimal
Pot size . . . . . . . . . . . . 3–6 quarts

4 large red tomatoes

1 garlic clove

2 tablespoons fresh parsley, minced

½ teaspoon dried basil

1 teaspoon table salt

¼ teaspoon ground black pepper

1 teaspoon dried oregano

1 (6-ounce) can tomato paste

½ pound small- to medium-sized fresh shrimp

**1.** Chop the tomatoes into 1-inch pieces. Peel and mince the garlic with a sharp paring knife. Mince the parsley by chopping it into very small pieces. Add the tomatoes, garlic, parsley, basil, salt, pepper, oregano, and tomato paste to the slow cooker. Cook covered on low setting for 6 to 8 hours.

**2.** Cook the shrimp by boiling it in a large kettle for 10 minutes. Rinse with cold water. Remove the shells and tails. Devein by using the tine of a fork to remove the blackish membrane along the back of each shrimp. Add the shrimp to the slow cooker and stir well. Turn the setting to high. Cook covered for 15 minutes.

# Freshwater Fish Stew

*Use shark, sea bass, or other mild saltwater fish to give a lighter flavor to this dish.*

**SERVES 4**

| | |
|---|---|
| Cooking time | 4–6 hours |
| Preparation time | 20 minutes |
| Attention | Minimal |
| Pot size | 3–6 quarts |

1½ pounds freshwater fish (walleye, northern, trout, bass, etc.), cleaned, skinned, and deboned

¾ cup fresh mushrooms, sliced

1 clove garlic

1 large white onion

1 green bell pepper

2 small zucchini

4 large ripe tomatoes

2 tablespoons olive oil

½ teaspoon dried basil

½ teaspoon dried oregano

1 teaspoon table salt

¼ teaspoon ground black pepper

¼ cup dry white wine

**1.** Cut the fish into 1-inch cubes. Clean the mushrooms by wiping with a damp cloth. Remove the stems and slice the mushroom heads paper-thin. Peel and mince the garlic. Peel the onion and slice into ¼-inch-thick rings. Remove the seeds and stem from the green pepper and chop into 1-inch pieces. Cut the tomatoes into 1-inch pieces.

**2.** Combine all ingredients in the slow cooker. Stir gently because the fish will break up if stirred too quickly. Cover and cook on low setting 4 to 6 hours.

# Lobster in Havarti and Cognac Cream Sauce

*Ladle over cooked spinach linguine noodles.*

**SERVES 4**

Cooking time . . . . . . . 1–2 hours
Preparation time . . . . 30 minutes
Attention . . . . . . . . . . Frequent
Pot size . . . . . . . . . . . . 3–6 quarts

1 pound fresh lobster meat
(approximately 3 whole lobsters)

4 garlic cloves

1 teaspoon fresh tarragon,
chopped

2 cups Havarti cheese, grated

1 cup light cream

¼ cup cognac

1 tablespoon ground black
pepper

½ teaspoon table salt

1 egg

**1.** Cook lobster by immersing them in boiling water head first. Cover and boil about 20 minutes.

**2.** Remove the meat from the lobster tails and claws and cut into 1-inch cubes. Peel and chop the garlic cloves into paper-thin slices. Chop the tarragon into ¼-inch lengths.

**3.** Combine the cheese, cream, cognac, garlic, pepper, salt, and tarragon in the slow cooker on low temperature setting; stir constantly with a wooden spoon until all the cheese has melted.

**4.** Pour the sauce into a blender and add the egg. Purée for 2 minutes on medium speed. Return the sauce to the slow cooker. Add the lobster meat. Cook covered on low setting for 30 to 60 minutes.

# Citrus Fish Fillets

*Serve with a vegetable medley of broccoli, cauliflower, and carrot slices about ¼-inch thick, steamed and drizzled with lemon juice.*

 **stats**

**SERVES 6**

Cooking time . . . . . . . 1½ hours

Preparation time. . . . 15 minutes

Attention. . . . . . . . . . Minimal

Pot size . . . . . . . . . . . . 3–6 quarts

1 fresh orange

1 fresh lemon

1 white onion

5 tablespoons fresh chopped parsley

¼ teaspoon butter

2 pounds fresh fish fillets, skinned and deboned

½ teaspoon table salt

¼ teaspoon ground black pepper

4 teaspoons vegetable oil

**1.** Before peeling, run the orange and lemon over the smallest teeth on a vegetable grater to yield 2 teaspoons of grated rind from each. Peel the remaining rind from the orange and lemon, discard, and slice the fruit into ¼-inch-thick pieces. Peel and chop the onion into ¼-inch pieces. Wash the parsley under cold water and chop into ¼-inch lengths.

**2.** Rub the butter on the bottom of the slow cooker. Add the fish fillets. Sprinkle salt and pepper over the fillets. Put the onion, parsley, and grated rinds on top of fish. Drizzle with vegetable oil. Cover and cook on low setting for 1½ hours. Ten minutes before serving, add the orange and lemon slices on top.

# Shrimp Creole

*Serve over long-grain brown rice. Top with fresh chopped chives.*

 **stats**

**SERVES 4**

Cooking time . . . . . . . 7–9 hours
Preparation time. . . . 20 minutes
Attention. . . . . . . . . . Minimal
Pot size . . . . . . . . . . . . 2–6 quarts

1 pound fresh shrimp

1¼ cup yellow onion, chopped

1 medium-sized green bell pepper

1½ cups celery, chopped

6 large ripe tomatoes

1 (8-ounce) can tomato sauce

1 teaspoon garlic salt

¼ teaspoon ground black pepper

½ teaspoon Tabasco or other hot pepper sauce

**1.** Cook the shrimp by boiling it for 20 minutes. Immerse in cold water until cool. Remove the shells and tails. Devein by using a fork tine to remove the blackish membrane on the back of each shrimp.

**2.** Peel and chop the onion into ¼-inch pieces. Remove the stem and seeds from the green pepper and chop the pepper into ¼-inch pieces. Cut the celery into ¼-inch pieces. Cut the tomatoes into 1-inch cubes. Add the celery, onion, green pepper, fresh tomatoes, tomato sauce, garlic salt, black pepper, and hot pepper sauce to the slow cooker. Cover and cook on low setting 6 to 8 hours. Add the shrimp, stir well, cover and cook an additional 1 hour.

# Vegetable Seafood Chowder

*Add 1 additional cup vegetable stock and 1 cup assorted other fresh seafood such as scallops, oysters, shrimp, and shark meat to make this a diverse, surprising treat.*

 **stats**

**SERVES 4**

| | |
|---|---|
| Cooking time | 8–10 hours |
| Preparation time | 20 minutes |
| Attention | Minimal |
| Pot size | 2–6 quarts |

*3 large potatoes*

*1 medium-sized white onion*

*1 cup fresh carrots, chopped*

*½ cup celery, chopped*

*1 cup fresh broccoli, chopped*

*1 cup frozen or fresh peas*

*1 cup fresh haddock, cubed*

*2 cups vegetable stock*

*1 teaspoon table salt*

*½ teaspoon ground black pepper*

**1.** Peel the potatoes and chop into 1-inch cubes. Peel and chop the onion in ¼-inch pieces. Cut the carrots, celery, and broccoli into ¼-inch pieces.

**2.** Add all the ingredients except fresh peas and fish to the slow cooker. Cover and cook on low setting for 7 to 8 hours. Add peas and fish, cook for 1 to 2 hours more.

# Manhattan Clam Chowder

*Everyone has their favorite type of chowder.*
*Why not experiment with your family and try different kinds?*

 **stats**

**SERVES 4**

Cooking time . . . . . . . 8–10 hours
Preparation time. . . . 20 minutes
Attention. . . . . . . . . . Minimal
Pot size . . . . . . . . . . . . 2–6 quarts

¼ pound bacon

1 large Vidalia onion

2 medium carrots

1 celery rib

8 medium-sized ripe tomatoes

3 medium potatoes

1 tablespoon dried parsley

3 cups fresh or canned clams

½ teaspoon table salt

½ teaspoon ground black pepper

1 teaspoon dried thyme

4 cups water

**1.** Brown the bacon in a medium-sized skillet on medium-high heat until crisp. Drain the grease. Lay the bacon on paper towels to cool. Crumble the bacon and add it to the slow cooker. Peel the onion and cut into ¼-inch pieces. Peel and slice the carrots into ¼-inch rounds. Cut the celery into ¼-inch pieces. Cut the tomatoes into ½-inch cubes. Peel the potatoes and cut into ½-inch cubes.

**2.** Add all ingredients to the slow cooker. Cover and cook on low setting for 8 to 10 hours.

# Cioppino

*Serve with some chunks of bread for sopping up the wonderful juice.*

## stats

**SERVES 8**

| | |
|---|---|
| Cooking time | 7–8 hours |
| Preparation time | 20 minutes |
| Attention | Minimal |
| Pot size | 4–8 quarts |

12 mussels

12 clams

12 large shrimp

1 pound cod

1 large yellow onion

1 medium-sized green bell pepper

2 medium-sized ripe tomatoes

2 garlic cloves

2 tablespoons fresh minced parsley

3 tablespoons olive oil

2 cups clam juice

½ cup dry white wine

1 bay leaf

1 teaspoon table salt

1 teaspoon ground black pepper

4 soft-shell crabs

1. Leave the mussels and clams in their shells. Remove the shells from the shrimp and devein the shrimp by running a fork tine along the back of each shrimp. Cut the cod into 1-inch cubes. Peel the onion and chop into ¼-inch pieces. Remove the stem and seeds from the green pepper; chop into ¼-inch pieces. Chop the tomatoes into ½-inch pieces. Peel the garlic and mince with a sharp kitchen knife. Mince the parsley with a sharp kitchen knife.

2. Heat the olive oil in a large skillet on medium heat. Add the onions, green pepper, and garlic and sauté for about 5 minutes, or until the onions are translucent; pour into the slow cooker. Stir in the tomatoes, parsley, clam juice, wine, and bay leaf. Cover and cook on low setting for 6 to 7 hours.

3. Remove the bay leaf. Add the salt, pepper, mussels, clams, shrimp, fish, and crab; stir gently. Cover and cook on low setting for 1 hour. Discard any mussels or clams that remain closed.

# Tuna Tomato Bake

*You can serve this as a sandwich spread too!*

## *stats*

### SERVES 4

Cooking time . . . . . . . 8–10 hours
Preparation time . . . . 20 minutes
Attention . . . . . . . . . . Minimal
Pot size . . . . . . . . . . . . 2–6 quarts

1 medium-sized green bell pepper

1 small yellow onion

1 celery rib

2 cups (16 ounces) water-packed tuna, drained

2 cups (16 ounces) tomato juice

2 tablespoons Worcestershire sauce

3 tablespoons vinegar

2 tablespoons sugar

1 tablespoon Dijon mustard

¼ teaspoon chili powder

½ teaspoon cinnamon

¼ teaspoon hot pepper sauce

**1.** Remove the seeds and stem from the green pepper and chop the pepper into ¼-inch pieces. Peel the onion and chop into ¼-inch pieces. Cut the celery stalk into ¼-inch pieces.

**2.** Combine all ingredients; mix gently. Cover and cook on low setting for 8 to 10 hours.

# Salmon Casserole

*Simple and delicious, try this meal tonight!*

**SERVES 4**

Cooking time . . . . . . . 3–4 hours
Preparation time . . . . 15 minutes
Attention . . . . . . . . . . Minimal
Pot size . . . . . . . . . . . 3–6 quarts

*8 ounces (1 cup) fresh
mushrooms, quartered*

*1 small yellow onion*

*1 cup shredded Cheddar cheese*

*2 eggs*

*2 cups (16 ounces) canned
salmon with liquid*

*1½ cups bread crumbs*

*1 tablespoon lemon juice*

**1.** Clean the mushrooms by wiping with a damp cloth; cut into quarters. Peel the onion and chop into ¼-inch pieces. Shred the Cheddar cheese with a vegetable grater. Beat the eggs by stirring quickly with a fork.

**2.** Put the fish in a medium-sized mixing bowl and flake with a fork, removing any bones. Mix together all the ingredients; pour into the slow cooker. Cover and cook on low setting for 3 to 4 hours.

# Peppery Salmon Chowder

*Serve with fresh chunky bread for a nice complement
to the spicy vegetables in this chowder.*

**SERVES 6**

| | |
|---|---|
| Cooking time | 6–7 hours |
| Preparation time | 20 minutes |
| Attention | Minimal |
| Pot size | 4–6 quarts |

1 pound fresh salmon

1 medium-sized red bell pepper

1 medium-sized green bell
pepper

1 medium-sized yellow bell
pepper

4 medium potatoes

3 medium carrots

1 celery rib

2 medium-sized white onions

2 cups sweet corn

3 cups vegetable broth

1 teaspoon whole black
peppercorns

**1.** Remove the skin and bones from the salmon and cut the meat into 1-inch cubes. Remove the stems and seeds from the bell peppers and chop the peppers into ½-inch pieces. Leave the peels on the potatoes and cut the potatoes into ½-inch cubes. Peel and chop the carrots and celery into ¼-inch pieces. Peel the onions and chop into ¼-inch pieces.

**2.** Combine all ingredients in the slow cooker. Cover and cook on low for 6 to 7 hours.

# Hot Chili Crab Soup

*This soup will require cold beverages to clear the palate before the next dish.*
*Be sure to have mild lemonade and sparkling water on hand.*

**stats**

**SERVES 6**

Cooking time . . . . . . . 2–3 hours
Preparation time . . . . 60 minutes
Attention . . . . . . . . . . Minimal
Pot size . . . . . . . . . . . . 3–5 quarts

3 cloves garlic

½ jalapeño pepper

1 onion

1 tablespoon vegetable oil

2 pounds Italian plum tomatoes

4 cups chicken broth

1 cup tomato sauce

2 teaspoons chili powder

2 teaspoons cumin

¼ teaspoon salt

3 tablespoons lime juice

1½ cups corn kernels

½ pound crabmeat

10 corn tortillas

1 bunch cilantro

1 avocado

½ pound Cheddar cheese

1 lime

1 jalapeño pepper

**1.** Finely mince the garlic and ½ jalapeno, and chop the onion. Sauté the onion, garlic, and jalapeño in the oil in a pan over low heat until the onion is soft.

**2.** Chop the tomatoes. Put the onion mixture, tomatoes, broth, tomato sauce, spices, salt, lime juice, and corn in the slow cooker.

**3.** Cover and heat on a low setting for 2 to 3 hours.

**4.** Shred the crabmeat. Before serving, stir in the crabmeat.

**5.** Prepare the garnishes as follows: Slice the tortillas into strips and brown on a baking sheet in a 300°F oven. Chop the cilantro, slice the avocado, shred the cheese, slice the lime, and mince the jalapeño. Serve in separate dishes near the slow cooker.

# Fillet of Sole with Grapes and White Wine

*Fillet of sole is a delicate fish, and this dish is nice and mild.*

**SERVES 6**

| | |
|---|---|
| Cooking time | 2–3 hours |
| Preparation time | 60 minutes |
| Attention | Minimal |
| Pot size | 3–5 quarts |

¼ pound mushrooms

½ pound seedless grapes

2 white onions

2 tablespoons butter

4 tablespoons butter

4 tablespoons flour

¼ teaspoon salt

¼ teaspoon pepper

1 cup milk

2 cups cream

1 cup white wine

3 pounds fillet of sole

¼ cup buttered toast crumbs

**1.** Quarter the mushrooms, halve the grapes, and finely slice the onions. Sauté mushrooms, grapes, and onions in 2 tablespoons butter in a pan over low heat until the onions are soft. Set aside the mushroom mixture, retaining the juices in the pan.

**2.** Add the remaining butter to the pan and melt. Mix the flour in slowly, then the salt, pepper, milk, and cream. Let thicken over low heat. Remove from the heat and stir in the wine.

**3.** Layer the mushroom mixture, fillets, and cream sauce in the slow cooker.

**4.** Cover and heat on a low setting for 2 to 3 hours.

**5.** Before serving, sprinkle the buttered crumbs over the top as a garnish.

# Chef's Fish Broth

*Keep a resealable container in the freezer for miscellaneous fish bones.*
*When you have enough, make a broth just like the chefs do.*

 **stats**

**MAKES ABOUT 4 CUPS**

Cooking time ....... 3–4 hours
Preparation time.... 15 minutes
Attention.......... Minimal
Pot size ............ 3–5 quarts

1 onion

1 carrot

3 cups fish bones

3 cups water

1 bouquet garni

1 cup white wine

1. Coarsely chop the onion and carrot. Add the onion, carrot, bones, water, bouquet garni, and wine to the slow cooker.

2. Cover and heat on a low setting for 3 to 4 hours.

3. Strain and use in soups, chowders, or sauces, or freeze.

# Pasta with Cheese and Oysters

*This is not the macaroni and cheese you ate as a kid.*
*Oysters give this dish party appeal and a delicious twist.*

 **SERVES 8**

| | |
|---|---|
| Cooking time....... | 3–4 hours |
| Preparation time.... | 45 minutes |
| Attention.......... | Minimal |
| Pot size............ | 3–5 quarts |

½ cup butter

½ pound Colby cheese

1 pound uncooked macaroni

½ pound salted oyster crackers

½ pound oyster meats

6 cups milk

**1.** Butter the inside of the slow cooker with half of the butter.

**2.** Shred the cheese. Make several layers each of the macaroni, cheese, crackers, and oysters in the slow cooker. Pour the milk over the layers and dot with the remaining butter. Cover and heat on a low setting for 3 to 4 hours.

# Seafood and Sherry Chowder

*Serve this with toasted slices of Classic Brown Bread (page 64)*
*for a nice contrast in colors and textures.*

 **stats**

**SERVES 6**

Cooking time . . . . . . . 3–4 hours
Preparation time. . . . 45 minutes
Attention. . . . . . . . . . Minimal
Pot size . . . . . . . . . . . . 3–5 quarts

1 onion

4 stalks celery

¼ pound mushrooms

3 tablespoons butter

3 tablespoons flour

3 cups milk

½ pound lobster meat

½ pound shrimp

1 cup cream

2 tablespoons parsley

¼ cup dry sherry

**1.** Chop the onion, celery, and mushrooms; sauté in butter in a pan over medium heat until the onions are soft.

**2.** Blend the flour into the melted butter, then add 1 cup of the milk and stir over low heat until the sauce is smooth and thickened.

**3.** Shred the lobster meat. Clean and devein shrimp. Transfer the onion mixture, remaining milk, cream, and seafood to the slow cooker.

**4.** Cover and heat on a low setting for 2 to 3 hours.

**5.** Chop the parsley. Half an hour before serving, stir in the sherry and the parsley.

# Tomato Shrimp Supreme

*Provide your family with soft white bread or hunks of a
crunchy baguette to soak up the juices of this dish.*

*stats*

**SERVES 6**

Cooking time . . . . . . . 2–3 hours
Preparation time . . . . 45 minutes
Attention . . . . . . . . . . Minimal
Pot size . . . . . . . . . . . . 3–5 quarts

1 pound mushrooms

½ green bell pepper

½ onion

2 tablespoons butter

1 tablespoon flour

¼ teaspoon salt

¼ teaspoon pepper

¼ teaspoon cayenne pepper

6 tomatoes

6 stalks celery

1 teaspoon sugar

1 pound shrimp, peeled and
deveined

1 cup white wine

**1.** Quarter the mushrooms; chop the green
pepper and onion. Sauté the mushrooms,
green pepper, and onion in butter in a pan
over low heat until the onion is soft. Add
the flour, salt, pepper, and cayenne pepper
to the mushroom mixture; stir over low heat
until the sauce thickens. Transfer to the slow
cooker.

**2.** Coarsely chop the tomatoes and thinly
slice the celery. Add the tomatoes, celery,
sugar, and shrimp to the slow cooker.

**3.** Cover and heat on a low setting for 2 to
3 hours.

**4.** Half an hour before serving, add the wine.

# Pimento Shrimp Pot

*This is a good all-in-one dish with lots of color.*
*Add fresh cilantro as a garnish, or fresh mint if cilantro isn't available.*

**stats**

**SERVES 8**

Cooking time . . . . . . . 2–3 hours
Preparation time . . . . 45 minutes
Attention . . . . . . . . . . Minimal
Pot size . . . . . . . . . . . . 3–5 quarts

1 pound mushrooms

¼ cup butter

2 ounces pimento

1 cup chopped green pepper

1 cup finely sliced celery

2½ cups coarsely chopped tomatoes

2 pounds shrimp, peeled and deveined

2 cups cooked rice

1 teaspoon salt

½ teaspoon chili powder

1. Quarter the mushrooms; sauté in butter in a pan over medium heat until lightly browned.

2. Cut the pimento into thin strips.

3. Add the mushrooms, green pepper, celery, tomatoes, pimento, shrimp, rice, salt, and chili powder to the slow cooker.

4. Cover and heat on a low setting for 2 to 3 hours.

# Delta Shrimp

*Shrimp come in several different sizes. For some visual variety,
try using more than one size in your shrimp dishes.*

 **SERVES 4**

Cooking time . . . . . . . 2–3 hours
Preparation time. . . . 45 minutes
Attention. . . . . . . . . . Minimal
Pot size . . . . . . . . . . . . 3–5 quarts

2 onions

1 cup chopped celery

2 tablespoons butter

1 tablespoon flour

1 teaspoon salt

1 cup water

4 tomatoes

1 green pepper

1 tablespoon vinegar

2 tablespoons chili powder

1 teaspoon sugar

1 pound shrimp, peeled and
deveined

**1.** Slice the onions. Sauté the onions with the chopped celery in butter in a pan over medium heat until the onion is soft. Add the flour and salt; stir to thicken. Add the water slowly and mix well.

**2.** Coarsely chop the tomatoes and green pepper. Transfer the onion mixture, tomatoes, green pepper, vinegar, chili powder, and sugar to the slow cooker.

**3.** Cover and heat on a low setting for 2 to 3 hours.

**4.** Half an hour before serving, add the shrimp.

# Silky Shrimp Soup

*Use fresh shrimp, if possible. The fresh shrimp shells add a little
extra flavor while cooking, so leave them on until the end.*

**stats**

**SERVES 6**

Cooking time . . . . . . . 2–3 hours
Preparation time . . . . 30 minutes
Attention . . . . . . . . . . Moderate
Pot size . . . . . . . . . . . . 3–5 quarts

1 clove garlic

1 onion

1½ pounds shrimp

4 cups fish stock

½ teaspoon thyme

½ teaspoon black pepper

1 cup heavy cream

¼ cup dry sherry

**1.** Finely chop the garlic and onion. Put the garlic, onion, and shrimp into the slow cooker with the stock and spices.

**2.** Cover and heat on a low setting for 2 to 3 hours.

**3.** Half an hour before serving, remove the shrimp from the broth using a slotted spoon. Shell the shrimp and discard the shells.

**4.** Puree half of the shrimp meats with the cream. Add the whole shrimp, the pureed shrimp mixture, and the sherry to the broth in the slow cooker.

# Tented Tilapia

*For extra flavor, add some fresh basil or mint leaves
to the tents before heating in the slow cooker.*

**SERVES 6–8**

Cooking time . . . . . . . 1–2 hours
Preparation time . . . . 15 minutes
Attention . . . . . . . . . . Minimal
Pot size . . . . . . . . . . . . 3–5 quarts

3 *cloves garlic*

2 *tomatoes*

2 *pounds tilapia fillets*

½ *teaspoon seasoned salt*

¼ *cup butter*

1 *cup white wine*

**1.** Mince the garlic and thinly slice the tomatoes. Lay each fillet in a rectangle of aluminum foil large enough to fold over and seal. Put this on each fillet: seasoned salt, dabs of butter, garlic, tomato, wine. Seal packages.

**3.** Arrange the wrapped fish on a trivet or rack in the slow cooker. Pour water around the base of the trivet. Cover and heat on high setting for 1 to 2 hours.

# Kids' Favorites

# Sloppy Joes

*Add potato chips and carrot sticks to the plate and you have a true all-American lunch that is perfect for chilly outings or teen get-togethers.*

**SERVES 12**

| | |
|---|---|
| Cooking time | 2–3 hours |
| Preparation time | 20 minutes |
| Attention | Minimal |
| Pot size | 4–6 quarts |

1 medium-sized yellow onion

2 celery ribs

2 pounds extra-lean hamburger

2 cups tomato sauce

½ cup can tomato paste

¼ cup white vinegar

3 teaspoons Worcestershire sauce

2 tablespoons brown sugar

1 teaspoon garlic salt

½ teaspoon pepper

1. Peel the onion and chop into ¼-inch pieces. Chop the celery into ¼-inch pieces. Put the onion, celery, and hamburger in a medium-sized skillet on medium-high heat. Cook until the hamburger is brown and no pink remains. Drain off the grease.

2. Combine all ingredients in the slow cooker. Cook covered on low setting for 2 to 3 hours.

# Pizza Meatballs

*Make these ahead of time and freeze them. They can be thawed in the
microwave for those last-minute lunch demands or as an after-school snack.*

### stats

**SERVES 6–8**

| | |
|---|---|
| Cooking time | 2 hours |
| Preparation time | 30 minutes |
| Attention | Minimal |
| Pot size | 5–6 quarts |

**Meatballs:** *½ pound (1 cup)
Swiss cheese*

*1 medium-sized yellow onion*

*½ of a green bell pepper*

*2 pounds extra-lean hamburger*

*2¾ cups bread crumbs*

*1 teaspoon salt*

*¼ teaspoon basil*

*¼ teaspoon pepper*

*1 cup canned condensed
vegetable soup*

*¼ cup skim milk*

**Sauce:** *1 garlic clove*

*1 medium-sized yellow onion*

*6 large ripe tomatoes*

*1 cup beef broth*

*½ cup (4 ounces) tomato paste*

*1 teaspoon salt*

*1 teaspoon oregano*

**1.** To make the meatballs, cut the cheese into
¼-inch cubes. Peel and chop the onion into
¼-inch pieces. Remove the stem and seeds
from the green pepper and chop the pepper
into ¼-inch pieces. Mix all the meatball ingredients together well and form into firm balls
no larger than 2 inches in diameter. Lay the
meatballs in the bottom of the slow cooker.

**2.** To make the sauce, peel the garlic and
slice thinly with a paring knife. Peel and
chop the onions into ½-inch pieces. Peel the
tomatoes with a sharp paring knife, gently
lifting the skin off, quarter them, and mix in
a blender on low speed for 2 minutes. Combine all sauce ingredients and pour over the
meatballs.

**3.** Cook covered on low setting for 2 hours.

# Real Baked Beans and Franks

*To add interest to the meal, serve with apple slices sprinkled with cinnamon.*

**SERVES 6**

Cooking time . . . . . . . 7–9 hours
Preparation time . . . . 15 minutes
Attention . . . . . . . . . . Minimal
Pot size . . . . . . . . . . . . 5–6 quarts

3 cups dried navy beans

6 cups water

1 medium-sized yellow onion

1 large tomato

½ cup brown sugar

½ cup maple-flavored syrup

1 cup ketchup

2 teaspoons dried mustard

2 teaspoons vinegar

1 cup water

12 all-beef hotdogs, cut into
½-inch round slices

**1.** Wash the beans then soak them in 6 cups of water for 12 hours before cooking. Drain and wash the beans again.

**2.** Peel the onion and cut into ⅛-inch pieces. Chop the tomato. Combine the brown sugar, maple-flavored syrup, ketchup, mustard, vinegar, tomato, and onion in the slow cooker. Cook uncovered on high setting until the brown sugar has dissolved; stir well. Add 1 cup water, beans, and hotdogs. Stir to cover the beans and hot dogs with sauce.

**3.** Cook covered on low setting for 7 to 9 hours. One hour before serving, remove the cover and continue cooking on low setting.

# Halftime Chili

*Place small bowls of shredded Cheddar cheese, diced jalapeño peppers, sour cream, and diced green onion tops on the table and let kids top their own chili.*

**SERVES 8**

Cooking time . . . . . . . 8 hours
Preparation time . . . . 20 minutes
Attention . . . . . . . . . . Minimal
Pot size . . . . . . . . . . . . 3–6 quarts

*2 pounds lean ground beef*

*1 medium-sized yellow onion*

*3 medium tomatoes*

*2 cups (16 ounces) canned or frozen corn*

*4 cups (32 ounces) precooked or canned red kidney beans*

*1 cup water*

*2 tablespoons chili powder*

*2 teaspoons table salt*

*1 teaspoon ground black pepper*

*¼ teaspoon dried red pepper flakes*

**1.** Brown the meat in a large skillet on the stove. Continue browning at medium heat until no pink remains in the meat. Drain off the fat and lay the meat on paper towels to absorb remaining fat.

**2.** Peel and dice the onion into ¼-inch pieces. Dice the tomatoes into ¼-inch pieces. Drain and rinse the kidney beans. Combine the onion, tomatoes, corn, kidney beans, water, chili powder, salt, black pepper, and dried red peppers; stir to combine. Cook covered on low setting for 8 hours.

# Macaroni and Cheese with Hamburger

*Try different pastas such as rotini or alphabet shapes.*
*Substitute hot dog or sausage slices for the hamburger*

**SERVES 8**

Cooking time . . . . . . . 3 hours
Preparation time. . . . 20 minutes
Attention. . . . . . . . . . Minimal
Pot size . . . . . . . . . . . . 4–6 quarts

*1 pound lean hamburger*

*6 cups elbow macaroni*

*2 cups whole milk*

*2 cups shredded Cheddar cheese*

*2 teaspoons dry mustard*

*¼ teaspoon garlic salt*

*¼ teaspoon ground black pepper*

**1.** Brown the hamburger in a skillet on medium-high heat on the stove. Drain off the fat and spread the hamburger on paper towels to absorb remaining grease. Cook the macaroni in boiling water until soft.

**2.** Combine the milk, Cheddar cheese, dry mustard, garlic salt, and black pepper in the slow cooker. Cook uncovered on high setting until the cheese has melted completely. Add the cooked macaroni and hamburger; stir well. Cook uncovered on low setting for 3 hours.

# Mom's Cold Cure: Easy Chicken Noodle Soup

*Spicy dill pickles, Cheddar cheese, and saltine crackers
are the perfect complement to chicken noodle soup.*

**stats**

**SERVES 10**

Cooking time ....... 8–10 hours
Preparation time.... 30 minutes
Attention .......... Medium
Pot size ............ 4–6 quarts

1 chicken, cleaned, with skin and bones

1 medium-sized yellow onion

8 carrots

4 celery ribs

6 cups water

2 chicken bouillon cubes

1 teaspoon table salt

½ teaspoon ground black pepper

8 ounces dried egg noodles

**1.** Cut the chicken into serving portions— legs, wings, thighs, breasts. Peel and dice the onions and carrots into about ¼-inch pieces. Slice the celery ribs into ¼-inch pieces.

**2.** Combine the water, bouillon cubes, salt, pepper, and chicken pieces in the slow cooker. Cook covered on high for 4 to 5 hours. Remove the chicken and discard the bones and skin. Place the meat back in the slow cooker. Add the noodles, carrots, celery, and onions in the slow cooker. Cook covered on high setting for 4 to 5 additional hours.

# Barbecued Chicken Drummies

*This is a perfect food for slumber parties or teen get-togethers. Add the optional ingredients for older teens to get the flavor of Buffalo wings. Remember to serve them with celery sticks and blue cheese dressing!*

**stats**

**SERVES 12**

Cooking time . . . . . . . 5 hours
Preparation time. . . . 15 minutes
Attention. . . . . . . . . . Minimal
Pot size . . . . . . . . . . . 3–6 quarts

1 teaspoon yellow onion, grated

2 garlic cloves

1 cup water

¼ cup honey

2 teaspoons soy sauce

2 tablespoons vinegar

1 cup bottled barbecue sauce

2 tablespoons hot pepper sauce (optional)

½ teaspoon table salt

½ teaspoon ground black pepper

1 teaspoon cayenne pepper (optional)

36 chicken drummies (the fleshy part of the wing that attaches to the breast)

**1.** Peel and grate the onion using a vegetable grater. Peel the garlic cloves and slice paper-thin. Combine the onion, garlic, water, honey, soy sauce, vinegar, barbecue sauce, hot pepper sauce (if using), salt, black pepper, and cayenne (if using) in the slow cooker.

**2.** Cook on high setting about 15 minutes, until all ingredients are well combined. Stir well and add the chicken drummies. Cook covered on low setting for 5 hours.

# Sicilian Potatoes

*Good on their own or with a meat entrée, these potatoes are sure to please.*

**SERVES 4**

Cooking time . . . . . . . 4–5 hours
Preparation time . . . . 20 minutes
Attention . . . . . . . . . . Medium
Pot size . . . . . . . . . . . . 4–6 quarts

1 small yellow onion

4 garlic cloves

4 ripe tomatoes

¼ teaspoon oregano

2 teaspoons salt

3 tablespoons olive oil

14 small new potatoes

6 links Italian sausage

**1.** Peel and chop the onions and garlic into ¼-inch pieces. Chop the tomatoes into ½-inch pieces. Turn the slow cooker on high setting. Add the olive oil, garlic, and onions. Cook for 10 minutes. Add the tomatoes, oregano, and salt. Reduce heat to low, cover, and cook for 15 minutes.

**2.** Peel and wash the potatoes. Cut each Italian sausage link into 4 equal pieces. Place the potatoes and sausage in the slow cooker. Cook on low setting for 4 hours, or until the potatoes are tender.

# I Did It Myself Ham and Vegetable Soup

*Even a preschooler will be proud to make this tasty soup—
all Mom or Dad did was open the cans! Serve it with cheese
sandwiches and olives for a complete do-it-yourself meal.*

**SERVES 8**

Cooking time . . . . . . . 2–3 hours
Preparation time . . . . 10 minutes
Attention . . . . . . . . . . Minimal
Pot size . . . . . . . . . . . . 2–6 quarts

4 cups water

1 can sliced carrots

1 can corn

1 can peas

1 can sliced potatoes

1 can green beans

1 ham soup bone

A dash of ground black pepper

**1.** Add the water to the slow cooker and turn on low setting.

**2.** Empty all ingredients into the slow cooker, including the juices from the canned vegetables; stir well. Cook covered on low setting for 2 to 3 hours.

**3.** Remove the soup bone and take off all of the meat that hasn't already fallen off. Tear the meat into bite-sized pieces if necessary. Return the meat to the slow cooker and discard the bone.

# Vegetarian Stone Soup

*This is a fun party recipe for preschoolers or kindergarteners. Have each child bring one or two ingredients and let them stir their own ingredients into the soup! Serve with crackers and American cheese for a healthy lunch.*

**stats**

### SERVES 8

| | |
|---|---|
| Cooking time | 8–10 hours |
| Preparation time | 30 minutes |
| Attention | Minimal |
| Pot size | 3–6 quarts |

1 large white onion

1 cup rutabaga, chopped

1 turnip

2 large potatoes

1 cup baby carrots

2 celery ribs

1 cup broccoli, chopped

1 small zucchini

1 stone, about the size of an egg

4 cups water

1 cup fresh or frozen green beans

1 teaspoon table salt

½ teaspoon ground black pepper

**1.** Peel and chop the onion, rutabaga, turnip, and potatoes into 1-inch pieces. Slice the carrots in half. Chop the celery into ¼-inch pieces. Chop the broccoli and zucchini into ½-inch pieces. Clean the stone well—it's best to run it through the dishwasher!

**2.** Put the stone and water in the slow cooker. Add one ingredient at a time to the slow cooker, stirring as each ingredient is added. Cook covered on low setting for 8 to 10 hours. Remove the stone before serving.

CHAPTER

9

# All-In-One Meals

# Hamburger Potato Casserole

*The best of both worlds, this meal is easy and delicious!*

**SERVES 4**

Cooking time . . . . . . . 7–9 hours
Preparation time. . . . 20 minutes
Attention. . . . . . . . . . Minimal
Pot size . . . . . . . . . . . . 4–6 quarts

1 pound lean ground beef

3 medium potatoes

4 medium carrots

1 medium-sized yellow onion

1 cup fresh peas

2 tablespoons dry white rice

1 teaspoon table salt

½ teaspoon ground black pepper

1 cup tomato juice

1. Brown the beef in a medium skillet on medium-high heat; drain off the grease. Peel the potatoes and cut into ¼-inch slices. Peel the carrots and slice into ¼-inch rounds. Peel the onion and cut into ¼-inch pieces.

2. Combine all ingredients except peas in the slow cooker; stir well. Cover and cook on low setting for 5 to 7 hours. Add peas and cook for 2 hours.

# Spinach, Cheese, and Egg Casserole

*Try this for an elegant Sunday brunch. Complement it with champagne and buttery croissants. Your guests will never believe you made it in the slow cooker!*

**stats**

**SERVES 8**

Cooking time . . . . . . . 5–6 hours
Preparation time. . . . 20 minutes
Attention. . . . . . . . . . Medium
Pot size . . . . . . . . . . . . 3–6 quarts

2 bunches fresh spinach

2 cups cottage cheese

1½ cups Cheddar cheese, grated

3 eggs

¼ cup flour

1 teaspoon table salt

½ cup butter, melted

**1.** Clean the spinach in cold water and remove the stems. Tear the leaves into 1-inch pieces. Place the spinach leaves, cottage cheese, and Cheddar cheese in a large mixing bowl.

**2.** In a small bowl, combine the eggs, flour, table salt, and butter, mixing well until all the ingredients are melded; pour over the spinach mixture. Mix well with a wooden spoon.

**3.** Pour mixture into the slow cooker and cook covered on high setting for 1 hour. Stir well after the hour is up and reduce heat to low setting.

**4.** Cover and cook 4 to 5 additional hours.

# Corned Beef Dinner

*Arrange the meat and vegetables on a large platter.*
*Use the juice left in the bottom of the slow cooker as you would gravy.*

 **SERVES 6**

Cooking time . . . . . . . 8–9 hours
Preparation time . . . . 20 minutes
Attention . . . . . . . . . . Minimal
Pot size . . . . . . . . . . . 4–6 quarts

2 *yellow onions*

6 *small potatoes*

12 *carrots*

1 *rutabaga, peeled and quartered*

6 *ribs celery*

1 *head cabbage*

3 *pounds corned beef brisket*

2 *bay leaves*

20 *black peppercorns*

2 *cups water*

**1.** Peel the onions and slice into quarters. Peel the potatoes and slice in halves. Peel the carrots and cut into quarters. Peel the rutabaga and slice into eight pieces. Cut the celery ribs into quarters. Cut the cabbage into eight pieces.

**2.** Place the corned beef brisket in the bottom of the slow cooker. Put the bay leaves and peppercorns on top. Layer the vegetables in the following order: onions, potatoes, celery, carrots, cabbage, and rutabaga. Add water. Cook covered on low setting for 8 to 9 hours, or until the rutabaga is soft.

**3.** Remove the bay leaves before serving. Cut the meat into thin slices across the grain.

# Sausage and Fall Vegetable Harvest

*This is a hearty dish. Squash has very tough skin, so when peeling the squash use a large, sharp knife and work on a hard surface.*

**SERVES 4**

| | |
|---|---|
| Cooking time | 6–8 hours |
| Preparation time | 20 minutes |
| Attention | Minimal |
| Pot size | 3–6 quarts |

1 pound acorn squash

2 medium potatoes

4 carrots

4 ribs celery

¼ cup green bell pepper, chopped

2 yellow onions

1 cup zucchini, sliced

1 cup fresh or frozen peas

1 cup fresh or frozen green beans

2 cups fresh or canned beef broth

2 tablespoons red wine

¼ teaspoon ground black pepper

1 teaspoon dried, crushed rosemary

½ pound sausage in large round links or patties

2 tablespoons flour

½ cup warm water

1. Peel the squash and cut into ½-inch cubes. Peel the potatoes and cut into ½-inch cubes. Peel the carrots and cut into 1-inch lengths. Cut the celery into 1-inch lengths. Core the green pepper and chop into pieces ¼-inch square. Peel the onions and quarter. Cut the zucchini into slices about ¼-inch thick.

2. Combine the squash, potatoes, carrots, celery, zucchini, green beans, broth, wine, black pepper, and rosemary in slow cooker.

3. Cut the sausage into ½-inch slices or break patties into marble-sized chunks. Combine the sausage, green peppers, and onions in a frying pan and cook on medium-high heat until the sausage is browned. Drain off grease and lay the mixture on paper towels for 2 minutes. Add the sausage, onions, and green peppers to the vegetables in the slow cooker. Cook covered on low heat for 6 to 8 hours.

4. One hour before serving, add the peas, and use a fork to mix 2 tablespoons flour and ½ cup water in a bowl until smooth; add this to the vegetables and sausage, stirring until it is mixed. Cook covered for 1 additional hour.

# Mixed Meat Tetrazzini

*Scoop out of the slow cooker with a large serving spoon
and sprinkle with Parmesan cheese before serving.*

**SERVES 8**

Cooking time....... 6–8 hours
Preparation time.... 30 minutes
Attention.......... Minimal
Pot size............ 4–6 quarts

1 bunch small green onions

1 cup celery

½ cup pimiento-stuffed green
olives, chopped

1 green bell pepper

½ pound fresh mushrooms

1 cup chicken, precooked and
cubed

1 cup turkey, precooked and
cubed

1 cup ham, precooked and cubed

1 pound package spaghetti

1 tablespoon dried parsley

3 cups chicken broth

**1.** Peel and chop the green onions into ¼-inch pieces. Chop the celery and olives into ¼-inch pieces. Remove the stem and seeds from the green pepper and chop pepper into ¼-inch pieces. Clean the mushrooms by wiping them with a damp cloth, then slice paper-thin. Precook meat in the microwave or use leftover meats; cut into 1-inch cubes. Break the spaghetti noodles into approximately 1-inch lengths.

**2.** Layer ingredients in the slow cooker in the following order:
  1. Spaghetti
  2. Meats
  3. Onions
  4. Olives
  5. Celery and parsley
  6. Mushrooms

**3.** Pour the chicken broth over the top. Cover and cook on low setting for 6 to 8 hours.

# Smoky Beef and Beans Dinner

*The smoky flavor adds a delicious spin on a regular beef and bean dinner.*

**stats**

**SERVES 4**

| | |
|---|---|
| Cooking time | 4–6 hours |
| Preparation time | 15 minutes |
| Attention | Minimal |
| Pot size | 3–6 quarts |

*1 pound lean ground beef*

*1 large yellow onion*

*¾ pound bacon*

*2 cans pork and beans*

*1 can lima beans*

*1 can kidney beans*

*1 cup ketchup*

*¼ cup brown sugar*

*1 tablespoon liquid smoke flavoring*

*3 tablespoons white vinegar*

*1 teaspoon salt*

*½ teaspoon ground black pepper*

**1.** Place the ground beef in a medium-sized skillet on the stove; cook on medium-high heat, stirring until the meat is brown. Drain off grease and place the meat in the slow cooker.

**2.** Peel and chop the onion into ¼-inch pieces. Slice the bacon into 1-inch pieces. Place the bacon and onion in skillet and cook on medium-high heat, stirring until the bacon is crisp.

**3.** Put all ingredients in the slow cooker; stir well. Cook covered on low setting 4 to 6 hours.

# New Orleans–Style Jambalaya

*Get a taste of the South with this fantastic and fret-free meal.*

**SERVES 8**

Cooking time . . . . . . . 7–8 hours
Preparation time . . . . 45 minutes
Attention . . . . . . . . . . Medium
Pot size . . . . . . . . . . . . 4–8 quarts

1 (3-pound) chicken

1 pound hot smoked sausage

3 tablespoons olive oil

1 cup celery, chopped

¾ cup fresh parsley, chopped

1 large yellow onion

⅔ cup green pepper, chopped

2 garlic cloves

**1.** Place the chicken in a large pot on the stove; cover with water and boil for 1 hour. Remove the chicken and cut the meat off the bones; discard the skin. Cut the meat into bite-size pieces and place in the slow cooker.

**2.** Cut the sausage into ¼-inch-thick pieces. Place in a large frying pan with the olive oil on the stove and cook on medium heat until brown. Remove the meat with a slotted spoon and place it on paper towels to absorb remaining grease.

**3.** Chop the celery and parsley into ¼-inch pieces. Peel the onion and chop into ¼-inch pieces. Remove the seeds and stem from the green pepper and chop the pepper into ¼-inch pieces. Mince the garlic using a sharp kitchen knife. Place the celery, parsley, onion, green pepper, and garlic in the frying pan and sauté in the sausage grease on medium heat for five minutes. Drain grease.

# New Orleans–Style Jambalaya

## (continued)

8 whole tomatoes

1 cup green onions, chopped

2 cups chicken broth

1 (6-ounce) can tomato paste

1½ teaspoons thyme

2 bay leaves

2 teaspoons oregano

1 teaspoon chili powder

1 teaspoon salt

½ teaspoon cayenne pepper

1 teaspoon ground black pepper

1 teaspoon garlic powder

2 cups uncooked long grain rice, washed and rinsed

3 pounds raw shrimp

**4.** Cut the tomatoes into quarters. Remove the roots and outer layer of skin from the green onions and chop into ¼-inch pieces, including the green stems. Place all the ingredients except the shrimp in slow cooker; stir to combine and cook covered on low setting 6 to 7 hours.

**5.** One hour before serving, boil the shrimp in water for 10 minutes. Remove shells and devein by running a fork tine up the back of the shrimp. Add shrimp to slow cooker; stir well. Cook covered on low setting for 1 hour.

# Chicken and Dumplings

*Serve immediately after the dumplings are cooked to ensure they don't become rubbery and tasteless. Sprinkle parsley flakes over individual servings.*

**stats**

**SERVES 4**

| | |
| --- | --- |
| Cooking time | 8½–10 hours |
| Preparation time | 15 minutes |
| Attention | Minimal |
| Pot size | 4–6 quarts |

1 (3-pound) chicken, cut up

½ cup chicken broth or bouillon

2 teaspoons salt

½ teaspoon ground black pepper

½ teaspoon poultry seasoning

3 stalks celery

3 medium carrots

1 small yellow onion

2 cups packaged biscuit mix

¾ cup milk

1 teaspoon dried parsley flakes

**1.** Wash the chicken pieces and cut away excess fat. Place the chicken pieces in the slow cooker. Add broth. Sprinkle with salt, pepper, and poultry seasoning.

**2.** Chop the celery and carrots into 1-inch lengths. Peel and chop the onion into ¼-inch pieces; place celery, carrots, and onion on top of the chicken. Cover and cook on low setting 8 to 10 hours.

**3.** About a half-hour before serving, combine the biscuit mix, milk, and parsley flakes; stir until all the biscuit mix is moistened. Drop by teaspoonfuls onto top of the mixture in the slow cooker. Cover and cook for 30 minutes.

# New England Dinner

*Serve with a dip made of half horseradish and half sour cream.*

**stats**

**SERVES 6**

| | |
|---|---|
| Cooking time | 7–9 hours |
| Preparation time | 15 minutes |
| Attention | Minimal |
| Pot size | 3–6 quarts |

6 medium carrots

2 medium-sized yellow onions

4 celery ribs

1 small head cabbage

3-pound boneless chuck roast

½ teaspoon table salt

½ teaspoon ground black pepper

1 envelope dry onion soup mix

2 cups water

1 tablespoon vinegar

1 bay leaf

1. Clean the carrots and cut in half. Peel the onions and slice into quarters. Cut the celery ribs in half. Remove outer leaves from the cabbage, then cut the head into eighths.

2. Place the carrots, onion, and celery in the slow cooker. Put the roast on top. Sprinkle with salt and pepper, then add the soup mix, water, vinegar, and bay leaf on top. Add the cabbage. Do not mix ingredients. Cover and cook on low setting for 7 to 9 hours.

# Ten-Story Casserole

*Ten sounds like a lot, but this filling meal is fantastic and surprisingly unfancy.*

**stats**

**SERVES 6**

Cooking time . . . . . . . 4 hours

Preparation time . . . . 20 minutes

Attention . . . . . . . . . . Minimal

Pot size . . . . . . . . . . . . 3–6 quarts

*1½ pounds ground turkey*

*6 medium potatoes*

*2 medium-sized white onions*

*½ teaspoon table salt*

*½ teaspoon ground black pepper*

*1 (15-ounce) can corn*

*1 (15-ounce) can peas*

*1 (10¾-ounce) can cream of celery condensed soup*

*¼ cup water*

**1.** Brown the turkey in a medium-sized skillet on medium-high heat. Drain off grease and spread the turkey on paper towels to cool. Peel the potatoes and cut into ¼-inch slices. Peel the onions and slice into ¼-inch rings.

**2.** Place ingredients in the slow cooker in the following layers:

1. One-fourth of potatoes, half of onions, sprinkle of salt and pepper
2. Half can of corn
3. One-fourth of potatoes
4. Half can peas
5. One-fourth of potatoes, remaining half of onions, sprinkle of salt and pepper
6. Half can corn
7. One-fourth of potatoes
8. Half can peas
9. Turkey
10. Cream of celery soup and water

**3.** Cover and cook on high setting for 4 hours.

# Black Forest Sausage and Sauerkraut

*Another delicious treat from abroad, this recipe is great year-round.*

**SERVES 6**

Cooking time . . . . . . . 8–9 hours

Preparation time . . . . 20 minutes

Attention . . . . . . . . . . Minimal

Pot size . . . . . . . . . . . . 3–6 quarts

2½ pounds fresh Polish sausage

6 medium carrots

6 medium potatoes

2 medium yellow onions

3 cloves garlic

4 cups sauerkraut

1½ cups dry white wine

1 teaspoon caraway seeds

½ teaspoon ground black pepper

**1.** Cut the Polish sausage into 3-inch pieces. Peel the carrots and cut into 3-inch lengths. Peel the potatoes and cut into 1-inch cubes. Peel the onions and cut into ¼-inch rings. Peel the garlic and mince with a sharp kitchen knife. Rinse and drain the sauerkraut.

**2.** Brown the sausage in a skillet at medium-high heat; drain off grease and transfer sausage to the slow cooker. Add remaining ingredients to the slow cooker. Cover and cook on low setting for 8 to 9 hours.

# Wyoming Cowboy Casserole

*Take the family out West for some good ol' cowboy eatin'—they'll love it!*

**stats**

**SERVES 4**

Cooking time . . . . . . . 4 hours

Preparation time. . . . 15 minutes

Attention. . . . . . . . . . Minimal

Pot size . . . . . . . . . . . 3–6 quarts

1 pound lean ground beef

1 cup Colby cheese, cubed

1 (10¾-ounce) can condensed tomato soup

1 (16-ounce) can whole kernel corn

1 (16-ounce) can red kidney beans

¼ cup milk

1 teaspoon dry onion flakes

½ teaspoon chili powder

1. Brown the beef in a medium-sized skilled on medium-high heat; drain off grease. Spread the beef on paper towels to cool. Cut the cheese into ½-inch cubes.

2. Add all ingredients to the slow cooker. Cover and cook on low for 4 hours.

# Shepherd's Pie

*A classic favorite that doubles as comfort food,*
*check out this super-simple recipe.*

**stats**

**SERVES 4**

Cooking time . . . . . . . 6–8 hours

Preparation time. . . . 15 minutes

Attention. . . . . . . . . . Minimal

Pot size . . . . . . . . . . . . 3–6 quarts

*1 pound beef steak*

*3 medium carrots*

*1 cup fresh green beans*

*1 medium-sized yellow onion*

*1 cup fresh peas*

*1 cup canned or frozen sweet corn*

*1 teaspoon table salt*

*1 teaspoon ground black pepper*

*2 cups beef gravy*

*6 cups leftover mashed potatoes*

**1.** Cut the meat into 1-inch cubes. Peel and chop the carrots into ¼-inch rounds. Remove the stems from the beans and cut the beans in half. Peel the onion and chop into ¼-inch pieces.

**2.** Combine the vegetables, salt, pepper, meat, and gravy in the slow cooker. Top with mashed potatoes. Cover and cook on low setting for 6 to 8 hours.

# Kielbasa and Cabbage Dinner

*Zesty and tangy, this kielbasa dinner is sure to delight.*

**stats**

**SERVES 6**

Cooking time . . . . . . . 7–8 hours
Preparation time. . . . 15 minutes
Attention. . . . . . . . . . Minimal
Pot size . . . . . . . . . . . . 4–6 quarts

1½ pounds kielbasa

2 medium yellow onions

4 medium potatoes

1 red bell pepper

4 large ripe tomatoes

2 garlic cloves

1½ heads green cabbage

1 cup dry white wine

1 tablespoon Dijon mustard

¾ teaspoon caraway seeds

½ teaspoon ground black pepper

¾ teaspoon table salt

**1.** Cut the kielbasa into 3-inch pieces. Peel the onions and chop into ¼-inch pieces. Peel the potatoes and cut into 1-inch cubes. Remove the stem and seeds from the red pepper and chop into ¼-inch pieces. Chop the tomatoes into ½-inch pieces. Peel the garlic and mince with a sharp paring knife. Shred the cabbage into ¼-inch strips with a sharp kitchen knife.

**2.** Combine all ingredients in the slow cooker. Cover and cook on low setting for 7 to 8 hours.

# Smoky Little Sausage Hot Dish

*These smoky weiners will wow your kids and prompt many "thanks"!*

**stats**

**SERVES 4**

Cooking time . . . . . . . 6–7 hours
Preparation time . . . . 15 minutes
Attention . . . . . . . . . . Minimal
Pot size . . . . . . . . . . . . 3–6 quarts

1 pound smoky wieners

2 cups cooked macaroni

1 medium-sized yellow onion

¾ cup American cheese

3 tablespoons pimientos, chopped

3 tablespoons flour

¾ teaspoon table salt

¼ teaspoon ground black pepper

1 cup milk

1 cup water

½ tablespoon vinegar

1 cup fresh peas

1 teaspoon dry parsley

**1.** Cut the wieners into 1-inch lengths. Cook the macaroni in boiling water until soft but not mushy. Peel the onion and chop into ¼-inch pieces. Grate the cheese using a vegetable grater. Chop the pimientos into ¼-inch pieces.

**2.** Combine the cheese, flour, salt, pepper, milk, water, and vinegar in a medium-sized saucepan on the stove; cook on medium heat, stirring frequently, until the mixture is smooth and thick. Pour into the slow cooker. Add the wieners, macaroni, peas, onions, parsley, and pimientos; stir well. Cover and cook on low setting for 6 to 7 hours.

# 10

# Vegetarian Options

# Mexican-Style Stuffed Red Peppers

*Spread butter on flour tortillas, sprinkle on garlic salt, and bake in a 350°F oven for 10 minutes to create a crunchy complement to this meal.*

**stats**

**SERVES 4**

Cooking time . . . . . . . 4–6 hours
Preparation time . . . . 30 minutes
Attention . . . . . . . . . . Minimal
Pot size . . . . . . . . . . . . 4–6 quarts

*4 large red bell peppers*

*2 cloves garlic*

*½ cup green chives, chopped*

*1 large tomato*

*2 sprigs fresh cilantro*

*½ cup cooked rice*

*½ cup cooked black beans (fresh or canned)*

*½ cup fresh, canned, or frozen corn*

*½ teaspoon dried crushed basil*

*¼ teaspoon ground black pepper*

*½ teaspoon chili powder*

*½ cup tomato sauce*

*2 cups water*

*¼ cup Cheddar cheese, shredded*

**1.** Remove the stem and seeds from the red peppers. Peel the garlic and mince with a sharp kitchen knife. Chop the chives into ¼-inch pieces. Chop the tomato into ¼-inch pieces. Crush the cilantro or mince with a sharp knife.

**2.** Combine the rice, beans, chives, corn, diced tomatoes, garlic, cilantro, basil, black pepper, and chili powder in a bowl; mix well with a large spoon. Use an ice cream scoop to spoon a portion of the mixture into each red pepper. The mixture should come to the top of the peppers but should not overflow.

**3.** Pour the tomato sauce and water into the slow cooker. Place the stuffed red peppers in the slow cooker so they stand upright. Cook covered on low setting for 4 to 6 hours. Five minutes before serving, sprinkle Cheddar cheese on the top of each red pepper. Cover and cook on low setting until cheese melts.

# Garlicky Red Beans

*Serve over brown rice with a side of fresh-steamed broccoli for a complete, healthy meal.*

 **stats**

**SERVES 8**

Cooking time . . . . . . . 8–10 hours
Preparation time. . . . 20 minutes
Attention. . . . . . . . . . Medium
Pot size . . . . . . . . . . . . 5–6 quarts

1 pound red beans

3 cups water

1 medium-sized yellow onion

1 bunch green onions

7 cloves garlic

1 celery rib

1 green bell pepper

½ cup fresh parsley

½ cup ketchup

1 tablespoon Worcestershire sauce

2 tablespoons Tabasco sauce

2 bay leaves

1 teaspoon thyme

½ teaspoon table salt

½ teaspoon ground black pepper

**1.** Soak the beans overnight in six cups water. Drain and rinse the beans. Place them in slow cooker and add 3 cups of fresh water. Cook covered on low setting for 3 hours.

**2.** Peel and chop the yellow onion into ¼-inch pieces. Clean and cut the green onions into ½-inch lengths. Be sure to use all of the green stems. Peel and slice the garlic paper-thin, using a sharp paring knife. Chop the celery into ¼-inch pieces. Remove the seeds from the bell pepper and cut the pepper into ¼-inch pieces.

**3.** Add the yellow onion, green onion, garlic, celery, bell pepper, parsley, ketchup, Worcestershire, Tabasco, bay leaves, thyme, salt, and pepper to slow cooker; stir until ingredients are well mingled with beans. Cook covered on low setting for 5 to 7 hours.

# Caribbean Black Beans and Rice

*With this tasty tropical meal, you and your family will be dreaming of sunshine!*

**stats**

**SERVES 6**

Cooking time . . . . . . . 7–9 hours
Preparation time. . . . 30 minutes
Attention. . . . . . . . . . Medium
Pot size . . . . . . . . . . . . 3–6 quarts

1 large red bell pepper

Olive oil for basting red pepper, plus 1½ teaspoons more

½ green bell pepper

2 cloves garlic

1 cup raw white rice (yields 3 cups cooked)

2 (16-ounce) cans of black beans

2 tablespoons white vinegar

2 teaspoons Tabasco or other hot sauce

3 tablespoons cilantro, chopped

1 teaspoon table salt

½ teaspoon ground black pepper

**1.** Remove the stems and seeds from the red bell pepper and cut into quarters. Lightly cover the inside "meat" of the pepper with olive oil. Bake in 350°F oven for 1 hour; remove and cut into ¼-inch-long strips. Remove the seeds from the green bell pepper and cut into ¼-inch-long strips. Peel and slice the garlic paper-thin with a sharp paring knife. Prepare the rice according to package directions to yield 3 cups of cooked rice.

**2.** Sauté the red pepper, green pepper, and garlic in 1½ teaspoons olive oil for 2 minutes on medium-high heat in a large skillet on the stove. Drain off the oil; combine with cilantro, salt, and black pepper and place mixture in the slow cooker. Drain and rinse the black beans; add them to the slow cooker. Add vinegar, Tabasco, and rice to slow cooker. Stir until all ingredients are well mingled. Cook covered on low setting for 6 to 8 hours. Because this meal does not have a great deal of liquid, you may need to add ¼ to ½ cup water about halfway through the cooking process.

# Spinach, Rice, and Vegetable Casserole

*Pair this meal with fresh cantaloupe and honeydew
melon cubes to offset the robust tomato flavor.*

**stats**

**SERVES 8**

Cooking time . . . . . . . 6–8 hours
Preparation time. . . . 20 minutes
Attention. . . . . . . . . . Medium
Pot size . . . . . . . . . . . . 3–6 quarts

1 large yellow onion

3 cloves of garlic

1 bunch parsley

2 bunches spinach

1 cup fresh tomatoes, chopped

2 tablespoons olive oil

3 cups water

2 tablespoons tomato paste

⅛ teaspoon table salt

⅛ teaspoon ground black pepper

1 cup uncooked white rice

**1.** Peel and chop the onion into ¼-inch pieces. Peel and slice the garlic paper-thin with a sharp paring knife. Chop the parsley into ¼-inch lengths. Wash the spinach and remove the stems. Chop the tomatoes into ¼-inch pieces.

**2.** Heat the oil over medium-high heat in a medium-sized skillet. Add the onions, parsley, and garlic; sauté for 3 to 5 minutes, until the onions are translucent. Drain off oil and transfer the mixture to the slow cooker. Add the water, tomato paste, chopped tomatoes, salt, and pepper. Mix well so ingredients are well mingled. Add spinach and rice; stir. Cook covered on low setting for 6 to 8 hours, or until rice is done.

# Creamy Roasted Corn with Rice

*Creamy and rich, this dish is great on its own or with a beef entrée.*

**stats**

**SERVES 6**

Cooking time . . . . . . . 7–9 hours
Preparation time. . . . 20 minutes
Attention . . . . . . . . . . Medium
Pot size . . . . . . . . . . . 3–6 quarts

3 tablespoons olive oil

1 cup uncooked white rice

4 cups vegetable broth

½ cup skim milk

½ cup dry white wine

½ teaspoon table salt

½ teaspoon ground black pepper

½ teaspoon nutmeg

2 cups fresh or frozen corn, cooked

⅓ pound cream cheese

4 fresh scallions

**1.** Heat the olive oil on medium-high in a medium-sized skillet. Sauté the rice, stirring constantly for 3 to 5 minutes, until slightly browned. Drain and place in the slow cooker.

**2.** Add the chicken broth, milk, white wine, salt, pepper, and nutmeg to the slow cooker. Cook covered on low setting for 6 to 8 hours, or until rice is soft.

**3.** Cut the cream cheese into ½-inch cubes. Peel and slice the scallions paper-thin, using a sharp paring knife.

**4.** Add the corn, scallions, and cream cheese to the slow cooker; stir well. Cook covered 30 to 60 minutes, stirring every 10 minutes. The cheese should be fully melted and integrated into the sauce.

# Lemony Bulgur Garbanzo Pilaf

*For a creamy alternative, add ½ cup of grated mild*
*Cheddar cheese and eliminate the parsley and lemon juice.*

**stats** — **SERVES 6**

| | |
|---|---|
| Cooking time | 6–9 hours |
| Preparation time | 30 minutes |
| Attention | Medium |
| Pot size | 3–6 quarts |

1 cup medium-grind bulgur

2 cups cooked chickpeas, or
1 cup dried

½ teaspoon table salt

½ teaspoon ground black pepper

2 cups vegetable stock or
bouillon

1 small yellow onion

1 small green bell pepper

3 cloves garlic

1 tablespoon olive oil

½ teaspoon cumin

⅓ cup fresh lemon juice

1 cup fresh parsley, chopped

**1.** Wash the bulgur and chickpeas, then place them in the slow cooker along with the salt, pepper, and vegetable stock. Cook covered on low setting for 2 to 3 hours.

**2.** Peel and chop the onion into ¼-inch pieces. Remove the seeds from the green pepper and chop into ¼-inch pieces. Peel and mince the garlic, using a sharp kitchen knife.

**3.** Heat the olive oil to medium-high heat in a medium-sized skillet. Add the onion, green pepper, and garlic; sauté for 3 to 5 minutes, stirring constantly, until the onions are translucent. Drain off oil. Add the onions, green pepper, garlic, and cumin to the slow cooker; mix well. Cook covered on low setting for 4 to 6 additional hours.

**4.** Add the lemon juice and parsley to the slow cooker; mix well. Cook uncovered for 30 minutes more on low setting.

# Eggplant and Tomatoes with Pasta

*Complement this meal with tomato slices topped with goat cheese and fresh basil.*

**stats**

**SERVES 4**

| | |
|---|---|
| Cooking time | 3½–5 hours |
| Preparation time | 45 minutes |
| Attention | Frequent |
| Pot size | 3–6 quarts |

¾ cup yellow onion, chopped

3 cloves garlic

¾ pound of eggplant, cubed

2 tablespoons fresh basil, chopped

1 (16-ounce) can Italian plum tomatoes with juice

2 tablespoons olive oil

2 tablespoons balsamic vinegar

½ cup chicken broth

1 tablespoon tomato paste

½ teaspoon dried oregano

⅛ teaspoon hot red pepper flakes

½ teaspoon table salt

12 ounces pasta shells or pieces (rotini, wagon wheels, bow ties, etc.)

**1.** Peel and chop the onion into ¼-inch pieces. Peel and mince the garlic. Peel and cut the eggplant into 1-inch cubes. Chop the basil into ¼-inch lengths. Pour the tomatoes into a bowl and break into approximate quarters, using a wooden spoon.

**2.** In a skillet, heat the olive oil on medium-high heat; sauté the onions and garlic for 3 to 5 minutes, stirring constantly, until the onions are translucent. Drain and place in the slow cooker.

**3.** Add the eggplant, balsamic vinegar, chicken broth, tomato paste, and oregano to the slow cooker; stir well so that all the ingredients are well mingled. Cook uncovered on high setting for 3 to 4 hours, or until the sauce is slightly thickened.

**4.** Reduce the temperature setting to low. Add the basil and red pepper flakes to the sauce in the slow cooker; stir. Boil the pasta in water with the ½ teaspoon of salt in a pot for 10 minutes. Drain the water and add the pasta to the slow cooker; stir so that all of the pasta is covered with sauce. Cover and cook on low setting for 30 to 60 minutes, or until the pasta is soft.

# Minted Lentil and Tofu Stew

*Substitute 2 tablespoons of Italian seasoning for the spearmint and peppermint to create an herbed version of this lentil stew.*

**stats**

**SERVES 6**

| | |
|---|---|
| Cooking time | 8–9 hours |
| Preparation time | 10 minutes |
| Attention | Minimal |
| Pot size | 3–6 quarts |

2 cups dry yellow lentils

6 cups salted water (add 1 tablespoon table salt to water and stir until dissolved)

¼ cup fresh spearmint, chopped

1 tablespoon fresh peppermint, chopped

2 cups firm tofu, cubed

½ teaspoon soybean oil

1 teaspoon lemon juice

1 cup water

1 teaspoon table salt

**1.** Soak the lentils overnight in 6 cups salted water. Wash and drain. Cut the spearmint and peppermint into ¼-inch pieces. Cut the tofu into 1-inch cubes.

**2.** Add all ingredients except tofu to the slow cooker; stir until ingredients are well mixed. Cook covered on low setting 7 to 8 hours. Add tofu and cook 1 to 2 more hours.

# Creamy Vegetarian Chili

*Serve this chili with corn bread to create an almost-authentic Tex-Mex treat.*

**stats**

**SERVES 6**

Cooking time . . . . . . . 8–9 hours
Preparation time. . . . 15 minutes
Attention. . . . . . . . . . Minimal
Pot size . . . . . . . . . . . . 3–6 quarts

2 cups dried red kidney beans
2 cups firm tofu, cubed
2 large carrots
2 large yellow onions
1 tablespoon chili powder
1 teaspoon garlic salt
1 teaspoon ground black pepper
1 cup fresh or frozen corn
½ cup low-fat sour cream

**1.** Soak the beans overnight in 6 cups water. Cut the tofu into 1-inch cubes. Peel and slice the carrots into ¼-inch rounds. Peel and slice the onions into ¼-inch squares.

**2.** Drain and wash the beans. Add all ingredients except tofu to the slow cooker; mix with a wooden spoon until all the ingredients are well mingled. Cook covered on low setting 7 to 8 hours. Add tofu cook 1 to 1½ hours. Approximately 30 minutes before serving, stir the chili, then add the sour cream; stir well. Cook uncovered on low setting for the remaining half-hour.

# Nutty Barley Pilaf

*Serve with fresh apple and orange slices to
complement the nutty flavors in this dish.*

 *stats*

**SERVES 4**

Cooking time . . . . . . . 6 hours
Preparation time . . . . 20 minutes
Attention . . . . . . . . . . Medium
Pot size . . . . . . . . . . . . 3–6 quarts

1¾ cup pearl barley

½ cup butter, divided

2 medium-sized yellow onions

8 ounces (1 cup) fresh
mushrooms, sliced

4 cups vegetable broth

¼ cup toasted macadamia nuts,
chopped

¼ cup toasted pecans, chopped

½ cup fresh parsley, chopped

**1.** On the stove, sauté the barley in four tablespoons of the butter in a medium-sized skillet on medium heat until the barley is golden; stir often. Pour the mixture into the slow cooker.

**2.** Peel and chop the onions into ¼-inch pieces. Clean the mushrooms by wiping with a damp cloth; slice paper-thin with a sharp paring knife. Put the onions and mushrooms in the skillet and sauté, stirring often, in the remaining butter on medium heat for about 5 minutes. Add this to the slow cooker and stir well. Pour 2 cups of vegetable broth over the mixture. Cover and cook on low setting for 4 hours.

**3.** Add the remaining broth and cook uncovered for 2 hours, stirring occasionally.

**4.** Chop the nuts finely with a sharp paring knife. Place on a cookie sheet in the oven and heat for 15 minutes at 350°F. Roughly chop the parsley. Fifteen minutes before serving, stir the nuts and parsley into the mixture.

# Buddhist Monk's Soup

*Serve with brown bread and three-year-old*
*Cheddar cheese for an authentic monastery meal.*

**stats**

**SERVES 6**

Cooking time........ 7–9 hours
Preparation time.... 40 minutes
Attention........... Medium
Pot size............. 3–6 quarts

1 pound butternut squash

1 large sweet potato

1 quart water

½ cup raw peanuts, shelled and skinned

⅓ cup dried mung beans

3 tablespoons vegetable oil

1 square of tofu

1 quart unsweetened coconut milk

1 teaspoon table salt

1 (12-ounce) package cellophane noodles

**1.** Peel the squash and sweet potato and cut into 3-inch pieces. Put them into the slow cooker with 1 quart of water and salt. Cook covered on high setting for 6 to 8 hours or until soft.

**2.** Soak the mung beans and peanuts in water until soft, about 30 minutes. Sauté the tofu in the vegetable oil on medium-high heat until brown; drain off grease and cut the tofu into ¼-inch strips. Add beans, peanuts, tofu, coconut milk, salt, and cellophane noodles. Cover and cook on low setting for 1 hour.

# Vidalia Onion and Lentil Casserole

*Peel and slice another onion into ¼-inch rings. Sauté rings until crisp and place them on top of the casserole before serving.*

**stats**

**SERVES 4**

| | |
|---|---|
| Cooking time | 6 hours |
| Preparation time | 15 minutes |
| Attention | Minimal |
| Pot size | 3–6 quarts |

1 large Vidalia onion, chopped

2 cups dried lentils

1 teaspoon table salt

3 cups water

2 cups tomato sauce

¼ cup brown sugar

2 tablespoons Dijon mustard

⅓ cup dark molasses

Peel the onion and chop into ¼-inch pieces. Rinse the lentils and place in the slow cooker. Add the onion, salt, water, tomato sauce, brown sugar, mustard, and molasses; stir well. Cover and cook on low setting for 6 hours.

# Root Vegetable Soup

*This is an excellent complement to grilled-vegetable sandwiches or veggie burgers.*

 **stats**

**SERVES 6**

Cooking time ....... 6–8 hours
Preparation time.... 15 minutes
Attention.......... Minimal
Pot size ............ 3–8 quarts

2 medium-sized yellow onions

3 medium carrots

1 medium rutabaga

1 large beet

1 medium turnip

3 medium potatoes

¼ teaspoon ground black pepper

1 teaspoon ground nutmeg

3 cups vegetable broth

Peel all the vegetables and chop into ¼-inch cubes. Combine all ingredients in the slow cooker. Cover and cook on low setting for 6 to 8 hours.

# Portobello-Stuffed Artichokes

*These are fun to eat and easy to make—a great combination for busy cooks!*

**SERVES 4**

Cooking time ....... 7–9 hours
Preparation time.... 30 minutes
Attention.......... Minimal
Pot size ............ 3–8 quarts

4 large artichokes

4 large portobello mushrooms

3 garlic cloves

2 tablespoons grated Parmesan cheese

½ teaspoon ground black pepper

1 tablespoon olive oil

1 teaspoon salt

**1.** Remove the stems from the artichokes and discard the outer 2 to 3 layers of leaves. Trim the base so that the artichokes stand flat. Cut off the top of the artichoke and hollow out the center, removing all purple-tinged leaves and fuzzy material.

**2.** Chop the mushrooms into ¼-inch pieces. Peel the garlic and mince with a sharp kitchen knife. Combine the mushrooms, garlic, Parmesan cheese, black pepper, and olive oil in a medium-sized mixing bowl. Stuff the mixture into the artichoke centers.

**3.** Pour water into the slow cooker (so it is about 1½ inches deep) and stir in the salt. Set the artichokes in the water. Cover and cook on low setting for 7 to 9 hours. The leaves should be tender when done.

# Farmer Peas

*For the best flavor, use fresh peas or spring peapods in this dish. This goes well with a crisp salad and crusty bread, as well as with chicken or seafood.*

**SERVES 6**

| | |
|---|---|
| Cooking time | 2–3 hours |
| Preparation time | 30 minutes |
| Attention | Minimal |
| Pot size | 3–5 quarts |

*1 onion*

*6 small carrots*

*1 head romaine lettuce*

*2 cups fresh green peas*

*12 asparagus tips*

*1 cup vegetable or mushroom broth*

*1 cup water*

*½ teaspoon salt*

*½ teaspoon sugar*

*3 tablespoons butter*

**1.** Coarsely chop the onion, carrots, and lettuce.

**2.** Combine the chopped vegetables with the peas, asparagus tips, broth, water, salt, sugar, and butter in the slow cooker.

**3.** Cover and heat on a high setting for 2 to 3 hours.

# Carrots in Dill and Wine

*The aromatic flavor of dill blends well with carrot.*
*If you have fresh dill, save some to add just before serving.*

**SERVES 6**

| | |
|---|---|
| Cooking time | 3–4 hours |
| Preparation time | 30 minutes |
| Attention | Moderate |
| Pot size | 3–5 quarts |

1 onion

2 cloves garlic

8 medium carrots

½ cup chicken broth

½ teaspoon dried dill weed

¼ teaspoon salt

1 tablespoon lemon juice

2 tablespoons cornstarch

2 tablespoons cold water

½ cup dry white wine

**1.** Mince the onion; crush the garlic. Cut the carrots into small sticks.

**2.** Combine the onion, garlic, carrots, broth, dill weed, salt, and lemon juice in the slow cooker.

**3.** Cover and heat on a high setting for 2 to 3 hours.

**4.** An hour before serving, mix the cornstarch into the cold water, stir into the slow cooker, and turn the temperature to low. Add the wine.

# Home Sweet Potatoes

*This is possibly the simplest potato recipe you'll ever use.*
*There's no need to even peel the potatoes!*

**SERVES 6**

Cooking time . . . . . . . 5–6 hours
Preparation time . . . . 15 minutes
Attention . . . . . . . . . . Minimal
Pot size . . . . . . . . . . . . 3–5 quarts

6 sweet potatoes
3 tablespoons butter
¼ cup brown sugar

1. Wash the potatoes, and put them in the slow cooker while still wet.

2. Cover and heat on a low setting for 5 to 6 hours.

3. Before serving, top with butter and brown sugar.

# Stuffed Baked Potatoes

*Did you know you can freeze baked potatoes?*
*Keep a tub of these in the freezer, then thaw and restuff as needed.*

**SERVES 6**

Cooking time . . . . . . . 1–2 hours
Preparation time. . . . 15 minutes
Attention. . . . . . . . . . Minimal
Pot size . . . . . . . . . . . . 3–5 quarts

¼ pound Cheddar cheese

6 baked potatoes

1 cup sour cream

½ teaspoon salt

½ teaspoon pepper

1. Shred the cheese. Halve the potatoes. Scoop most of the insides of the potatoes into a mixing bowl. Add the sour cream, cheese, salt, and pepper and mix well. Return the mixture to the potatoes.

2. Wrap the potatoes in foil and arrange on a trivet in the slow cooker. Pour water around the base of the trivet.

3. Cover and heat on a high setting for 1 to 2 hours.

# Spiced Orange Vegetables

*For extra zing, you can set aside a dash of the fresh
orange juice to add at the very end, just before serving.*

**stats**

**SERVES 6**

Cooking time . . . . . . . 2–3 hours
Preparation time. . . . 30 minutes
Attention. . . . . . . . . . Minimal
Pot size . . . . . . . . . . . . 3–5 quarts

2 pounds baby carrots

½ pound yellow squash

¼ cup butter

3 tablespoons brown sugar

1 teaspoon ground cinnamon

½ teaspoon ground cumin

¼ teaspoon cayenne pepper

¼ teaspoon pepper

½ teaspoon salt

2 cups peas

1¼ cups orange juice

1. Cube the squash.

2. Melt the butter in a pan and stir in the sugar, spices, and salt; add the carrots, squash, and peas and stir until coated.

3. Transfer the vegetable mix to the slow cooker. Add the orange juice.

4. Cover and heat on a medium setting for 2 to 3 hours.

# Dallas Beans

*This is the dish to serve when having friends over to watch old Westerns.*
*Serve with grilled veggie burgers and root beer.*

**stats**

**SERVES 9**

| | |
|---|---|
| Cooking time | 8–10 hours |
| Preparation time | 30 minutes |
| Attention | Minimal |
| Pot size | 3–5 quarts |

2 cups dry pinto beans

1 onion

1 clove garlic

1 teaspoon salt

½ cup water

¼ pound soy sausage
(or salt pork)

1 green pepper

5 tomatoes

¼ teaspoon white pepper

1 teaspoon salt

6 drops hot pepper sauce

2 tablespoons sugar

**1.** Cover the beans with water and soak overnight in the slow cooker, then drain and discard the water.

**2.** Coarsely chop the onion and garlic. Add onion, garlic, and salt to the beans in the slow cooker and stir in ½ cup water.

**3.** Cover and heat on a low setting for 6 to 8 hours.

**4.** Chop the soy sausage, green pepper, and tomatoes. Two hours before serving, add the soy sausage, green pepper, tomatoes, white pepper, salt, pepper sauce, and sugar to the slow cooker.

# Red Cabbage with Wine

*Red cabbage becomes sweet and tender after slow cooking,*
*and in this recipe, the red wine helps it retain its rich red color.*

**SERVES 6**

| | |
|---|---|
| Cooking time | 4–5 hours |
| Preparation time | 15 minutes |
| Attention | Minimal |
| Pot size | 3–5 quarts |

1 head red cabbage

1 teaspoon salt

½ teaspoon coarsely ground black pepper

2 cups beef broth

1 tablespoon vegetable oil

1 cup red wine

**1.** Finely slice the red cabbage.

**2.** Combine the cabbage, salt, pepper, broth, and oil in the slow cooker.

**3.** Cover and heat on a low setting for 3 to 4 hours.

**4.** An hour before serving, add the wine.

# Spiced Tomatoes

*This tangy and colorful dish goes well with
any entrée and it can be served hot or cold.*

**SERVES 6**

Cooking time . . . . . . . 2–3 hours
Preparation time . . . . 30 minutes
Attention . . . . . . . . . . Minimal
Pot size . . . . . . . . . . . . 3–5 quarts

2 pounds red and yellow pear
tomatoes

1 teaspoon ground cloves

1 teaspoon ground allspice

1 teaspoon coarsely ground
black pepper

1 tablespoon sugar

2 cups cider vinegar

**1.** Pierce the tomatoes and arrange them in the slow cooker.

**2.** Sprinkle the tomatoes with the spices. Dissolve the sugar in the vinegar and pour it over the tomatoes.

**3.** Cover and heat on a low setting for 2 to 3 hours.

# Simple Beans

*Still not sure what to feed your guests? Go ahead and make
a batch of beans while you decide, and you'll be a step ahead.*

 **YIELDS ABOUT 4 CUPS**

Cooking time ....... 4–6 hours
Preparation time.... 30 minutes
Attention.......... Minimal
Pot size ............ 3–5 quarts

1 cup dried beans

2 cups water

**1.** Soak the beans in water overnight, then drain and rinse.

**2.** Add soaked beans and 2 cups fresh water to the slow cooker.

**3.** Cover and heat on a low setting for 8 to 10 hours or overnight.

# Easy Pickle Beans

*This is a good Super Bowl menu item. It's easy to make, very popular, and best of all, you can watch the game while it cooks.*

**stats**

**SERVES 8**

Cooking time . . . . . . . 3–4 hours
Preparation time . . . . 30 minutes
Attention . . . . . . . . . . Minimal
Pot size . . . . . . . . . . . . 3–5 quarts

6 slices bacon

½ onion

½ cup sweet pickle relish

4 cups baked beans

2 tablespoons molasses

½ teaspoon salt

**1.** Cut the bacon into 1-inch pieces. Sauté in a pan over medium heat until crisp. Transfer the bacon pieces to the slow cooker, leaving the drippings in the pan.

**2.** Coarsely chop the onion. Sauté the onion in the pan with the bacon drippings until the onion is tender but not brown. Drain; transfer the onion to the slow cooker.

**3.** Drain the relish. Add the relish, beans, molasses, and salt to the slow cooker.

**4.** Cover and heat on a low setting for 3 to 4 hours.

# Wild Game

# Bing Cherry Pheasant

*Cherries have a rich, savory taste that is especially delicious when coupled with a buttery pheasant.*

*stats*

**SERVES 8**

Cooking time . . . . . . . 4–6 hours
Preparation time. . . . 60 minutes
Attention. . . . . . . . . . Minimal
Pot size . . . . . . . . . . . . 3–5 quarts

4 pounds pheasant

½ teaspoon salt

½ teaspoon pepper

2 tablespoons flour

¼ cup butter

1 pound fresh Bing cherries

1 cup red wine

6 whole cloves

½ cup water

½ cup sugar

1 cup cream

**1.** Cut the pheasant into serving-size pieces. Combine the salt, pepper, and flour. Roll the pheasant pieces in the flour mixture; sauté in butter in a pan over medium heat until browned. Transfer to the slow cooker.

**2.** Pit and halve the cherries. Add half of the cherries, half of the wine, the cloves, and the water to the slow cooker. Cover and heat on a low setting for 4 to 6 hours.

**3.** Mix the sugar, remaining cherries, and remaining wine in a saucepan over low heat; stir until partly reduced.

**4.** An hour before serving, add the cream to the slow cooker.

**5.** When serving, provide the reduced cherry mixture as a sauce.

# Pheasant with Orange

*This goes well with Orange Raisin Bread (page 68), or you can cream some orange pulp into a soft spread and serve it with crusty French bread.*

**stats**

**SERVES 6**

Cooking time . . . . . . . 4–6 hours
Preparation time . . . . 45 minutes
Attention . . . . . . . . . . Minimal
Pot size . . . . . . . . . . . 3–5 quarts

3 pounds pheasant

⅔ cup flour

½ teaspoon salt

¼ teaspoon pepper

2 tablespoons butter

2 tablespoons olive oil

1 cup orange juice

½ cup white raisins

2–4 sprigs fresh rosemary

1 small bunch fresh parsley

1 cup white wine

**1.** Cut the pheasant into serving-size pieces and remove the skin. Shake the pieces in flour, salt, and pepper to coat; sauté in butter and olive oil in a pan over medium heat until browned. Transfer to the slow cooker.

**2.** Add the orange juice and raisins to the meat.

**3.** Cover and heat on a low setting for 4 to 6 hours.

**4.** Coarsely chop the rosemary and parsley. Half an hour before serving, add the herbs and wine to the slow cooker.

# Pheasant with Sauerkraut

*Pheasant can be very dry, but the sauerkraut in
this recipe keeps the meat moist and tender.*

**stats**

### SERVES 4–6

Cooking time . . . . . . . 4–6 hours
Preparation time . . . . 30 minutes
Attention . . . . . . . . . . Minimal
Pot size . . . . . . . . . . . 3–5 quarts

2 *pounds pheasant*

1 *onion*

2 *tablespoons vegetable oil*

2 *pounds sauerkraut*

2 *bay leaves*

6 *cloves*

16 *ounces beer*

**1.** Cut the pheasant meat into serving-size pieces; thinly slice the onion. Sauté the meat and onion in oil in a pan over medium heat until lightly browned.

**2.** Drain the sauerkraut. Layer the meat, sauerkraut, and spices in the slow cooker. Pour the beer over the top.

**3.** Cover and heat on a low setting for 4 to 6 hours. Remove bay leaves before serving.

# Cinnamon Apple Pheasant

*Use good baking apples, like Rome or Granny Smith, for some*
*extra tartness. You can leave the peels on for a little more color.*

**SERVES 8**

Cooking time . . . . . . . 4–6 hours
Preparation time . . . . 30 minutes
Attention . . . . . . . . . . Minimal
Pot size . . . . . . . . . . . 3–5 quarts

4 pounds pheasant

½ teaspoon salt

½ teaspoon black pepper

¼ cup butter

4 apples

2 cups apple cider

2 sticks cinnamon bark

**1.** Cut the pheasant into serving-size pieces and roll in the salt and pepper. Sauté in butter in a pan over medium heat until lightly browned.

**2.** Core and slice the apples. Layer the pheasant with the apple slices in the slow cooker. Add the cider and cinnamon.

**3.** Cover and heat on a low setting for 4 to 6 hours.

# Reindeer Stew

*Reindeer is actually domesticated caribou. This recipe can also be made with venison if you don't have any reindeer on hand.*

**stats**

**SERVES 10–12**

Cooking time . . . . . . . 4–6 hours
Preparation time . . . . 60 minutes
Attention . . . . . . . . . . Minimal
Pot size . . . . . . . . . . . . 3–5 quarts

1 pound baby potatoes
1 pound mushrooms
2 tablespoons olive oil
5 pounds reindeer
½ teaspoon salt
½ teaspoon pepper
¼ cup butter
¼ cup flour
1 cup water
2 cups red wine
1 bouquet garni

**1.** Halve the baby potatoes and mushrooms. Sauté them in oil in a pan over medium heat until the mushrooms are slightly browned. Transfer to the slow cooker.

**2.** Cube the meat. Roll in the salt and pepper, then sauté in the butter in a pan over medium heat until lightly browned. Add the flour and stir over medium heat until the flour browns, then stir in the water and mix while the sauce thickens. Transfer the meat and sauce to the slow cooker.

**3.** Add the wine and bouquet garni to the meat.

**4.** Cover and heat on a low setting for 4 to 6 hours.

# Country Hare Stew

*This recipe takes some advance planning, but it's a sure way to impress your guests. Serve this with small black bread rolls.*

*stats*

**SERVES 4–6**

Cooking time . . . . . . . 6–8 hours
Preparation time. . . . 90 minutes
Attention. . . . . . . . . . Moderate
Pot size . . . . . . . . . . . . 3–5 quarts

2 pounds rabbit

1 carrot

1 onion

1 cup white wine

1 cup water

1 bouquet garni

1 teaspoon whole black peppercorns

½ pound butter

2 tablespoons flour

1 cup water

¼ pound salt pork

10 pearl onions

½ pound mushrooms

1 tablespoon chopped parsley

**1.** Cut the rabbit meat into pieces. Scrub, peel, and chop the carrot and peel and chop the onion. Marinate the meat in the refrigerator with the carrot, onion, wine, 1 cup water, bouquet garni, and peppercorns. After 2 days, remove the meat; strain the marinade and save the juice, discarding the vegetables and spices.

**2.** Melt the butter in a pan over medium heat and mix in the flour. Add the marinated meat, stir for a few minutes, then slowly stir in the strained marinade and the remaining 1 cup of water. Transfer to the slow cooker. Cover and heat on a low setting for 4 to 6 hours.

**3.** Cube the salt pork and peel the onions. Heat the pork with the onions in water in a covered pot over high heat until boiling; drain and discard the liquid.

**4.** Halve the mushrooms. Sauté the boiled pork, boiled onions, and mushrooms in a pan over medium heat until pork is browned. Drain, then transfer to the slow cooker with the meat.

**5.** Cover the slow cooker and heat on a low setting another 2 hours. Before serving, stir in the parsley.

# Hungarian Rabbit

*Rabbit and paprika are a delicious combination.*
*This dish goes well with fresh sourdough bread.*

**stats**

**SERVES 8**

Cooking time . . . . . . . 4–6 hours
Preparation time . . . . 60 minutes
Attention . . . . . . . . . . Minimal
Pot size . . . . . . . . . . . . 3–5 quarts

*1 egg*
*1 teaspoon milk*
*4 pounds rabbit*
*⅓ cup flour*
*1 tablespoon paprika*
*½ teaspoon salt*
*¼ teaspoon pepper*
*2 onions*
*3 tablespoons butter*
*1 cup white wine*
*¼ cup water*
*1 cup sour cream*
*2 teaspoons paprika*

**1.** Beat the egg and milk together.

**2.** Cut the rabbit meat into pieces. Dip the pieces in the egg mixture, then coat the pieces by shaking them in a mixture of the flour, 1 tablespoon paprika, salt, and pepper.

**3.** Thinly slice the onions. Sauté the meat and onions in butter in a pan over medium heat until the meat is lightly browned. Transfer the meat and onions to the slow cooker. Add the wine and water.

**4.** Cover and heat on a low setting for 4 to 6 hours.

**5.** Half an hour before serving, add the sour cream and remaining 2 teaspoons paprika to the slow cooker.

# Venison with Gingered Sauerkraut

*Serve big, buttery pumpernickel croutons with this dish.*
*Cube the bread, dunk in melted butter, sprinkle with herbs, and toast.*

**SERVES 4–6**

| | |
|---|---|
| Cooking time | 4–6 hours |
| Preparation time | 30 minutes |
| Attention | Minimal |
| Pot size | 3–5 quarts |

*2 pounds venison*

*1 pound mushrooms*

*2 tablespoons vegetable oil*

*1 onion*

*1½ pounds sauerkraut*

*½ cup water*

*2 tablespoons brown sugar*

*½ cup red wine vinegar*

*1 teaspoon soy sauce*

*½ teaspoon ground ginger*

**1.** Cube the meat and quarter the mushrooms. Sauté meat and mushrooms in oil in a pan over medium heat until the meat is lightly browned.

**2.** Thinly slice the onion. Drain the sauerkraut. Mix the water, sugar, vinegar, soy sauce, and ginger in a small mixing bowl.

**3.** Layer the meat mixture, onion, and sauerkraut in the slow cooker. Pour the vinegar mixture over the top.

**4.** Cover and heat on a low setting for 4 to 6 hours.

# Venison Roast in Orange

*If you don't have access to venison, substitute beef or pork.*
*Use an inexpensive cut; the acidic orange juice will tenderize it during cooking.*

*stats* **SERVES 9**

Cooking time . . . . . . . 6–8 hours
Preparation time . . . . 30 minutes
Attention . . . . . . . . . . Moderate
Pot size . . . . . . . . . . . . 3–5 quarts

*1 slice bacon*

*2 cloves garlic*

*3 pounds venison roast*

*½ teaspoon salt*

*½ teaspoon pepper*

*1 bay leaf*

*2 whole cloves*

*1 cup orange juice*

**1.** Cut the bacon into small pieces; crush and mince the garlic. Cut the meat into serving-size pieces.

**2.** Sauté the meat with the bacon, garlic, salt, and pepper over medium heat until the meat is lightly browned.

**3.** Transfer the meat and juices, bay leaf, cloves, and orange juice to the slow cooker.

**4.** Cover and heat on low setting for 6 to 8 hours. Open the slow cooker twice to baste, but no more.

# Campfire Duck

*Fresh duck should hang to age for about six days in the cold before cooking.*
*Ask a butcher or hunter for help with this.*

**stats**

**SERVES 6–8**

Cooking time....... 4–6 hours
Preparation time.... 30 minutes
Attention.......... Minimal
Pot size............ 3–5 quarts

*3 pounds duck, aged*
*1 teaspoon seasoning salt*
*½ cup flour*
*4 slices bacon*
*½ cup water*
*½ cup heavy cream*

**1.** Cut the meat into serving-size pieces. Rub with the salt and roll in the flour. Mince the bacon. Sauté the duck and bacon in a pan over high heat until browned. Adjust the heat to low. Stir in the water and mix to thicken.

**2.** Transfer the meat and juices to the slow cooker. Cover and heat on low setting for 4 to 6 hours. Half an hour before serving, stir in the cream.

# Slow Venison

*As with wild poultry, the secret to cooking wild game is to age the meat.*
*Do this by marinating it in your refrigerator for an extra-long time.*

**SERVES 6–8**

Cooking time . . . . . . . 4–6 hours
Preparation time . . . . 30 minutes
Attention . . . . . . . . . . Moderate
Pot size . . . . . . . . . . . . 3–5 quarts

3 pounds venison roast

3 cups red wine

3 tablespoons olive oil

3 bay leaves

10 whole cloves

1. Slice the meat. Cover with wine and marinate in the refrigerator for 3 to 4 days. Strain and save 1 cup of marinade. Sauté the meat in oil in a pan over medium heat until browned. Transfer to the slow cooker with saved marinade and spices.

2. Cover and heat on low setting for 4 to 6 hours. Baste twice.

# Hot BBQ Squirrel

*If you don't have squirrel, you could substitute chicken or pork.*
*But if you can get squirrel meat, give it a try.*

 **stats**

**SERVES 8–10**

Cooking time....... 5–7 hours
Preparation time.... 30 minutes
Attention.......... Minimal
Pot size............ 3–5 quarts

*4 pounds squirrel*

*2 slices bacon*

*1 clove garlic*

*1 cup catsup*

*½ cup water*

*½ cup brown sugar*

*⅓ cup Worcestershire sauce*

*1 teaspoon chili powder*

*3 drops red pepper sauce*

**1.** Cut the squirrel meat into pieces. Cut the bacon into 1-inch pieces, and crush the garlic.

**2.** Sauté the meat, bacon, and garlic in a pan over medium heat until the meat is lightly browned. Transfer to the slow cooker.

**3.** Add the catsup, water, sugar, and Worcestershire sauce.

**4.** Cover and heat on low setting for 4 to 6 hours.

**5.** An hour before serving, add the chili powder and pepper sauce.

# Dove with Herbs

*Dove has a dark, rich flavor. Complement this*
*by providing your guests with mild sides.*

 **stats**

**SERVES 6**

Cooking time . . . . . . . 4–6 hours
Preparation time . . . . 60 minutes
Attention . . . . . . . . . . Minimal
Pot size . . . . . . . . . . . . 3–5 quarts

1 onion

1 pound mushrooms

3 tablespoons butter

12 dove breasts

3 tablespoons flour

½ cup water

2 cups red wine

2 sprigs fresh thyme

2 sprigs fresh sage

**1.** Chop the onion and slice the mushrooms. Sauté the onion and mushrooms in butter in a pan over medium heat until the onion is soft. Add the dove and sauté over medium heat until the meat is lightly browned.

**2.** Transfer the meat and vegetables to the slow cooker, leaving the juices in the pan. Add the flour to the pan. Stir over low heat to blend and thicken, then mix in the water. Transfer to the slow cooker with half the wine.

**3.** Cover and heat on low setting for 4 to 6 hours.

**4.** Coarsely chop the herbs. Half an hour before serving, add the herbs and the remaining wine to the slow cooker.

# Pepper Duck

*This goes well with fresh whole wheat bread, or sections of whole wheat pita loaves. Also, use wild mushrooms, if possible.*

**SERVES 6–8**

| | |
|---|---|
| Cooking time | 4–6 hours |
| Preparation time | 30 minutes |
| Attention | Minimal |
| Pot size | 3–5 quarts |

3 *pounds duck*

½ *cup flour*

1 *teaspoon salt*

1 *teaspoon pepper*

1 *onion*

½ *pound mushrooms*

¼ *cup butter*

1 *cup water*

½ *cup dry red wine*

2 *bay leaves*

1 *green pepper*

**1.** Remove the bones and skin from the duck; cube the meat. Shake the meat in flour, salt, and pepper to coat. Thinly slice the onion and halve the mushrooms.

**2.** Sauté the duck, onion, and mushrooms in butter in a pan over medium heat until the duck is lightly browned. Put the duck mixture, water, wine, and bay leaves in the slow cooker.

**3.** Cover and heat on low setting for 4 to 6 hours.

**4.** Mince the green pepper. Half an hour before serving, stir in the green pepper.

# Sherry Duck with Dill

*Use fresh dill if possible, and add it at the end for the best flavor.*

**SERVES 4–6**

Cooking time . . . . . . . 4–6 hours
Preparation time . . . . 60 minutes
Attention . . . . . . . . . . Minimal
Pot size . . . . . . . . . . . . 3–5 quarts

2 pounds duck
1 cup cider vinegar
½ cup water
2 tablespoons olive oil
1 teaspoon salt
¼ teaspoon pepper
¼ cup flour
3 tablespoons butter
¼ cup flour
½ cup olives
1 tablespoon sugar
½ cup white wine
2 sprigs fresh dill weed
½ cup dry sherry

**1.** Cut the meat into serving-size pieces and marinate for 24 hours, refrigerated, in the vinegar, water, oil, salt, and pepper. Strain the marinade and set aside.

**2.** Coat the meat with ¼ cup flour, then sauté in butter in a pan over medium heat until lightly browned. Transfer the meat to the slow cooker.

**3.** Add the remaining ¼ cup flour to the juices in the pan and, while heating, stir until thick. Add the marinade slowly to this and mix until smooth. Mince the olives. Add the marinade sauce, sugar, white wine, and olives to the meat in the slow cooker.

**4.** Cover and heat on low setting for 4 to 6 hours.

**5.** Coarsely chop the dill. Half an hour before serving, add the dill and sherry.

# Duck with Sauerkraut

*Duck is a rich, dark meat; it goes well with the light tang of sauerkraut.*
*You can also substitute goose in this recipe.*

**stats**

**SERVES 8–10**

Cooking time ....... 4–6 hours
Preparation time.... 30 minutes
Attention.......... Minimal
Pot size ............ 3–5 quarts

*4 pounds duck*
*½ teaspoon salt*
*½ teaspoon pepper*
*3 tablespoons sugar*
*½ cup water*
*8 cups sauerkraut*

**1.** Cut the duck into serving-size pieces. Wash and dry with paper towels. Rub the meat with salt and pepper.

**2.** Dissolve the sugar in the water. Layer the duck and sauerkraut in the slow cooker; add the water mixture.

**3.** Cover and heat on a low setting for 4 to 6 hours.

# Hassenpfeffer

*Hassenpfeffer, or "pepper rabbit" in German, is a classic rabbit dish.*
*Be sure to use whole peppercorns when cooking this.*

**stats**

**SERVES 6–8**

Cooking time . . . . . . . 4–6 hours
Preparation time . . . . 30 minutes
Attention . . . . . . . . . . Minimal
Pot size . . . . . . . . . . . . 3–5 quarts

3 pounds rabbit meat

1 onion

10 peppercorns

1½ cups vinegar

1½ cups water

½ teaspoon salt

6 cloves

2 bay leaves

3 tablespoons butter

1 cup sour cream

**1.** Cut the rabbit into serving-size pieces. Slice the onion, and crack (but do not crush) the peppercorns.

**2.** Marinate the rabbit in the onion, vinegar, water, salt, peppercorns, cloves, and bay leaves for 2 days, turning the meat several times. Save 1 cup of the marinade, including the onion slices and spices.

**3.** Sauté the meat in butter in a pan over medium heat until lightly browned; transfer to the slow cooker with the reserved 1 cup of marinade.

**4.** Cover and heat on a low setting for 4 to 6 hours.

**5.** Half an hour before serving, add the sour cream and remove the bay leaves.

# Elk in Wine Sauce

*If a member of your family happens to hunt elk, this is a great way to use it.*
*But if you don't have elk on hand, you can substitute beef.*

*stats*

**SERVES 6–8**

Cooking time . . . . . . . 4–6 hours
Preparation time . . . . 45 minutes
Attention . . . . . . . . . . Minimal
Pot size . . . . . . . . . . . . 3–5 quarts

3 pounds boneless elk roast
¼ cup flour
½ teaspoon salt
¼ teaspoon white pepper
¾ cup butter
2 onions
1 pound mushrooms
¼ pound leeks
1 cup dry wine

**1.** Trim the meat and cut into serving-size pieces; pat dry with a paper towel. Coat in a mixture of the flour, salt, and pepper. Sauté in half of the butter in a pan over high heat until browned. Set aside the meat, leaving the juices in the pan.

**2.** Finely chop the onions. Add the remaining butter to the pan and sauté the onions over medium heat until brown. Lift out the onions with a slotted spoon, leaving the juices in the pan, and transfer to the slow cooker. Put the meat over the onions.

**3.** Chop the mushrooms and leeks (white parts only) and add to the pan; sauté over low heat until soft, then transfer to the slow cooker.

**4.** Cover and heat on low setting for 4 to 6 hours.

**5.** Half an hour before serving, add the wine.

# Rabbit in Coconut Sauce

*The flavors of rabbit and coconut work wonderfully together in this dish.*
*Serve with a side of rice.*

**SERVES 6–8**

Cooking time . . . . . . . 4–6 hours
Preparation time . . . . 30 minutes
Attention . . . . . . . . . . Moderate
Pot size . . . . . . . . . . . . 3–5 quarts

1 coconut

1 cup water

3 tomatoes

2 onions

1 teaspoon salt

½ teaspoon pepper

3 pounds rabbit meat

**1.** Puncture and drain the coconut, setting aside the milk. Crack the coconut; remove the meat. Pare off the brown lining and cut the coconut meat into chunks.

**2.** Put the coconut meat, coconut milk, and water into a blender; blend until smooth. Heat to a boil in a large saucepan and simmer 15 minutes to thicken slightly. Transfer to the slow cooker.

**3.** Mince the tomatoes and onions. Add the tomatoes, onions, salt, and pepper to the coconut.

**4.** Cut the rabbit meat into serving-size pieces. Add to the coconut mixture. Cover and heat on a low setting for 4 to 6 hours, basting often.

# Wild Duck Gumbo

*You can substitute other dark, rich wild fowl for duck in this recipe.*
*Serve with wild rice, barley, or polenta.*

*stats*

**SERVES 6**

| | |
|---|---|
| Cooking time | 4–5 hours |
| Preparation time | 60 minutes |
| Attention | Moderate |
| Pot size | 3–5 quarts |

3 pounds duck

1½ teaspoons salt

1 teaspoon black pepper

½ teaspoon Tabasco sauce

¼ cup oil

3 tablespoons butter

3 tablespoons flour

1 onion

4 cloves garlic

6 cups water

2 dozen oysters, with liquor

**1.** Cut the duck into serving-size pieces. Roll the pieces in the salt and pepper and sprinkle with Tabasco. Sauté the duck in the oil in a pan over medium heat until the meat is browned, then transfer to the slow cooker.

**2.** Melt the butter in a pan over low heat. Blend in the flour and stir until lightly browned.

**3.** Mince the onion and garlic. Add to the browned flour mixture and stir over low heat until the onion is soft.

**4.** Add the onion mixture and water to the slow cooker. Cover and heat on a low setting for 4 to 5 hours.

**5.** Half an hour before serving, take out the pieces of duck and remove the bones, then put the meat back in the slow cooker. Add the oysters and oyster liquor.

# Hot & Spicy

# South o' the Border Chicken Casserole

*Serve over a bed of lettuce and baked tortilla chips.*

*stats* **SERVES 4**

Cooking time....... 4–5 hours
Preparation time.... 15 minutes
Attention.......... Minimal
Pot size........... 3–6 quarts

4 boneless, skinless chicken breasts

1 small yellow onion

1½ cups grated Cheddar cheese

12 flour tortillas

1 (10¾-ounce) can cream of mushroom condensed soup

1 (10¾-ounce) can cream of chicken condensed soup

1 cup sour cream

½ cup (4 ounces) canned chopped jalapeño peppers

1 cup salsa

**1.** Cut the chicken into 1-inch cubes. Peel the onion and grate using the fine side of a vegetable grater. Grate the cheese using the larger side of the vegetable grater. Tear the tortillas into eighths.

**2.** Combine the onion, cheese, soups, sour cream, and jalapeño peppers in a medium-sized bowl. Make layers in the slow cooker using a third of the torn tortillas, soup mixture, chicken, then salsa. Repeat twice more. Cover and cook on low setting for 4 to 5 hours. Gently stir before serving.

# Mexican Beef

*Serve over white rice with fresh-sliced oranges—yum!*

**SERVES 6**

| | |
|---|---|
| Cooking time | 6–8 hours |
| Preparation time | 15 minutes |
| Attention | Minimal |
| Pot size | 3–6 quarts |

2 pounds round steak

1 yellow onion

4 fresh tomatoes

1 beef bouillon cube

1 (16-ounce) can kidney beans

¼ teaspoon ground black pepper

½ teaspoon garlic salt

1 tablespoon chili powder

1 tablespoon prepared mustard

½ cup (4 ounces) canned chopped jalapeño peppers

**1.** Cut the beef into 1-inch cubes. Peel and chop the onion into ¼-inch pieces. Cut the tomatoes into quarters. Crush the bouillon cube. Drain the kidney beans.

**2.** Mix meat, pepper, garlic salt, chili powder, and mustard in slow cooker. Cover with onion, crushed bouillon cube, tomatoes, jalapeño peppers and beans; mix well. Cover and cook on low setting 6 to 8 hours. Mix well before serving.

# Mexican Chicken Chowder

*Serve with corn bread for an authentic Mexican meal.*

**stats**

**SERVES 4**

Cooking time ....... 7–8 hours
Preparation time.... 20 minutes
Attention.......... Medium
Pot size ............ 3–6 quarts

1½ pounds boneless, skinless
chicken breasts

2 medium-sized white onions

2 garlic cloves

2 celery ribs

½ cup (4 ounces) canned or fresh
green chilies, chopped

1 cup (8 ounces) Velveeta cheese,
cubed

1 tablespoon olive oil

4 cups chicken broth

1 package dry chicken gravy mix

2 cups milk

2 cups salsa

1 (32-ounce) bag frozen hash
brown potatoes

**1.** Cut the chicken into ½-inch cubes. Peel the onion and cut into ¼-inch pieces. Peel the garlic and mince with a sharp kitchen knife. Cut the celery into ¼-inch pieces. Cut the chilies into ⅛-inch pieces. Cut the cheese into ½-inch cubes.

**2.** Combine the chicken, onions, garlic, celery, oil, and broth in the slow cooker. Cover and cook on low for 3 to 4 hours.

**3.** Dissolve the gravy mix in the milk in a medium-sized mixing bowl. Stir into chicken mixture. Add the salsa, potatoes, chilies, and cheese; mix well. Cover and cook on low for 4 hours.

# Chicken Creole

*Serve this over white rice for a simple, delicious, and complete meal.*

**stats**

### SERVES 8

Cooking time . . . . . . . 6½–8 hours

Preparation time . . . . 30 minutes*

Attention . . . . . . . . . . Medium

Pot size . . . . . . . . . . . . 4–6 quarts

*plus 1 hour soaking time

*4 large chicken breasts (about four cups of meat)*

*4 tablespoons dehydrated onion*

*1 tablespoon dehydrated green onion*

*1 tablespoon dehydrated parsley flakes*

*1 teaspoon garlic powder*

*2 cups warm water*

*2 cups chicken or vegetable stock (or water)*

*1 cup dry white wine*

*3 tablespoons steak sauce*

*2 teaspoons hot sauce*

*4 cups (32 ounces) canned, peeled tomatoes*

*½ cup (4 ounces) canned, chopped jalapeño peppers*

**1.** Boil the chicken for 20 minutes in water in a large pot on the stove. Cut the meat off the bones.

**2.** Mix the dehydrated onions, green onions, parsley, and garlic powder in 2 cups of water and set aside; let this soak for about 1 hour. Combine the water, wine, steak sauce, hot sauce, tomatoes, and jalapeño peppers in the slow cooker. Cook uncovered on high for 30 minutes. Add the soaked dehydrated ingredients to the slow cooker; stir well. Add the chicken and mint to the seasoned water and stir well. Cover and cook on low setting for 6 to 8 hours.

# Southwestern Beef Roast with Peppers

*Serve with vegetables like asparagus and carrots for a wonderful mix of flavors.*

 **stats**

**SERVES 6**

Cooking time . . . . . . . 8–10 hours
Preparation time . . . . 20 minutes
Attention . . . . . . . . . . Minimal
Pot size . . . . . . . . . . . . 3–6 quarts

*4 garlic cloves*

*3 medium-sized yellow onions*

*1 green bell pepper*

*1 red bell pepper*

*1 yellow bell pepper*

*2 tablespoons jalapeño pepper, minced*

*5 large ripe tomatoes*

*1 tablespoon olive oil*

*3-pound chuck roast*

*2 cups hot salsa*

**1.** Remove the peel and mince the garlic with a sharp kitchen knife. Remove the peels from the onions and slice into ¼-inch-thick rings. Remove the stems and seeds from the peppers and slice lengthwise into ¼-inch-wide strips. Mince the jalapeño pepper with a paring knife. Chop the tomatoes into ½-inch pieces.

**2.** Place the olive oil, garlic, onions, bell and jalapeño peppers, and roast in a large skillet on the stove. Cook on medium-high heat until the roast is browned. Flip it so both sides are browned. Scoop the mixture into the slow cooker. Do not drain the oil. Pour the salsa over the ingredients in the slow cooker. Add the tomatoes on top. Cover and cook on low setting for 8 to 10 hours.

# Tex-Mex Pork and Potatoes

*Take pork and potatoes to a new horizon with some hot spices and zesty flavors.*

*stats*

**SERVES 6**

Cooking time . . . . . . . 4–5 hours
Preparation time . . . . 20 minutes
Attention . . . . . . . . . . Medium
Pot size . . . . . . . . . . . . 3–8 quarts

*3-pound pork roast*

*3 large white onions*

*4 garlic cloves*

*10 assorted whole chili peppers*

*5 medium-sized new potatoes*

*10 whole cloves*

*1 cinnamon stick*

*10 black peppercorns*

*1 teaspoon whole cumin seeds*

*2 tablespoons white vinegar*

1. Trim the fat from the pork roast. Peel the onions and cut into quarters. Peel the garlic and mince with a sharp kitchen knife. Remove the stems from the chili peppers; cut in half lengthwise. Peel the potatoes and cut in half.

2. Place the pork in the slow cooker. Cover with onions, garlic, chili peppers, cloves, cinnamon, peppercorns, and cumin. Add just enough water to cover ingredients. Cover and cook on low setting for 3 hours.

3. Stir mixture. Add the potatoes. Cover and cook for 1 to 2 hours, or until the potatoes are soft. Ten minutes before serving, remove the spices and add vinegar.

# Mexican Pork Carnitas

*Steam corn tortillas by placing them in the microwave with a cup of water and cooking on high for 20 seconds. Ladle the meat into the tortillas and top with chopped tomatoes and onions.*

 **SERVES 4**

Cooking time . . . . . . . 4–6 hours
Preparation time . . . . 15 minutes
Attention . . . . . . . . . . Minimal
Pot size . . . . . . . . . . . . 3–6 quarts

*4 garlic cloves*

*2–4-pound pork butt roast*

*1 bunch fresh cilantro*

*1 fresh jalapeño pepper, seeded and chopped*

*1 (12-ounce) can or bottle lager beer*

**1.** Peel and slice the garlic cloves about ⅛-inch thick. Using a sharp paring knife, cut slices into the butt roast and insert the garlic cloves, one slice in each opening. Place the butt roast in the slow cooker.

**2.** Chop the cilantro into ¼-inch lengths. Place the cilantro and jalapeño pepper on top of the butt roast. Pour the beer over the top and cook on high setting for 4 to 6 hours. Remove the meat and shred it. Discard the jalapeño pepper and cilantro.

# Spicy Chicken Chili Stew

*Instead of adding rice, create a wonderful chicken chili stew by mixing 2 tablespoons of flour with 2 cups of water until well blended; then add the mixture to the ingredients in the slow cooker about 20 minutes before serving.*

*stats*

**SERVES 4**

Cooking time . . . . . . . 1–3 hours
Preparation time . . . . 20 minutes
Attention . . . . . . . . . . Minimal
Pot size . . . . . . . . . . . . 4–6 quarts

4 chicken breasts

1 large white onion

2 stalks celery

2 (4-ounce) cans of tomato paste

2 (12-ounce) cans of tomato sauce

2 (15-ounce) cans of red chili beans, with juice

6 tablespoons chili powder

2 tablespoons cumin

3 teaspoons dried hot red peppers

4 tablespoons hot red pepper sauce

4 bay leaves

8 cups cooked rice

**1.** Remove the skin from the chicken and boil the chicken for about 15 minutes in water on the stove. Remove the bone and shred the chicken meat, using 2 forks.

**2.** Peel and chop the onion into ⅛-inch pieces. Chop the celery into ⅛-inch pieces. Place all ingredients in the slow cooker and stir well. Cook on low setting for 1 to 3 hours. Remove the bay leaves.

**3.** Prepare the rice as per package directions to yield 8 cups cooked. Add the rice to the slow cooker and mix together all the ingredients well.

# Hot as a Devil Green Chili

*Let people make their own chili tacos by serving this with warm flour tortillas, fresh chopped lettuce, grated Colby cheese, and sour cream.*

 **stats**

**SERVES 6**

Cooking time . . . . . . . 4–6 hours
Preparation time . . . . 20 minutes
Attention . . . . . . . . . . Minimal
Pot size . . . . . . . . . . . . 4–6 quarts

1 large yellow onion

4 garlic cloves

4 large potatoes

1 cup (8 ounces) fresh or canned green chiles, diced

1 pound lean ground beef

½ pound ground pork

1½ cups whole kernel corn

3 cups chicken broth

1 teaspoon ground black pepper

1 teaspoon crushed dried oregano

½ teaspoon ground cumin

1 teaspoon table salt

2 teaspoons red pepper sauce

**1.** Remove the peel from the onion and cut into ¼-inch pieces. Remove the peel from the garlic cloves and mince with a sharp paring knife. Peel the potatoes and cut into ½-inch cubes. Dice the green chilies with a sharp paring knife.

**2.** Put the meat, onion, and garlic in a large skillet and cook on medium-high heat until the meat is well browned; drain off grease. Put all ingredients in the slow cooker; stir well. Cover and cook on low setting for 4 to 6 hours.

# Super Taco Filling

*Let people make their own tacos by serving this with warm flour tortillas, grated cheese, refried beans, shredded lettuce, chopped tomatoes, and sour cream.*

**stats**

**SERVES 8**

Cooking time . . . . . . . 10 hours

Preparation time . . . . 10 minutes

Attention . . . . . . . . . . Minimal

Pot size . . . . . . . . . . . 3–6 quarts

1 medium-sized yellow onion

1½ cups fresh or canned green chilies, minced

4-pound beef chuck roast

1 envelope dry taco seasoning

1 tablespoon white vinegar

2 teaspoons red pepper sauce

½ teaspoon garlic salt

**1.** Peel the onion and chop into ¼-inch pieces. Mince the green chilies with a sharp paring knife. Add all ingredients to the slow cooker. Cover and cook on low setting for 9 hours.

**2.** Remove the meat and shred with a fork. Return the meat to the slow cooker and stir into the other ingredients. Cover and cook on low setting for 1 additional hour.

# Szechuan Chicken

*Serve over white rice and sprinkle with chopped peanuts.*

**stats**

**SERVES 4**

Cooking time . . . . . . . 7–8 hours
Preparation time . . . . 20 minutes
Attention . . . . . . . . . . Minimal
Pot size . . . . . . . . . . . . 4–6 quarts

4 chicken breasts

3 green onions

2 garlic cloves

1 tablespoon peanut oil

¼ cup sesame paste

3 tablespoons strong-brewed green tea

2 tablespoons wine vinegar

2½ tablespoons soy sauce

1½ tablespoons rice wine

2 teaspoons crushed red pepper

1 teaspoon dried ginger

½ teaspoon cayenne pepper

**1.** Remove the skin and bones from the chicken and slice the meat into ¼-inch strips. Remove the roots and first layer of green onion and chop the onion into ¼-inch pieces, including the stems. Peel the garlic and chop into eighths.

**2.** Place the peanut oil in a medium-sized skillet on medium heat. Add the chicken, sauté until browned and set aside. Add the garlic and onions; sauté until the onions are limp and translucent. Pour into the slow cooker. Add the remaining ingredients; stir well. Cover and cook on low setting for 6 to 7 hours, add chicken and cook for another hour.

# Barbecueless Chicken

*Tastes like barbecue, but it's from your slow cooker—how easy!*

 *stats*

**SERVES 4**

Cooking time ....... 8 hours
Preparation time .... 30 minutes
Attention .......... Minimal
Pot size ............ 6–8 quarts

*1 whole chicken*

*½ cup onion, chopped*

*4 garlic cloves*

*1 can tomato sauce*

*¼ cup vinegar*

*¼ cup dark brown sugar*

*2 tablespoons Bourbon*

*1 tablespoon Worcestershire sauce*

*½ teaspoon table salt*

*2 tablespoons hot sauce*

**1.** Cut the chicken into serving portions (legs, thighs, wings, breasts).

**2.** Peel and chop the onion into ¼-inch pieces. Peel the garlic and smash each clove with the broad side of a large knife. Combine the onion, garlic, tomato sauce, vinegar, dark brown sugar, Bourbon, Worcestershire sauce, salt, and hot sauce in a small mixing bowl.

**3.** Place the chicken in the slow cooker. Pour the prepared barbecue sauce over the chicken. Cover and cook on low setting for 8 hours.

# Recipes from Around the World

# Congo Stew

*Add no-salt, skinless peanuts to the top of the bowl before serving.*

*stats*
**SERVES 8**

| | |
|---|---|
| Cooking time . . . . . . . | 7–9 hours |
| Preparation time . . . . | 20 minutes |
| Attention . . . . . . . . . . | Minimal |
| Pot size . . . . . . . . . . . . | 3–8 quarts |

*2-pound pork roast*

*1 large white onion*

*1 green bell pepper*

*2 garlic cloves*

*2 plum tomatoes*

*½ teaspoon curry powder*

*½ teaspoon ground coriander*

*½ teaspoon ground cumin*

*½ teaspoon ground black pepper*

*1 teaspoon crushed red pepper flakes*

*½ teaspoon ground ginger*

*¼ teaspoon cinnamon*

*1 bay leaf*

*1 teaspoon table salt*

*2 cups chicken broth*

*1 tablespoon tomato paste*

*½ cup chunky peanut butter*

**1.** Cut the pork into 1-inch cubes. Peel and chop the onion into ¼-inch pieces. Remove the stems and seeds from the green pepper and chop into ¼-inch pieces. Peel and mince the garlic using a sharp kitchen knife. Chop the plum tomatoes into ¼-inch pieces.

**2.** Brown the pork in a large skillet at medium-high heat. Add the onions, garlic, curry powder, coriander, cumin, black pepper, and crushed red pepper; stir well and cook for 1 minute. Transfer the mixture to the slow cooker. Add the ginger, cinnamon, salt, bay leaf, chicken broth, and tomato paste. Cover and cook on low setting for 6 to 8 hours.

**3.** Add the peanut butter and stir well to blend. Stir in the chopped tomato and bell pepper. Cover and cook on low setting for 1 hour.

# Mexican Green Chile Burros

*Try topping these with diced avocado too.*

*stats*

**SERVES 4**

Cooking time . . . . . . . 8–10 hours

Preparation time . . . . 15 minutes

Attention . . . . . . . . . . Minimal

Pot size . . . . . . . . . . . . 3–6 quarts

2-pound beef rump roast

1 cup chopped yellow onions

1 (10-ounce) can diced green chiles

1 (16-ounce) can tomato sauce

1 package taco seasoning mix

1 tablespoon oregano

1 teaspoon garlic powder

8 flour tortillas

½ cup sour cream

1 large green onion, diced

¼ cup chopped black olives

1. Add the meat to the slow cooker. Peel and chop the onions into ¼-inch pieces. Add all ingredients on top of the meat. Cook on low setting for 7 hours. Remove the meat and shred it using 2 forks. Return the meat to the slow cooker and stir together all the ingredients. Cook on low setting for an addition 1 to 3 hours.

2. Serve on flour tortillas that have been warmed in a 250°F oven for 10 minutes. Top with sour cream, diced green onions, and olives.

# Egyptian Chicken

*With its peanut-buttery taste, this ethnic chicken dish
is special but not too out of the ordinary.*

*stats*

**SERVES 6**

Cooking time . . . . . . . 5–6 hours
Preparation time . . . . 20 minutes
Attention . . . . . . . . . . Minimal
Pot size . . . . . . . . . . . . 3–6 quarts

12 chicken legs

2 medium-sized yellow onions

1 red bell pepper

1 green bell pepper

2 celery ribs

2 cups chicken broth

½ cup crunchy peanut butter

1 teaspoon crushed red chili pepper

**1.** Remove the skin from the chicken legs. Peel and slice the onion into ¼-inch-thick rings. Remove the stems and seeds from the peppers and slice into ¼-inch-thick rings. Slice the celery into ¼-inch pieces.

**2.** Combine the onions, peppers, celery, and chicken broth in the slow cooker. Spread the peanut putter over the chicken legs and sprinkle with chili pepper. Place on top of the onions and peppers; do not stir. Cover and cook on low setting for 5 to 6 hours.

# Chicken from the French Countryside

*Serve on a platter with a dry white wine.*

**stats**

**SERVES 4**

Cooking time . . . . . . . 7–9 hours
Preparation time . . . . 45 minutes
Attention . . . . . . . . . . Minimal
Pot size . . . . . . . . . . . . 6 quarts

1 whole chicken

2 teaspoons table salt

¼ teaspoon coarsely ground pepper

4 carrots

1 large Bermuda onion

2 cups fresh green beans

½ cup fresh mushrooms, sliced

8 garlic cloves

2 bay leaves

6 ripe tomatoes

⅓ cup brown rice

½ cup water

**1.** Cut the chicken into serving portions (legs, thighs, wings, breasts), then rinse off the pieces and dry them. Peel and dice the carrots and onions. Wash the green beans and cut into 2-inch pieces. Clean the mushrooms by wiping individually with a moistened paper towel; slice the mushrooms. Smash, peel, and dice the garlic. Wash, core, and chop the tomatoes into ¼-inch pieces.

**2.** Place the chicken in the slow cooker. Add the carrots, onions, green beans, mushrooms, garlic, tomatoes, salt, pepper, and bay leaves to the slow cooker. Cover and cook on low for 4 to 5 hours.

**3.** Stir in the rice and water. Cover and cook on low for 3 to 4 more hours.

# Savory Chinese Beef

*For an adventurous audience, serve in individual bowls
over Chinese noodles with chopsticks.*

**SERVES 6**

Cooking time . . . . . . . 6–7 hours
Preparation time . . . . 30 minutes
Attention . . . . . . . . . . Minimal
Pot size . . . . . . . . . . . . 3–6 quarts

1½ pounds sirloin tip

1 bunch (approximately 8) green
onions or 1 large leek

8 ounces (1 cup) bean sprouts

8 ounces (1 cup) Chinese pea
pods

1 cup low-fat beef broth

¼ cup low-sodium soy sauce

2 tablespoons cornstarch

2 tablespoons lukewarm water

¼ teaspoon ground ginger or ½
teaspoon fresh minced ginger

½ teaspoon hot sauce (optional)

1 small can water chestnuts,
drained

1 small can bamboo shoots,
drained

**1.** Thinly slice the sirloin tip (slicing is easier if the meat is frozen and then cut when partially thawed). Wash all the fresh vegetables. Cut off the roots at the ends of the green onions (or leek); finely chop the onions (or leek).

**2.** Place the sliced sirloin in the slow cooker with the beef broth, soy sauce, ginger, and chopped green onions (or leeks). Cover and cook on low for 6 to 7 hours.

**3.** Uncover and turn setting to high. Mix the cornstarch with the water in a small measuring cup. Stir the cornstarch mixture and the hot sauce into the slow cooker. Cook on high for 15 minutes, or until thickened; stir periodically. During the last 5 minutes of cooking add the remaining canned and fresh vegetables.

# Native American Pudding

*Serve in small bowls with a dollop of low-fat whipping cream.*

 **stats**

**SERVES 4**

Cooking time . . . . . . . 4–5 hours
Preparation time . . . . 45 minutes
Attention . . . . . . . . . . Medium
Pot size . . . . . . . . . . . . 3–6 quarts

2 tablespoons butter, plus ¼
tablespoon for greasing

3 cups 1 percent milk

½ cup cornmeal

½ teaspoon salt

3 large eggs, beaten

¼ cup packed light brown sugar

⅓ cup molasses

½ teaspoon cinnamon

¼ teaspoon allspice

½ teaspoon ginger

**1.** Lightly grease the slow cooker with ¼ tablespoon butter by putting butter on a paper towel and rubbing it along the inside of the slow cooker. Preheat the slow cooker on high for 15 minutes. In a medium-sized saucepan bring the milk, cornmeal, and salt to boil. Boil, stirring constantly, for 5 minutes. Cover and simmer on low for 10 minutes.

**2.** In a large bowl, combine the remaining ingredients. Gradually whisk the cornmeal mixture into the combined ingredients until thoroughly mixed and smooth. Pour into slow cooker. Cook covered on medium for 4 to 5 hours.

# Brazilian Paella

*Serve with fresh-sliced oranges and bananas sprinkled*
*with coconut to achieve a true Brazilian flavor.*

**SERVES 8**

Cooking time . . . . . . . 8–9 hours
Preparation time. . . . 45 minutes
Attention. . . . . . . . . . Minimal
Pot size . . . . . . . . . . . . 4–6 quarts

½ pound medium-spicy pork sausage

2–3-pound chicken

2 large yellow onions

1 pound (16 ounces) canned tomatoes

½ teaspoon table salt

½ teaspoon ground black pepper

1½ cups uncooked long-grain brown rice

3 chicken bouillon cubes

2 cups hot water

**1.** Form the sausage into balls about the size of large marbles. Clean and cut the chicken into serving size pieces. Peel and chop the onions into ¼-inch pieces. Drain the tomatoes, retaining the liquid, and cut into 1-inch pieces.

**2.** Using a large skillet on medium-high heat, fry the sausage balls until they are well browned and crisp. Place them on paper towels to absorb the grease. Sprinkle the chicken with salt and pepper. Without emptying the grease from the skillet, fry the chicken pieces for about 10 minutes. Place the chicken on paper towels to absorb the grease.

**3.** Drain all but 3 tablespoons of grease from the skillet. Sauté the onions on medium heat in the skillet until translucent. Add the rice to the skillet and continue to sauté, stirring constantly for 10 minutes.

**4.** Place the sausage balls, chicken, the onion and rice mixture, tomato juice, and tomatoes in the slow cooker. Mix the bouillon in 2 cups of hot water; add to the slow cooker. Cover and cook on low setting for 8 to 9 hours.

# Mongolian Mixed Meat Stew

*Mixed meat stew is a great way to clean out your freezer—and with the Mongolian twist you'll have a mouth-watering meal in no time.*

 **stats**

**SERVES 8**

Cooking time . . . . . . . 8–9 hours
Preparation time . . . . 20 minutes
Attention . . . . . . . . . . Minimal
Pot size . . . . . . . . . . . . 3–6 quarts

¼ cup A-1 Steak Sauce

2 chicken bouillon cubes

1 teaspoon table salt

½ teaspoon ground black pepper

1 teaspoon sugar

½ cup hot water

3 pounds chicken thighs

1 pound lean stewing beef

1 medium-sized yellow onion

2 medium potatoes

8 ounces (1 cup) baby carrots

1 (16-ounce) can stewed tomatoes, liquid retained

¼ cup flour

**1.** Combine steak sauce, bouillon cubes, salt, pepper, sugar, and hot water in the slow cooker; stir well. Remove the skin from the chicken thighs and discard. Cut the chicken meat into 1-inch cubes. Cut the stewing beef into 1-inch cubes. Peel and chop the onions into ¼-inch pieces. Peel the potatoes and cut into ½-inch cubes.

**2.** Add the chicken, beef, onion, potatoes, carrots, and tomatoes, including juice, to the slow cooker. Cover and cook on low setting for 8 to 9 hours. Before serving, mix the ¼ cup flour with enough water to make a paste; stir mixture into the stew. Cook on high setting uncovered until thick, about 15 to 30 minutes.

# Portuguese Sweet Bread

*This delicious bread is enjoyed all over the world,*
*why not at your dinner table too?*

**stats**

**SERVES 8**

| | |
|---|---|
| Cooking time | 2–3 hours |
| Preparation time | 10 minutes |
| Attention | Medium |
| Pot size | 3–8 quarts |

**Bread:** *½ cup milk*

*1 package active dry yeast*

*⅛ cup warm water*

*¾ cup sugar*

*½ teaspoon salt*

*3 eggs*

*¼ cup butter, softened*

*3 cups flour*

**Glaze:** *1 egg*

*1 teaspoon sugar*

**1.** To make the bread, put the milk in a small saucepan on the stove and heat on high until the milk is slightly yellowed. Let the milk cool to room temperature. Dissolve the yeast in warm water in large bowl. Stir in the milk, sugar, salt, eggs, and butter. Beat with an electric mixer until smooth and creamy. Stir in flour. Place the dough onto a lightly floured surface and knead until smooth and elastic, about 5 minutes. Place the dough in a greased bowl; cover and let rise in a warm place for about 2 hours. Shape a round, slightly flat loaf.

**2.** Grease the slow cooker by putting a small amount of shortening on a paper towel and rubbing it along the inside of the slow cooker. Place the loaf of bread in the slow cooker. To make the glaze, beat the egg until the yellow and white are well mixed brush over the loaf. Sprinkle with sugar.

**3.** Cover and cook on high setting for 2 to 3 hours. The loaf should be golden.

# Russian Vegetable Beef Borscht

*Add a dollop of sour cream to the top of each bowl right before serving.*

**SERVES 8**

| | |
|---|---|
| Cooking time | 8–10 hours |
| Preparation time | 20 minutes |
| Attention | Minimal |
| Pot size | 3–6 quarts |

*1 pound leftover beef roast*

*½ head cabbage*

*3 medium potatoes*

*4 carrots*

*1 large white onion*

*1 cup fresh tomatoes, chopped*

*1 cup green beans*

*1 cup diced beets*

*1 cup fresh sweet corn*

*2 cups beef broth*

*2 cups tomato juice*

*¼ teaspoon garlic powder*

*¼ teaspoon dill seed*

*2 teaspoons salt*

*½ teaspoon pepper*

**1.** Cut the beef roast into 1-inch cubes. Slice the cabbage into ¼-inch strips. Peel the potatoes and dice into ½-inch cubes. Peel and slice the carrots into ¼-inch pieces. Remove the skin from the onion and chop into ¼-inch pieces. Chop the tomatoes into ½-inch pieces. Remove the stems from the green beans. Precook the beets by slicing the tops and roots off. Boil in water for ½ hour. Set beets in cool water and use a sharp paring knife to remove the skins. Cut into ½-inch pieces.

**2.** Add all ingredients to the slow cooker. Add enough water so that the slow cooker is ¾ full. Cook covered on low setting for 8 to 10 hours.

# Polish Sauerkraut Soup

*This scrumptious soup can be made in no time.*
*Enjoy a warm bowl, after work or school on a cold winter night.*

 **stats**

**SERVES 8**

Cooking time ....... 8–10 hours
Preparation time.... 10 minutes
Attention.......... Minimal
Pot size ............ 4–6 quarts

1 pound smoked Polish sausage

5 medium potatoes

2 large yellow onions

3 medium carrots

6 cups chicken broth

4 cups (32 ounces) canned or
bagged sauerkraut

1 (6-ounce) can tomato paste

**1.** Slice the Polish sausage into ½-inch-thick pieces. Do not remove the peel from the potatoes; slice into ½-inch cubes. Remove the peel from the onions and chop into ¼-inch pieces. Peel and slice the carrots ¼-inch thick.

**2.** Add all ingredients to the slow cooker. Cover and cook on low setting for 8 to 10 hours.

# Pepperoni Rigatoni

*Serve with a fresh green salad with Italian dressing.*

**SERVES 8**

Cooking time . . . . . . . 4–5 hours
Preparation time. . . . 15 minutes
Attention. . . . . . . . . . Minimal
Pot size . . . . . . . . . . . . 4–8 quarts

*12 ounces rigatoni*

*1 cup fresh mushrooms, sliced*

*1 large yellow onion*

*4 garlic cloves*

*1 medium-sized green bell pepper*

*2 pounds pepperoni slices*

*1 (28-ounce) jar spaghetti sauce*

*3 cups shredded mozzarella cheese*

**1.** Cook the rigatoni in boiling water until soft but not mushy. Clean the mushrooms by wiping with a damp cloth; slice ⅛-inch thick. Remove the peel from the onion and cut into ¼-inch pieces. Remove the peel from the garlic and mince with a sharp paring knife. Remove the stem and seeds from the green pepper; cut into ¼-inch pieces.

**2.** Add all the ingredients to the slow cooker; stir well. Cover and cook on low setting for 4 to 5 hours.

# East Indian Green Curried Chicken

*Serve with long-grain brown rice.*

**SERVES 6**

Cooking time . . . . . . . 6½–7 hours

Preparation time . . . . 20 minutes

Attention . . . . . . . . . . Medium

Pot size . . . . . . . . . . . . 4–6 quarts

6 chicken breasts

2 fresh green chili peppers

¼ cup fresh mint leaves, chopped

1½ cups unsweetened coconut milk, divided

1½ tablespoons green curry paste

1 cup sliced, canned bamboo shoots

¼ cup fish sauce

1 tablespoon sugar

**1.** Remove the skin and bones from chicken breast. Remove the stems and seeds from the chili peppers and chop into ⅛-inch pieces. Chop the mint leaves into ¼-inch pieces.

**2.** Heat ½ cup of the coconut milk and the green curry paste in a medium-sized skillet on medium heat; stir until well blended. Add the chicken and sauté for 10 minutes. Put the chicken breasts into the slow cooker. Stir in the remaining coconut milk, bamboo shoots, fish sauce, and sugar. Cover and cook on low setting for 6 to 7 hours. Stir in the mint and chili peppers. Cover and cook an additional 30 minutes.

# Mediterranean Couscous with Vegetables

*Serve with pocket bread and hummus for an authentic meal.*

**SERVES 8**

| | |
|---|---|
| Cooking time | 6½–7 hours |
| Preparation time | 30 minutes |
| Attention | Medium |
| Pot size | 3–8 quarts |

2 medium zucchini

6 plum tomatoes

½ pound (1 cup) fresh mushrooms

4 garlic cloves

2 medium-sized white onions

2 celery ribs

1 large red bell pepper

2 medium carrots

½ cup black olives, pitted and diced

¼ cup minced fresh basil

2 tablespoons olive oil

½ teaspoons dried oregano

1 teaspoon salt

¼ teaspoon cinnamon

¼ teaspoon ground black pepper

3 tablespoons balsamic vinegar

1½ cups whole-wheat couscous

**1.** Cut the zucchini into 1-inch pieces. Chop the tomatoes into ¼-inch pieces. Clean the mushrooms by wiping with a damp cloth; cut in half. Peel the garlic and mince with a sharp kitchen knife. Peel the onions and chop into ¼-inch pieces. Chop the celery into ¼-inch pieces. Remove the stem and seeds from the bell pepper and slice into ¼-inch strips. Peel and slice the carrots into ¼-inch rounds. Chop the black olives into ¼-inch pieces. Chop the basil into ¼-inch pieces.

**2.** Heat the olive oil in a large skillet at medium-high heat. Add the garlic, onion, and red pepper. Sauté until the onion is limp and translucent. Add the celery, carrots, mushrooms, zucchini, tomatoes, olives, and half the basil; sauté for 5 minutes. Transfer to slow cooker. Add half the remaining basil, oregano, salt, cinnamon, and black pepper. Cover and cook on low setting for 6 to 7 hours.

**3.** Stir in the vinegar and couscous. Cover and cook on low setting for an additional 30 minutes.

# Thai Shrimp and Scallop Soup

*This Thai treat will make kids come back for seconds without a doubt.*

 **stats**

**SERVES 8**

Cooking time . . . . . . . 8–9 hours
Preparation time . . . . 20 minutes
Attention . . . . . . . . . . Minimal
Pot size . . . . . . . . . . . . 3–8 quarts

1 small white onion

8 ounces (1 cup) fresh mushrooms, sliced

2 garlic cloves

6 green onions

⅓ cup fresh parsley, chopped

½ pound precooked popcorn shrimp

½ pound baby scallops

6 cups water

½ teaspoon thyme

1 teaspoon table salt

¼ teaspoon ground black pepper

2 teaspoons ground coriander

1½ teaspoons chili powder

1 teaspoon red pepper sauce

1 tablespoon soy sauce

2 cups uncooked white rice

**1.** Peel the onion and chop into ¼-inch pieces. Clean the mushrooms by wiping with a damp cloth; cut into paper-thin slices with a sharp kitchen knife. Peel the garlic and mince with a sharp kitchen knife. Remove the roots and first layer of skin from the green onions and chop into ¼-inch pieces. Chop the parsley into ½-inch pieces.

**2.** Combine all ingredients except the parsley, green onions, precooked shrimp, and baby scallops in the slow cooker. Cover and cook on low setting for 7 to 8 hours. Add shrimp and scallops and cook for 1 to 2 hours. Stir in the parsley and green onions right before serving.

# Turkish Pork Chops

*Make a sauce by combining 1 cup sour cream with 1 tablespoon dill.*
*Add dollops of the sauce to the top of each pork chop.*

**stats**

**SERVES 6**

| | |
|---|---|
| Cooking time | 8–9 hours |
| Preparation time | 30 minutes |
| Attention | Minimal |
| Pot size | 3–6 quarts |

*½ teaspoon salt*

*½ teaspoon pepper*

*2 tablespoons paprika*

*½ cup flour*

*6 lean pork chops*

*4 medium onions*

*2 garlic cloves*

*4 tablespoons butter*

*1 cup chicken stock*

**1.** Combine salt, pepper, paprika, and flour. Dredge the pork chops by smashing them into the flour. Peel the onions and chop into ¼-inch pieces. Peel the garlic and chop into eighths.

**2.** Heat the butter in large skillet at medium-high heat. Brown the pork chops. Remove the pork chops and put into the slow cooker. Add the onions and garlic to skillet and sauté until the onions are limp and translucent. Drain off the grease and place the onions and garlic on top of the pork chops. Add chicken stock. Cover and cook on low setting for 8 to 9 hours.

# Greek Lamb Chops with Lentils

*Serve with a fresh green salad with Greek dressing.*

**stats**

**SERVES 6**

Cooking time . . . . . . . 7–9 hours
Preparation time . . . . 30 minutes
Attention . . . . . . . . . . Minimal
Pot size . . . . . . . . . . . 3–6 quarts

6 medium lamb chops

1 medium-sized yellow onion

4 garlic cloves

3 medium carrots

2 medium-sized ripe tomatoes

1 cup black olives, chopped

1 cup lentils

3 cups water

½ cup vodka

2 tablespoons olive oil

1 teaspoon table salt

½ teaspoon ground black pepper

**1.** Trim the fat from the lamb chops. Peel and chop the onion into ¼-inch pieces. Peel the garlic and mince with a sharp kitchen knife. Peel and slice the carrots into ¼-inch rounds. Chop the tomatoes into ¼-inch pieces. Chop the olives into ¼-inch pieces.

**2.** Put the lentils in the slow cooker with the water and vodka. Add the carrots, onions, and tomatoes. Begin cooking on low setting. In the meantime, heat the olive oil in a large skillet at medium heat. Sprinkle the lamb chops with the salt and pepper and place in the skillet. Add the garlic. Cook until the lamb chops are browned on both sides. Transfer to the slow cooker. Sprinkle the black olives on top. Cover and cook on low setting for 7 to 9 hours.

# European & Mediterranean Family Favorites

# Hungarian Sauerkraut

*A taste of Hungary for your hungry clan!*

**stats**

**SERVES 6–8**

| | |
|---|---|
| Cooking time | 4–6 hours |
| Preparation time | 30 minutes |
| Attention | Minimal |
| Pot size | 3–5 quarts |

6 tomatoes

1 pound bacon

2 pounds sauerkraut

2 tablespoons paprika

1 tablespoon sugar

1 cup white wine

1 cup beef broth

1 bouquet garni

**1.** Chop the tomatoes; cut the bacon into 1-inch pieces. Drain the sauerkraut. Divide the tomatoes, bacon, sauerkraut, and paprika each into two equal portions.

**2.** Make two layers in the slow cooker as follows: Bacon on the bottom, then sauerkraut, paprika, tomatoes; repeat. Sprinkle the top with the sugar.

**3.** Pour the wine and broth over the top. Add the bouquet garni.

**4.** Cover and heat on low setting for 4 to 6 hours.

# Classic German Cabbage Rolls

*Serve with black bread and garlic butter. Save the broth from this recipe to use as a starter for some great soup.*

 **stats**

**SERVES 6–8**

| | |
|---|---|
| Cooking time | 6–8 hours |
| Preparation time | 90 minutes |
| Attention | Minimal |
| Pot size | 3–5 quarts |

1 head cabbage

1 onion

1 clove garlic

1 pound ground beef

1 pound ground sausage

¾ cup cooked rice

1½ teaspoons salt

½ teaspoon black pepper

1 cup water

2 cups vinegar

**1.** Boil one whole head of cabbage in a covered pot over high heat for 5 minutes. Cool; carefully separate the leaves and set aside.

**2.** Mince the onion and garlic. Mix with the meat, rice, salt, and pepper.

**3.** Put about ¼ cup of the meat mixture onto each cabbage leaf, roll, and tuck in the ends. Arrange in the slow cooker. To secure the mound, top it with an inverted glass plate or glass bowl as a weight.

**4.** Add the water and vinegar.

**5.** Cover and heat on a low setting for 6 to 8 hours.

# Country French Sauerkraut

*This isn't as rich as the original recipe, which calls for goose fat, not goose meat, but it's just as delectable.*

**SERVES 8–10**

| | |
|---|---|
| Cooking time | 5–6 hours |
| Preparation time | 30 minutes |
| Attention | Moderate |
| Pot size | 5 quarts |

2 pounds bacon

½ pound goose meat

2 pounds sauerkraut

1 tablespoon whole peppercorns

2 cups white wine

2 cups beef bouillon

**1.** Sauté two slices of the bacon in a pan over medium heat until browned. Cut the goose meat into 1-inch cubes; sauté in the pan with the bacon over medium heat until the goose is lightly browned. Drain the meat. Set aside the two cooked bacon strips.

**2.** Cut the remaining, uncooked bacon into 1-inch lengths. Divide the browned goose meat into two equal portions; do the same for the sauerkraut and bacon.

**3.** Assemble layers in the slow cooker, in this order: Raw bacon (on the bottom), goose, sauerkraut, raw bacon, goose, sauerkraut. Sprinkle each layer with a few peppercorns.

**4.** Pour the wine and bouillon over the layers. Cover and heat on low setting for 5 to 6 hours.

**5.** Before serving, remove the excess liquid from the slow cooker, enough to expose the top of the layered ingredients. Sprinkle the sauerkraut with the set-aside bacon, crumbled.

# Jacque's White Beans

*Depending on your schedule, you can complete some parts of this recipe in advance, and save the final assembly until just before your party.*

 *stats*

**SERVES 10–12**

Cooking time . . . . . . . 7–9 hours
Preparation time. . . . 45 minutes
Attention . . . . . . . . . . Moderate
Pot size . . . . . . . . . . . . 5 quarts

2 pounds white beans

2 cups water

1 ham bone

1 bouquet garni

1 teaspoon salt

3 onions

1 clove garlic

3 tablespoons butter

¼ cup parsley

1 cup tomato sauce

½ teaspoon black pepper

**1.** Soak the beans overnight in cold water, then drain.

**2.** Combine 2 cups fresh water, beans, ham bone, bouquet garni, and salt in the slow cooker.

**3.** Cover and heat on a low setting for 6 to 8 hours. Remove the bone and bouquet garni; drain.

**4.** Dice the onions; crush and slice the garlic. Sauté the onions and garlic in butter in a pan over medium heat until soft. Chop the parsley.

**5.** An hour before serving, add the onion, garlic, parsley, tomato sauce, and black pepper to the beans in the slow cooker.

# Spanish Beef Stew

*For extra flavor, use wrinkled Turkish or other olives, instead of the standard stuffed olives found in the grocery store.*

**stats**

**SERVES 4–6**

Cooking time . . . . . . . 4–6 hours
Preparation time . . . . 30 minutes
Attention . . . . . . . . . . Minimal
Pot size . . . . . . . . . . . . 3–5 quarts

2 cloves garlic

1 onion

3 slices bacon

1 pound beef

3 tomatoes

1 bay leaf

¼ teaspoon sage

¼ teaspoon marjoram

½ teaspoon paprika

½ teaspoon curry powder

1 teaspoon salt

2 tablespoons vinegar

1 cup stock

½ cup white wine

4 potatoes

⅓ cup olives

2 tablespoons parsley

**1.** Crush and slice the garlic; slice the onion. Cut the bacon into 1-inch lengths. Cube the beef. Sauté the garlic, onion, bacon, and beef in a pan over medium heat; drain and transfer the meat mixture to the slow cooker.

**2.** Dice the tomatoes. Crumble the bay leaf. Add the tomatoes, spices, salt, vinegar, stock, and wine to the slow cooker.

**3.** Cover and heat on a medium setting for 4 to 6 hours.

**4.** Dice the potatoes, slice the olives, and chop the parsley. An hour before serving, add the potatoes, olives, and parsley to the slow cooker.

# Spanish Saffron Rice

*This fragrant dish goes well with grilled chicken or fish and looks very festive alongside shish kebabs. Use saffron threads instead of powder, if possible.*

**stats**

**SERVES 6–8**

| | |
|---|---|
| Cooking time | 4–6 hours |
| Preparation time | 45 minutes |
| Attention | Minimal |
| Pot size | 3–5 quarts |

1 onion

4 stalks celery

2 tablespoons olive oil

3 tomatoes

1⅓ cups uncooked rice

4 cups water

2 teaspoons salt

¼ teaspoon cayenne pepper

1 green pepper

¼ pound Gruyère cheese

½ teaspoon saffron threads

**1.** Thinly slice the onion and celery. Sauté the onion and celery in oil in a pan over medium heat until soft. Transfer to the slow cooker.

**2.** Cube the tomatoes. Put the tomatoes, rice, water, salt, and cayenne pepper in the slow cooker.

**3.** Cover and heat on a low setting for 4 to 6 hours.

**4.** Mince the green pepper and grate the cheese. Half an hour before serving, stir in the green pepper, cheese, and saffron.

# Polish Bouja

*You can use your food processor to speed up this recipe, if you wish.*
*Serve with pumpernickel rolls to soak up the juices.*

**stats**

**SERVES 4–6**

Cooking time . . . . . . . 4–6 hours
Preparation time . . . . 90 minutes
Attention . . . . . . . . . . Minimal
Pot size . . . . . . . . . . . . 5 quarts

1 pound chicken meat, boneless

4 potatoes

4 carrots

1 onion

1 pound fresh green beans

4 stalks celery

½ head cabbage

¾ cup water

¼ cup pearl barley

½ teaspoon salt

½ teaspoon peppercorns

1 teaspoon pickling spices, in
cloth bag

**1.** Cube the chicken meat, potatoes, carrots, and onion. Cut the beans into ½-inch lengths. Thinly slice the celery. Shred the cabbage.

**2.** Add the cut ingredients, water, barley, salt, and peppercorns to the slow cooker.

**3.** Cover and heat on a low setting for 4 to 6 hours.

**4.** Half an hour before serving, add the bag of pickling spices. Remove the bag before serving.

# Chicken Mulligatawny Soup

*When serving this dish, also provide toasted strips of
fresh coconut, white raisins, and fruit chutney.*

**SERVES 6–8**

| | |
|---|---|
| Cooking time | 4–6 hours |
| Preparation time | 45 minutes |
| Attention | Minimal |
| Pot size | 3–5 quarts |

*1 pound boneless, skinless
chicken breast*

*3 tablespoons butter*

*2 apples*

*2 onions*

*¼ cup flour*

*1½ tablespoons curry powder*

*6 cups chicken broth*

*1 cup uncooked rice*

*½ teaspoon salt*

**1.** Cube the chicken. Sauté in butter in a pan over medium heat until lightly browned.

**2.** Core and cube the apples and mince the onions. Add the apples and onions to the chicken in the pan over medium heat and stir until the onions are soft. Add the flour and curry powder and stir to blend in.

**3.** Put the sautéed mixture, broth, rice, and salt in the slow cooker.

**4.** Cover and heat on a low setting for 4 to 6 hours.

# O'Riley's Lamb Stew

*Serve this hearty stew with warm hunks of*
*sourdough bread and herbed butter for dipping.*

*stats*

**SERVES 8–10**

Cooking time . . . . . . . 4–6 hours
Preparation time . . . . 30 minutes
Attention . . . . . . . . . . Moderate
Pot size . . . . . . . . . . . . 3–5 quarts

4 pounds lamb
1 pound baby carrots
1 pound red spring potatoes
½ pound pearl onions
½ teaspoon salt
2 cups water
1 bouquet garni
1 bunch parsley
½ cup flour
1 cup water
1 tablespoon Worcestershire
sauce

**1.** Cube the lamb. Heat it in water and boil 10 minutes, then drain. Transfer the meat to the slow cooker.

**2.** Scrub the potatoes. Halve the carrots and potatoes. Remove the outer layer from the pearl onions.

**3.** Combine the meat and vegetables with salt, 2 cups water, and the bouquet garni in the slow cooker.

**4.** Cover and heat on a low setting for 4 to 6 hours.

**5.** Chop the parsley. Half an hour before serving, remove the bouquet garni. Blend the flour and remaining water and stir slowly into the stew. Stir in the parsley and Worcestershire sauce.

# Hungarian Goulash #2

*This dish freezes well. Keep a batch set aside for unexpected
company, then reheat and add a fresh parsley garnish.*

*stats*

**SERVES 6–8**

Cooking time . . . . . . . 4–6 hours
Preparation time . . . . 45 minutes
Attention . . . . . . . . . . Minimal
Pot size . . . . . . . . . . . . 3–5 quarts

2 *onions*

3 *tablespoons butter*

1 *pound beef*

1 *pound pork*

2 *tablespoons flour*

½ *teaspoon salt*

½ *teaspoon pepper*

2 *tablespoons paprika*

¼ *cup celery*

3 *potatoes*

1 *cup beef stock*

1 *cup tomato sauce*

½ *teaspoon salt*

½ *teaspoon thyme*

1 *bay leaf*

2 *whole cloves*

¼ *cup parsley*

**1.** Chop the onions and sauté in butter in a pan over medium heat until browned. Cube the meat and add to the onions. Sauté over medium heat until browned.

**2.** Mix the flour with ½ teaspoon salt, pepper, and paprika. Stir the flour mixture into the meat and onions. Transfer the meat mixture to the slow cooker.

**3.** Chop the celery into ½-inch lengths; cut the potatoes into 1-inch cubes. Add the celery, potatoes, stock, tomato sauce, ½ teaspoon salt, and spices to the slow cooker. Cover and heat on a low setting for 4 to 6 hours.

**4.** Chop the parsley. Before serving, remove the bay leaf and stir in the parsley.

# Aromatic Paella

*This is a fun dish for a slow cooker. The mussels and clams open during the cooking and flavor the rice.*

**stats**

**SERVES 10–12**

| | |
|---|---|
| Cooking time | 4–6 hours |
| Preparation time | 60 minutes |
| Attention | Minimal |
| Pot size | 5 quarts |

2 onions

1 pound bulk spicy sausage

1 tablespoon olive oil

4 cloves garlic

2 pounds tomatoes

16 ounces clam juice

2 cups chicken broth

1 cup dry vermouth

2½ cups uncooked rice

2 teaspoons coriander

½ teaspoon cumin

1 teaspoon saffron

¼ teaspoon each white pepper and salt

1 pound each fish and shrimp

2 tablespoons olive oil

1 pound each fresh mussels and clams

1 green pepper

1 cup fresh green peas

**1.** Thinly slice the onions. Sauté with the sausage in oil in a pan over low heat until the sausage is crumbled and browned, then drain and transfer to the slow cooker.

**2.** Crush the garlic and dice the tomatoes; stir in with the sausage and onions. Add the liquids, rice, spices, and salt.

**3.** Cover and heat on a low setting for 4 to 6 hours.

**4.** Cube the fish. Sauté the fish and shrimp in the remaining oil. Clean the mollusk shells. Do not steam them.

**5.** Dice the green pepper. An hour before serving, add the seafood, green pepper, and peas to the slow cooker.

# German Eggs

*This dish is delicious on a crisp morning—or any time of day or night. Switch up your routine dinner with this delicious treat—serve these eggs with fried tomatoes and everyone will be wanting more.*

**stats**

**SERVES 6**

Cooking time . . . . . . . 3–4 hours
Preparation time . . . . 30 minutes
Attention . . . . . . . . . . Minimal
Pot size . . . . . . . . . . . . 3–5 quarts

6 potatoes
2 tablespoons butter
4 eggs
2 cups light cream
1 teaspoon salt
2 tablespoons flour
½ cup light cream

1. Shred the potatoes.

2. Butter the inside of the slow cooker.

3. Beat the eggs; mix in 2 cups light cream, salt, and flour.

4. Pour the egg mixture into the slow cooker. Add the potatoes. Pour the remaining ½ cup of cream over the top.

5. Cover and heat on a low setting for 3 to 4 hours.

# Chicken Budapest

*This goes well with a side dish of steamed baby asparagus,*
*baby carrots, and small red potatoes with cracked black peppercorns.*

**stats**

**SERVES 5–6**

Cooking time . . . . . . . 4–6 hours
Preparation time . . . . 45 minutes
Attention . . . . . . . . . . Moderate
Pot size . . . . . . . . . . . 3–5 quarts

1 cup flour

½ teaspoon salt

½ teaspoon white pepper

2½ pounds chicken

3 tablespoons oil

2 onions

3 cloves garlic

3 tablespoons paprika

2 cups water

½ cup water

2 tablespoons flour

2 cups sour cream

**1.** Mix the flour, salt, and pepper. Cut the chicken into serving-size pieces and coat with the flour mixture. Sauté the chicken pieces in oil in a pan over medium heat until the meat is lightly browned.

**2.** Slice the onions. Crush and slice the garlic. Add the onion and garlic to the pan with the chicken and stir over medium heat until the onion is soft. Add the paprika to the pan and stir to mix.

**3.** Add the chicken–and-onion mixture and 2 cups of water to the slow cooker.

**4.** Cover and heat on a low setting for 4 to 6 hours.

**5.** Mix the remaining water and flour in a mixing bowl, then add the sour cream and blend well. An hour before serving, slowly stir the sour cream mixture into the chicken.

# Royal Stew

*This classic recipe is a thrifty way to get the most use out of juicy soup bones. Ask your butcher to crack them for you.*

**stats**

**SERVES 5–6**

| | |
|---|---|
| Cooking time | 4–6 hours |
| Preparation time | 45 minutes |
| Attention | Moderate |
| Pot size | 3–5 quarts |

1 onion

1 leek

1 stalk celery

2 tablespoons olive oil

¼ pound butter

¼ cup flour

2 large carrots

1 cup green peas

5 pounds fresh beef bones

3 cups water

1 bouquet garni

½ cup sherry

**1.** Thinly slice the onion, leek, and celery and combine. Sauté the sliced onion mixture in oil in a pan over medium heat until soft. Transfer to the slow cooker.

**2.** Melt the butter in the same pan over medium heat. Add the flour to the melted butter and stir until the flour is lightly browned. Transfer to the slow cooker; stir into the onion mixture.

**3.** Slice the carrots. Add the carrots, peas, beef bones, water, and bouquet garni to the slow cooker.

**4.** Cover and heat on a low setting for 4 to 6 hours.

**5.** Half an hour before serving, remove the beef bones and bouquet garni, then add the sherry.

# 15

# From the Far East
# to Your Dinner Table

# Greek Dolmades

*Grape leaves are often sold pickled in jars. If you can't get them at your local market, you can substitute cabbage leaves.*

*stats*

**YIELDS ABOUT 20**

Cooking time . . . . . . . 3–4 hours
Preparation time. . . . 2 hours
Attention. . . . . . . . . . Moderate
Pot size . . . . . . . . . . . . 3–5 quarts

½ pound ground beef
½ pound ground lamb
1 egg
1 onion
1 bunch parsley
4–6 fresh mint leaves
½ cup uncooked rice
2 tablespoons olive oil
¼ cup water
¼ teaspoon salt
¼ teaspoon black pepper
20 grape leaves
1½ cups beef broth
1½ cups water
2 eggs
Juice of 1 lemon

**1.** Mix the beef, lamb, and egg. Mince the onion; chop the parsley and mint leaves. Add the onion, parsley, mint, rice, olive oil, water, salt, and pepper to the meat mixture.

**2.** Put 1 to 2 teaspoons of the meat mixture on each grape leaf, shiny side down, sealing the ends inside. Arrange the folded side down on a rack in the slow cooker. Place a glass plate or bowl on top to weight down the mound.

**3.** Pour the broth and water over the rolls.

**4.** Cover and heat on a high setting for 3 to 4 hours.

**5.** Before serving, beat the eggs in a large mixing bowl and stir the lemon juice into the eggs. Slowly add ½ cup of the hot broth from the slow cooker to the egg mixture and continue mixing. Drain most of the broth from the rolls and add it to the egg mixture. Provide this separately as a sauce.

# Japanese Custard

*This delicate custard-like soup goes well with grilled fish and vegetables,
or as part of a light meal with a green salad.*

 **SERVES 4**

| | |
|---|---|
| Cooking time | 1–2 hours |
| Preparation time | 45 minutes |
| Attention | Minimal |
| Pot size | 3–5 quarts |

2 eggs

2 cups chicken broth

¼ teaspoon salt

¼ pound mushrooms

¼ pound boneless, skinless chicken

4 green onions

1 teaspoon rice oil

¼ cup cooked rice

**1.** Beat the eggs well. Mix with the chicken broth and salt in a mixing bowl.

**2.** Dice the mushrooms, chicken, and green onions; sauté in rice oil in a pan over low heat until the mushrooms are soft.

**3.** Distribute the mushroom mixture and rice between 4 custard cups. Divide the broth mixture between the same custard cups; top each with a lid of glass.

**4.** Arrange the dishes on a trivet in the slow cooker. Pour water around the base.

**5.** Cover and heat on a high setting for 1 to 2 hours.

# Gingery Pumpkin Soup

*You can use raw butternut or acorn squash instead of pumpkin,
or add some brown sugar or maple syrup for an extra hint of autumn.*

 **stats**

**SERVES 6**

Cooking time . . . . . . . 5–6 hours
Preparation time. . . . 30 minutes
Attention . . . . . . . . . . Moderate
Pot size . . . . . . . . . . . . 3–5 quarts

2 *pounds raw pumpkin*

1 *onion*

2 *cloves*

3 *cups chicken stock*

¼ *teaspoon cinnamon*

2 *tablespoons fresh ginger*

½ *teaspoon black pepper*

¼ *teaspoon salt*

1 *cup heavy cream*

**1.** Peel the pumpkin; remove the seeds and cube the flesh. Peel the onion and stick the cloves in the whole, peeled onion.

**2.** Transfer the pumpkin, onion, stock, spices, and salt to the slow cooker.

**3.** Cover and heat on a low setting for 4 to 5 hours.

**4.** An hour before serving, remove the onion. Lift out some of the pumpkin chunks and puree with the cream in a blender or food processor. Add the creamed mixture to the slow cooker.

# Katie's Chai

*Chai is stewed to caramelize the milk sugars, which completely changes the taste. Enjoy this chai with one of the breads found in this book for a comforting, soothing meal.*

 *stats*

**SERVES 6**

Cooking time....... 3–4 hours
Preparation time.... 30 minutes
Attention.......... Moderate
Pot size........... 3–5 quarts

3 cups milk

3 cups water

½ cup loose tea leaves

¾ cup sugar

3 cardamom pods

4 whole cloves

¼ vanilla bean pod

**1.** Combine the ingredients in the slow cooker. Stir to be sure the sugar is dissolved.

**2.** Cover and heat on a low setting for 3 to 4 hours.

**3.** Remove the pods and skim the surface to remove any floating tea leaves before serving.

# Ginger Tomato Lamb

*You can substitute beef or pork for lamb in this recipe if you wish.*
*Serve with triangles of fresh pita bread.*

 **SERVES 4–6**

Cooking time . . . . . . . 4–5 hours
Preparation time . . . . 30 minutes
Attention . . . . . . . . . . Minimal
Pot size . . . . . . . . . . . . 3–5 quarts

2 pounds lamb

2 tablespoons butter

1 onion

1 clove garlic

3 tablespoons flour

1½ tablespoons curry powder

2 tomatoes

1 inch fresh gingerroot

1 teaspoon salt

¼ cup water

**1.** Cube the lamb. Sauté in butter in a pan over medium heat until slightly browned. Transfer the meat to the slow cooker; set aside the pan with the juices.

**2.** Chop the onion; crush and mince the garlic. Add the onion and garlic to the pan used for the lamb and sauté over medium heat until the onion is tender. Stir in the flour and curry and mix while heating. When thickened, add the onion mixture to the slow cooker.

**3.** Chop the tomatoes. Peel and grate the gingerroot. Add the tomatoes, ginger, salt, and water to the slow cooker.

**4.** Cover and heat on a low setting for 4 to 5 hours.

# Ginger Barbecue Beef

*Fresh ginger has a much more potent flavor than powdered, dried ginger.*
*Try to use the fresh root if available.*

**SERVES 6–8**

Cooking time . . . . . . . 4–5 hours
Preparation time . . . . 30 minutes
Attention . . . . . . . . . . Minimal
Pot size . . . . . . . . . . . 3–5 quarts

3 cloves garlic
1 inch fresh gingerroot
½ cup soy sauce
½ cup water
2 tablespoons sesame oil
2 tablespoons sugar
4 teaspoons sesame seeds
3 pounds beef
1 onion

**1.** Peel and mince the garlic and ginger. Mix in a small bowl with the soy sauce, water, oil, sugar, and sesame seeds.

**2.** Cut the beef in slices. Coarsely chop the onion.

**3.** Arrange the beef and onion in the slow cooker while sprinkling it throughout with the sauce mixture.

**4.** Cover and heat on a low setting for 4 to 5 hours.

# Almond Chicken Gifts

*Grated fresh gingerroot and mandarin orange segments are excellent condiments for these treats. Serve with white or stir-fried rice.*

 **SERVES 6–8**

Cooking time . . . . . . . 2–3 hours
Preparation time . . . . 30 minutes
Attention . . . . . . . . . . Minimal
Pot size . . . . . . . . . . . . 3–5 quarts

*1 pound boneless, skinless chicken*

*½ cup almonds*

*2 eggs*

*2 tablespoons soy sauce*

*30–35 large spinach leaves*

*½ cup white wine*

*1 cup water*

**1.** Mince the chicken and almonds. Beat the eggs and stir in the chicken, almonds, and soy sauce.

**2.** Clean the spinach leaves. Place a teaspoon of the chicken mixture on each leaf. Fold the leaves over the chicken mixture, forming a roll, and tie with cotton string.

**3.** Arrange the rolls on a rack in the slow cooker. Pour the wine and water around the base.

**4.** Cover and cook on a high setting for 2 to 3 hours.

# Tropical Bread Pudding

*Bread Pudding for dinner? Maybe once in a blue moon—what a tasty treat!*

**stats**

**YIELDS 2 LOAVES**

Cooking time . . . . . . . 3–4 hours
Preparation time . . . . 30 minutes
Attention . . . . . . . . . . Minimal
Pot size . . . . . . . . . . . . 3–5 quarts

6 eggs

½ cup brown sugar

1 teaspoon cinnamon

2 cups coconut milk

10 slices stale bread

½ pound pineapple, peeled and cored

2 tablespoons butter

Rind of ½ lemon

**1.** Beat the eggs. Add the sugar, cinnamon, and coconut milk; mix well.

**2.** Cube the bread. Dice the pineapple. Butter 2 loaf pans or the equivalent. Arrange the bread and pineapple in the baking dishes.

**3.** Grate the lemon rind. Sprinkle the grated rind and pour the milk mixture over the bread, filling the dishes no more than ½ full.

**4.** Loosely cover each dish with a foil or glass lid. Place on a trivet or rack in the slow cooker, and pour water around the base of the trivet.

**5.** Cover and heat on a high setting for 2 to 3 hours.

# Coconut Rice

*Try adding white raisins or pieces of fresh pineapple during the last hour of cooking.*

 **stats**

**SERVES 4–6**

Cooking time . . . . . . . 4–5 hours
Preparation time . . . . 15 minutes
Attention . . . . . . . . . . Minimal
Pot size . . . . . . . . . . . . 3–5 quarts

1 lemon

1 cup uncooked rice

2 cups coconut milk

½ cup water

½ teaspoon salt

½ teaspoon turmeric

¼ cup toasted pistachios

**1.** Squeeze the juice from the lemon. Put the lemon juice, rice, coconut milk, water, salt, and turmeric in the slow cooker.

**2.** Cover and heat on a low setting for 3 to 4 hours.

**3.** Chop the pistachios into coarse pieces. An hour before serving, stir in the pistachios.

# Ghee

*Ghee is used to replace butter in some Far East recipes, try it on bread or pasta tonight.*

 **stats**

**YIELDS ABOUT 3 CUPS**

Cooking time . . . . . . . 2–3 hours
Preparation time . . . . 15 minutes
Attention . . . . . . . . . . Moderate
Pot size . . . . . . . . . . . . 3–5 quarts

2 pounds butter, unsalted

**1.** Cut the butter into large cubes.

**2.** Cover and heat on a low setting for 2 to 3 hours. The butter should separate. Don't let it brown.

**3.** Skim off the clear liquid on the top; this is ghee. Store in glass jars, refrigerated and covered. Discard the butter solids, or use in cooking as a butter substitute.

# Indian Lentils

*Look for orange lentils in your local market or an international grocery.*
*Brown lentils give an entirely different taste and texture.*

**stats**

**SERVES 6**

| | |
|---|---|
| Cooking time | 3–4 hours |
| Preparation time | 30 minutes |
| Attention | Minimal |
| Pot size | 3–5 quarts |

*1 onion*

*3 cloves garlic*

*1 green pepper*

*1 teaspoon cumin*

*2 tablespoons Ghee (page 304)*

*2 cups cubed tomatoes*

*1½ cups orange lentils*

*3 cups water*

*2 teaspoons honey*

*¼ teaspoon salt*

**1.** Slice the onion and garlic; dice the green pepper. Sauté the onion, garlic, and green pepper with cumin in ghee in a pan over medium heat until the onion is soft.

**2.** Add the tomatoes, onion mixture, lentils, water, honey, and salt to the slow cooker.

**3.** Cover and heat on a low setting for 3 to 4 hours.

# Eastern Lamb Curry

*This should be served with rice, preferably basmati rice. Provide condiments,*
*including white raisins, toasted coconut shavings, and roasted cashews or pistachios.*

**stats**

**SERVES 6–8**

Cooking time . . . . . . . 3–4 hours
Preparation time. . . . 60 minutes
Attention . . . . . . . . . . Minimal
Pot size . . . . . . . . . . . . 3–5 quarts

3 pounds lamb

1 carrot

1 onion

3 cups water

1 bouquet garni

½ teaspoon salt

1 banana

5 tablespoons butter

2 tablespoons curry powder

2 tablespoons flour

1 apple

½ cup chutney

**1.** Cube the lamb. Clean and peel the carrot and onion. Put the meat in a stockpot with the carrot, onion, water, bouquet garni, and salt; boil for 20 minutes.

**2.** After boiling, remove and discard the carrot, onion, and bouquet garni. Skim the surface of the boiled water and discard any debris. Transfer the meat and liquid to the slow cooker.

**3.** Slice the banana in ½-inch slices. Sauté in 2 tablespoons of the butter in a pan over low heat until the banana is lightly browned. Transfer the banana and juices to the slow cooker.

**4.** In the same pan, melt the remaining butter. Add the curry and flour, then stir over low heat for 5 minutes. Core and cube the apple; stir the apple and chutney into the curry mixture. Transfer the curry mixture to the slow cooker.

**5.** Cover and heat on a low setting for 3 to 4 hours.

# Mountain Honey Lamb with Dates

*You can buy ghee for this recipe, or make your own Ghee (page 304).*
*Serve this with warm, fresh pita bread.*

 **stats**

**SERVES 6–8**

Cooking time . . . . . . . 5–6 hours
Preparation time. . . . 30 minutes
Attention. . . . . . . . . . Minimal
Pot size . . . . . . . . . . . . 3–5 quarts

2 pounds lamb

1 onion

5 tablespoons Ghee (page 304)

1 cup dates

1 teaspoon turmeric

1 teaspoon cinnamon

½ teaspoon salt

2 tablespoons honey

1 cup uncooked rice

2½ cups water

Rind of ¼ lemon

**1.** Cut the lamb into cubes; slice the onion. Sauté the lamb and onion in 3 tablespoons of the ghee in a pan over medium heat until the meat is lightly browned.

**2.** Pit and chop the dates. Add the meat mixture, dates, spices, salt, honey, rice, and water to the slow cooker.

**3.** Cover and heat on a low setting for 4 to 5 hours.

**4.** Finely grate the lemon rind. Half an hour before serving, add the lemon rind and the remaining ghee.

# Simple Curry Chicken

*This basic curry can be served with rice, preferably basmati.*
*Dress it up with a variety of condiments if your schedule allows.*

**SERVES 6–8**

Cooking time . . . . . . . 2–3 hours
Preparation time. . . . 15 minutes
Attention. . . . . . . . . . Minimal
Pot size . . . . . . . . . . . . 3–5 quarts

2 onions

3 pounds chicken breasts

¼ cup olive oil

⅓ cup curry powder

½ cup water

**1.** Dice the onions and cut the chicken into serving-size pieces. Sauté the onions in oil in a pan over medium heat until browned. Slowly stir in the curry powder, then add the chicken breasts and sauté over medium heat until lightly browned.

**2.** Put the chicken mixture and water in the slow cooker.

**3.** Cover and heat on a low setting for 2 to 3 hours.

# Soy and Chestnut Chicken

*Garnish this with roasted soy nuts and mung bean sprouts.*
*It's also very good chilled and sliced over salad greens.*

**stats**

**SERVES 6–8**

Cooking time . . . . . . . 2–3 hours
Preparation time . . . . 15 minutes
Attention . . . . . . . . . . Minimal
Pot size . . . . . . . . . . . 3–5 quarts

3 pounds chicken

1 pound canned water chestnuts

1 green bell pepper

1 cup soy sauce

½ cup vinegar

**1.** Cut the chicken into serving-size pieces. Thinly slice the water chestnuts and cube the green pepper. Put the chicken, cut vegetables, soy sauce, and vinegar in the slow cooker.

**2.** Cover and heat on a low setting for 2 to 3 hours.

# Nomad's Fruit and Nut Dish

*This flavorful dish, made from ingredients that store well, is served over rice.*
*This is also excellent served with lamb chops.*

**SERVES 4–6**

Cooking time . . . . . . . 4–5 hours
Preparation time. . . . 15 minutes
Attention. . . . . . . . . . Minimal
Pot size . . . . . . . . . . . 3–5 quarts

1 tablespoon dried orange rind

¼ cup shaved blanched almonds

¼ cup toasted pistachio nuts

¼ cup raisins

¼ cup dried apricots

4 carrots

¼ cup sugar

2 cups water

**1.** Use kitchen shears to finely mince the orange rind. Chop the nuts and fruits. Diagonally slice the carrots.

**2.** Combine the rind, nuts, fruits, carrots, sugar, and water in the slow cooker.

**3.** Cover and heat on a low setting for 4 to 5 hours.

CHAPTER

16

# Latin American Creations

# Equatorial Bread Pudding

*This bread pudding has fruits, nuts, and cheese instead*
*of eggs and milk as in the traditional continental U.S. version.*

**stats**

**SERVES 4–6**

Cooking time . . . . . . . 2–3 hours
Preparation time . . . . 15 minutes
Attention . . . . . . . . . . Minimal
Pot size . . . . . . . . . . . . 3–5 quarts

8 slices white bread

2 apples

½ pound cheese of choice

2 tablespoons butter

½ cup raisins

½ cup shelled peanuts

2 cups brown sugar

3 cups water

2 teaspoons cinnamon

½ teaspoon cloves

**1.** Remove the crusts from the bread; cube and toast it. Peel, core, and finely slice the apples. Shred the cheese.

**2.** Butter the inside of the slow cooker. Place half of the bread cubes in the bottom of the slow cooker. Then add the apples, raisins, and peanuts. Cover with the rest of the bread cubes, and put the cheese on top.

**3.** Combine the brown sugar, water, and spices. Pour this syrup over the whole mixture.

**4.** Cover and heat on a low setting for 2 to 3 hours.

# Colombian Beef Stew

*You can substitute pork for beef in this recipe, if you wish.*
*Use ears of fresh sweet corn, if possible.*

**SERVES 6–8**

Cooking time . . . . . . . 3–4 hours
Preparation time . . . . 45 minutes
Attention . . . . . . . . . . Minimal
Pot size . . . . . . . . . . . . 3–5 quarts

1 onion

3 cloves garlic

2 tablespoons oil

2 pounds beef

3 potatoes

4 carrots

1 cup chopped tomatoes

3 cups water

1 teaspoon cumin

4 ears corn

1 cup green peas

½ teaspoon salt

¼ teaspoon pepper

**1.** Coarsely chop the onion and finely chop the garlic. Heat the onion and garlic in oil in a pan over medium heat until soft.

**2.** Cube the beef. Add the beef to the onion mixture and continue stirring over medium heat until the beef is browned.

**3.** Chop the potatoes; slice the carrots. Put the beef mixture, chopped tomatoes, and cut vegetables in the slow cooker with the water and cumin.

**4.** Cover and heat on a low setting for 3 to 4 hours.

**5.** Cut the corn ears into 1-inch lengths. An hour before serving, add the corn, peas, salt, and pepper.

# Brazilian Meat Stew

*This goes well with fluffy white rice and a nice after-dinner coffee.*
*You can substitute salt pork for the bacon.*

**stats**

**SERVES 8-10**

Cooking time . . . . . . . 3–4 hours
Preparation time . . . . 30 minutes
Attention . . . . . . . . . . Minimal
Pot size . . . . . . . . . . . . 3–5 quarts

3 slices bacon

2 onions

3 cloves garlic

1 pound beef

1 pound pork

1 pound spicy link sausage

4 cups cooked black beans with liquid

2 cups chopped tomatoes

1 cup water

1 tablespoon prepared mustard

½ teaspoon salt

½ teaspoon pepper

**1.** Dice and sauté the bacon in a pan over medium heat until crispy.

**2.** Finely chop the onions and garlic. Add the onions and garlic to the bacon and continue heating until the onions are soft.

**3.** Cut the beef, pork, and sausage into bite-size pieces. Add the meat to the onion mixture and continue heating until the meat is browned. Transfer the meat-and-onion mixture to the slow cooker.

**4.** Mash 1 cup of the black beans and add both mashed and whole beans to the slow cooker. Add the tomatoes and the remaining ingredients to the slow cooker.

**5.** Cover and heat on a low setting for 3 to 4 hours.

# Spices-of-Life Beef Stew

*This is your chance to take advantage of your spice collection.
However, if you have fresh parsley, use it instead of dried.*

**SERVES 6–8**

| | |
|---|---|
| Cooking time | 4–5 hours |
| Preparation time | 30 minutes |
| Attention | Minimal |
| Pot size | 3–5 quarts |

1 pound beef

3 slices bacon

2 cloves garlic

1 onion

1 bay leaf

3 tomatoes

4 potatoes

¼ teaspoon sage

¼ teaspoon marjoram

½ teaspoon paprika

½ teaspoon curry powder

2 tablespoons vinegar

¾ cup stock

1 teaspoon salt

⅓ cup black olives

1 small bunch parsley

⅓ cup white wine

**1.** Cube the beef and dice the bacon. Crush the garlic and slice the onion. Sauté the beef, bacon, garlic, and onion in a pan over medium heat until the meat is browned. Transfer to the slow cooker.

**2.** Crumble the bay leaf. Dice the tomatoes and quarter the potatoes. Add the spices, tomatoes, potatoes, vinegar, stock, and salt to the slow cooker. Mix well.

**3.** Cover and heat on low setting for 3 to 4 hours.

**4.** Slice the olives and chop the parsley. Half an hour before serving, add the olives, parsley, and wine to the slow cooker.

# Mountain Garden Stew

*This is a good dish to provide for the vegetarians in your crowd,
or to serve with a grilled steak.*

**SERVES 8–10**

Cooking time . . . . . . . 4–5 hours
Preparation time . . . . 30 minutes
Attention . . . . . . . . . . Minimal
Pot size . . . . . . . . . . . . 3–5 quarts

3 onions

3 cloves garlic

2 tablespoons olive oil

1 pound squash

2 cups chopped tomatoes

1 teaspoon basil

1 teaspoon oregano

4 cups cooked navy beans

1 cup corn kernels

½ teaspoon salt

¼ teaspoon black pepper

**1.** Chop the onions and mince the garlic. Sauté the onions and garlic in oil in a pan over medium heat until soft.

**2.** Chop the squash and remove the squash seeds. Add the tomatoes, squash, and herbs to the slow cooker.

**3.** Cover and heat on a low setting for 3 to 4 hours.

**4.** An hour before serving, add the beans, corn, salt, and pepper to the slow cooker.

# Everything Stew

*This unusual dish blends sweet flavors, including peaches, with vegetables and meat. Serve with a simple green salad with oil and vinegar.*

### stats
**SERVES 12–14**

Cooking time . . . . . . . 4–5 hours
Preparation time . . . . 45 minutes
Attention . . . . . . . . . . Minimal
Pot size . . . . . . . . . . . . 3–5 quarts

2 onions
1 green pepper
2 tablespoons oil
2 pounds beef
1 pound tomatoes
1½ pounds sweet potatoes
1 pound squash
1 pound potatoes
2 cups corn kernels
2 cups water
4 peaches
½ teaspoon salt
¼ teaspoon pepper
2 tablespoons brown sugar

**1.** Finely chop the onions and green pepper. Sauté the onions and green pepper in oil in a pan over medium heat until soft.

**2.** Cube the meat. Add to the onion mixture and stir over medium heat until the meat is browned.

**3.** Cube the tomatoes, sweet potatoes, and squash; slice the potatoes. Add the cut vegetables, corn, and water to the slow cooker.

**4.** Cover and heat on a low setting for 3 to 4 hours.

**5.** Pit and slice the peaches. Half an hour before serving, add the peaches, salt, pepper, and sugar to the slow cooker.

# Coconut Soup

*This dish is simple but smooth and creamy. You can also add rice, chicken, or seafood to add other flavors and textures.*

**SERVES 6–8**

Cooking time . . . . . . . 3–4 hours

Preparation time. . . . 30 minutes

Attention. . . . . . . . . . Minimal

Pot size . . . . . . . . . . . . 3–5 quarts

1 onion

2 tablespoons butter

3 tablespoons flour

5 cups chicken broth

1¼ cups coconut milk

**1.** Finely chop the onion. Sauté in butter in a pan over medium heat until soft.

**2.** Blend the flour into ½ cup of the chicken broth. Add to the onion mixture and stir over medium heat until thickened.

**3.** Transfer to the slow cooker and add the remaining broth to the onion mixture.

**4.** Cover and heat on a low setting for 2 to 3 hours.

**5.** An hour before serving, add the coconut milk to the slow cooker.

# Banana Ribs

*Bananas add a subtle sweetness to the meat.*
*If available, try tiny red bananas instead of the standard yellow.*

**stats**

**SERVES 10–12**

Cooking time . . . . . . . 6–8 hours
Preparation time . . . . 30 minutes
Attention . . . . . . . . . . Minimal
Pot size . . . . . . . . . . . . 3–5 quarts

4 potatoes

2 ears corn

1 bunch cilantro

1 teaspoon dried oregano

½ teaspoon salt

½ teaspoon black pepper

2 pounds beef ribs

2 onions

2 tomatoes

1 green bell pepper

3 bananas

4 cups beef broth

**1.** Peel the potatoes and cut them into 2-inch cubes. Husk and quarter the ears of corn. Put the potatoes and corn in the bottom of the slow cooker.

**2.** Chop the cilantro. Mix it in a small bowl with the oregano, salt, and black pepper. Sprinkle the vegetables in the slow cooker with one-third of the cilantro mixture.

**3.** Cut the ribs into serving-size pieces. Arrange in the slow cooker over the potatoes and corn. Sprinkle with one-third of the cilantro mixture.

**4.** Chop the onions, tomatoes, and green pepper. Peel the bananas and cut them into ½-inch slices. Arrange the cut vegetables and fruit over the meat in the slow cooker. Sprinkle with the remaining cilantro mixture.

**5.** Add the broth.

**6.** Cover and heat on a low setting for 6 to 8 hours.

# Creamy Corn Soup

*This is a rich, delicious soup that is best served
with hunks of crusty bread for dipping.*

**SERVES 6–8**

Cooking time....... 4–5 hours
Preparation time.... 30 minutes
Attention.......... Minimal
Pot size........... 3–5 quarts

2 cloves garlic

1 pound tomatoes

3 cups chicken broth

2 cups corn kernels

1 teaspoon oregano

½ teaspoon salt

½ teaspoon black pepper

1 cup heavy cream

½ pound Romano cheese

1. Mince the garlic and chop the tomatoes.

2. Combine the ingredients, except cream
and cheese, in slow cooker.

3. Cover and heat on low setting for 3 to
4 hours.

4. Half an hour before serving, stir in the
cream.

5. Grate the cheese and provide as a garnish
for individual servings.

# Curry and Zucchini Soup

*If you or a neighbor has zucchini in the garden, use it in this soup.*
*Fresh garden vegetables always provide great flavor.*

**SERVES 6–8**

| | |
|---|---|
| Cooking time | 3–4 hours |
| Preparation time | 30 minutes |
| Attention | Moderate |
| Pot size | 3–5 quarts |

3 zucchini

2 onions

4 cups chicken broth

1 tablespoon curry powder

1 cup cream

½ teaspoon salt

½ teaspoon pepper

**1.** Coarsely chop the zucchini and onions.

**2.** Combine the zucchini, onions, broth, and curry powder in the slow cooker.

**3.** Cover and heat on a low setting for 2 to 3 hours.

**4.** Half an hour before serving, transfer some of the zucchini and onions with a slotted spoon to a blender or food processor and puree with the cream, salt, and pepper; return the pureed material to the slow cooker.

# Rancho Beef Casserole

*In this recipe, corn tortillas are used to thicken the casserole.*
*Try this in other recipes to add a nice hint of corn flavor.*

**stats**

**SERVES 6–8**

| | |
|---|---|
| Cooking time | 4–5 hours |
| Preparation time | 45 minutes |
| Attention | Minimal |
| Pot size | 3–5 quarts |

1 onion

3 cloves garlic

2 green peppers

2 pounds beef

1 teaspoon chili powder

2 tablespoons oil

1 pound tomatoes

2 cups water

2 bay leaves

1 teaspoon ground cloves

1 teaspoon oregano

½ teaspoon salt

½ teaspoon pepper

2 corn tortillas

**1.** Finely chop the onion and garlic. Chop the green peppers; cube the beef.

**2.** Sauté the onion, garlic, peppers, beef, and chili powder in oil in a pan over medium heat until the meat is browned. Transfer the meat mixture to the slow cooker.

**3.** Chop the tomatoes. Add the tomatoes, water, spices, salt, and pepper to the slow cooker.

**4.** Cover and heat on a low setting for 3 to 4 hours.

**5.** Half an hour before serving, crumble the tortillas and add to the slow cooker to thicken. Remove bay leaves before serving.

# Light Tortilla Soup

*Here, tortillas are used not as a thickener, but as a crackly garnish.*
*Set out extras with salsa for your guests to snack on.*

**stats**

**SERVES 6–8**

Cooking time . . . . . . . 3–4 hours
Preparation time . . . . 30 minutes
Attention . . . . . . . . . . Minimal
Pot size . . . . . . . . . . . . 3–5 quarts

½ onion
4 cups chicken broth
6 tablespoons tomato paste
½ teaspoon salt
¼ teaspoon white pepper
1 bunch cilantro
½ pound white cheese of choice
2 tortillas
¼ cup oil

**1.** Finely chop the onion. Combine the onion, broth, tomato paste, salt, and pepper in the slow cooker.

**2.** Cover and heat on a low setting for 2 to 3 hours.

**3.** Finely chop the cilantro. Half an hour before serving, add the cilantro to the slow cooker.

**4.** Shred the cheese. Slice the tortillas into strips and heat in oil in a pan over medium heat until browned. Transfer the tortilla strips to absorbent paper to drain. Provide the shredded cheese and tortilla strips as a garnish for individual servings.

# Spiced Okra

*This goes well with rice and grilled chicken.*
*Try using a bit of fresh gingerroot instead of ground ginger.*

 **SERVES 4–6**

Cooking time . . . . . . . 2–3 hours
Preparation time . . . . 30 minutes
Attention . . . . . . . . . . Minimal
Pot size . . . . . . . . . . . 3–5 quarts

*1 onion*

*3 tablespoons butter*

*2 pounds fresh okra*

*½ cup water*

*½ teaspoon cumin*

*½ teaspoon ginger*

*½ teaspoon coriander*

*¼ teaspoon black pepper*

*½ teaspoon salt*

**1.** Mince the onion. Sauté the onion in butter in a pan over medium heat until soft.

**2.** Slice the okra. Add the okra, onion, water, and spices, and salt to the slow cooker.

**3.** Cover and heat on a low setting for 2 to 3 hours.

CHAPTER

17

# Hot Sandwiches
# & Hearty Favorites

# Cheesy Melts

*You can make the sandwich filling and prepare the rolls the day before a party, then assemble these sandwiches right before heating.*

**stats**

**YIELDS 12**

Cooking time . . . . . . . 1–2 hours
Preparation time . . . . 30 minutes
Attention . . . . . . . . . . Minimal
Pot size . . . . . . . . . . . . 3–5 quarts

1½ pounds extra sharp Cheddar cheese

½ cup pitted black olives

¼ cup green chilies

1 onion

¾ cup tomato sauce

3 tablespoons olive oil

½ teaspoon black pepper

¼ teaspoon salt

12 large French rolls

**1.** Grate the cheese; slice the olives and chilies. Mince the onion.

**2.** Mix the cheese, olives, chilies, and onion with the tomato sauce, oil, pepper, and salt.

**3.** Cut the tops off the rolls. Stuff the rolls with the cheese mixture, replace the tops, and wrap the sandwiches in foil.

**4.** Arrange the wrapped sandwiches on a trivet or rack in the slow cooker. Pour water around the base of the trivet.

**5.** Cover and heat on a high setting for 1 to 2 hours.

# Steamers

*If you don't have fresh buns available on party day, don't worry.*
*Stale buns will soften with the steam.*

*stats*
**YIELDS 8**

Cooking time....... 1–2 hours
Preparation time.... 30 minutes
Attention.......... Minimal
Pot size............ 3–5 quarts

1 clove garlic

1 onion

1 pound ground beef

1 pound pork sausage

2 eggs

½ teaspoon salt

1 cup bread crumbs

¼ cup milk

8 hamburger buns

½ cup sliced pickles

**1.** Crush and mince the garlic; mince the onion. Mix the garlic and onion with the meat, eggs, salt, crumbs, and milk.

**2.** Form the mixture into 8 patties.

**3.** Briefly sear the patties on each side in a pan over high heat. Assemble the patties on hamburger buns, with pickles on each.

**4.** Wrap the sandwiches in aluminum foil. Arrange the wrapped sandwiches on a trivet or rack in the slow cooker. Pour water around the base of the trivet.

**5.** Cover and heat on a high setting for 1 to 2 hours.

# Bagel and Muenster Cheese Sandwich

*The drier your bagels are, the more juice they'll absorb from the tomatoes.*

**SERVES 6**

Cooking time . . . . . . . 1–2 hours
Preparation time . . . . 30 minutes
Attention . . . . . . . . . . Minimal
Pot size . . . . . . . . . . . . 3–5 quarts

6 bagels

2 tomatoes

½ pound Muenster cheese

½ pound cream cheese

1 onion

**1.** Slice the bagels, tomatoes, Muenster cheese, and cream cheese. Thinly slice the onion. Arrange the slices in this order: bagel, tomato, Muenster, onion, cream cheese, bagel.

**2.** Wrap the sandwiches in foil and arrange on a trivet in the slow cooker. Pour water around the base of the trivet.

**3.** Cover and heat on a high setting for 1 to 2 hours.

# Hot Corned Beef Sandwich

*Serve with dill pickles and cold cream soda on a hot afternoon with good friends.*

**SERVES 6**

Cooking time . . . . . . . 1–2 hours
Preparation time . . . . 30 minutes
Attention . . . . . . . . . . Minimal
Pot size . . . . . . . . . . . . 3–5 quarts

2 tablespoons horseradish

½ pound cream cheese

1 pound corned beef

12 slices rye bread

**1.** Cream the horseradish and the cream cheese together. Thinly slice the corned beef. Arrange the sandwich layers in this order: bread, beef, cheese, bread.

**2.** Wrap the sandwiches in foil and arrange on a trivet in the slow cooker. Pour water around the base of the trivet.

**3.** Cover and heat on a high setting for 1 to 2 hours.

# Classic Reuben

*These juicy sandwiches can be made ahead and frozen, then thawed*
*before heating. You can make half-size sandwiches, as well.*

 **stats**

**SERVES 6**

Cooking time ....... 1–2 hours
Preparation time.... 15 minutes
Attention.......... Minimal
Pot size ........... 3–5 quarts

12 slices rye bread

3 tablespoons butter

1 pound corned beef

½ pound Swiss cheese

1 pound sauerkraut

1 cup Russian dressing

**1.** Brown one side of each slice of bread in butter in a pan over medium heat.

**2.** Thinly slice the beef and the cheese. Drain sauerkraut until very dry. Arrange the sandwich layers in this order: bread (browned side out), beef, sauerkraut, dressing, cheese, bread.

**3.** Wrap the sandwiches in foil and arrange on a trivet in the slow cooker. Pour water around the base of the trivet.

**4.** Cover and heat on a high setting for 1 to 2 hours.

# Crab and Mushroom Kaiser Roll

*If you happen to have some fresh lobster, use it instead of crab.*
*Serve with a fresh green salad with vinaigrette.*

**SERVES 6**

Cooking time . . . . . . . 1–2 hours
Preparation time. . . . 30 minutes
Attention. . . . . . . . . . Minimal
Pot size . . . . . . . . . . . 3–5 quarts

1 cup crabmeat

½ pound mushrooms

1 small bunch parsley

¼ pound Parmesan cheese

¾ cup mayonnaise

1 teaspoon lemon juice

⅛ teaspoon rosemary

⅛ teaspoon thyme

⅛ teaspoon sage

6 Kaiser rolls

2 tablespoons butter

¼ cup toasted slivered almonds

1. Shred and blot dry the crabmeat, mince the mushrooms and parsley, and grate the cheese. Mix the crabmeat, mushrooms, parsley, cheese, mayonnaise, lemon juice, and herbs.

2. Split the rolls and toast the insides.

3. Arrange the sandwich layers in this order: bottom of roll (toasted side in), butter, crab mixture, almonds, butter, top of roll.

4. Wrap the sandwiches in foil and arrange on a trivet in the slow cooker. Pour water around the base of the trivet.

5. Cover and heat on a high setting for 1 to 2 hours.

# Chicken and Gherkin Sandwich

*Some people prefer sweet pickles, but dill pickles are the standard for guests.*
*Use the baby gherkins; they have a nicer texture.*

*stats*

**SERVES 6**

| | |
|---|---|
| Cooking time | 1–2 hours |
| Preparation time | 30 minutes |
| Attention | Minimal |
| Pot size | 3–5 quarts |

*12 slices rye bread*

*½ pound cooked chicken*

*6 baby dill pickles*

*¼ pound mozzarella cheese*

*2 tablespoons butter*

*½ teaspoon salt*

*½ teaspoon pepper*

**1.** Toast the bread on one side. Thinly slice the chicken, pickles, and cheese.

**2.** Arrange the sandwich layers in this order: bread (toasted side out), butter, chicken, salt, pepper, pickle, cheese, butter, bread.

**3.** Wrap the sandwiches in foil and arrange on a trivet in the slow cooker. Pour water around the base of the trivet.

**4.** Cover and heat on a high setting for 1 to 2 hours.

# Ham and Swiss Croissant

*Enhance this sandwich by using honey-baked ham, a fancy mustard,*
*or cherry tomatoes. You can also add a few leaves of raw spinach.*

**stats**

**SERVES 6**

Cooking time . . . . . . . 1–2 hours

Preparation time. . . . 30 minutes

Attention. . . . . . . . . . Minimal

Pot size . . . . . . . . . . . . 3–5 quarts

6 croissants

2 tomatoes

½ pound Swiss cheese

½ pound ham

3 tablespoons mustard

**1.** Slice the croissants and the tomatoes. Thinly slice the cheese and ham.

**2.** Arrange the sandwich layers in this order: bottom of croissant, ham, cheese, mustard, ham, tomato, top of croissant.

**3.** Wrap the sandwiches in foil and arrange on a trivet in the slow cooker. Pour water around the base of the trivet.

**4.** Cover and heat on a high setting for 1 to 2 hours.

# Bacon and Turkey Sandwich

*Fresh slices of avocado are an excellent addition to this sandwich.*

**stats**

**SERVES 6**

Cooking time . . . . . . . 1–2 hours
Preparation time. . . . 30 minutes
Attention . . . . . . . . . . Minimal
Pot size . . . . . . . . . . . . 3–5 quarts

12 slices bacon

12 slices rye bread

2 tomatoes

½ pound turkey

¼ pound Gruyère cheese

¼ cup mayonnaise

**1.** Brown the bacon in a pan over medium heat until crispy; drain.

**2.** Toast the bread; slice the tomatoes. Thinly slice the turkey and cheese.

**3.** Arrange the sandwich layers in this order: bread, mayonnaise, turkey, bacon, tomato, cheese, bread.

**4.** Wrap the sandwiches in foil and arrange on a trivet in the slow cooker. Pour water around the base of the trivet.

**5.** Cover and heat on a high setting for 1 to 2 hours.

# Steamed Turkey Sandwich

*Choose a nice, dense sourdough, then leave it out for a day to dry before toasting. Also, try substituting goose or duck for turkey.*

 **SERVES 6**

Cooking time . . . . . . . 1–2 hours
Preparation time . . . . 30 minutes
Attention . . . . . . . . . . Minimal
Pot size . . . . . . . . . . . . 3–5 quarts

12 slices bacon

12 slices sourdough bread

3 tomatoes

½ pound turkey

½ pound Cheddar cheese

2 tablespoons butter

2 teaspoons mustard

**1.** Sauté the bacon in a pan over medium heat until crispy; drain.

**2.** Toast the bread; slice the tomatoes. Thinly slice the turkey and the cheese.

**3.** Arrange the sandwich layers in this order: bread, butter, turkey, cheese, bacon, tomato, mustard, butter, bread.

**4.** Wrap the sandwiches in foil and arrange on a trivet in the slow cooker. Pour water around the base of the trivet.

**5.** Cover and heat on a high setting for 1 to 2 hours.

# Stromboli

*For a slight variation, substitute a nice olive relish*
*for the chopped olives on this sandwich.*

**SERVES 6**

Cooking time . . . . . . . 1–2 hours
Preparation time . . . . 30 minutes
Attention . . . . . . . . . . Minimal
Pot size . . . . . . . . . . . . 3–5 quarts

½ pound roast beef

2 tablespoons butter

12 slices French bread

½ cup olives

½ pound ham

½ pound mozzarella cheese

**1.** Thinly slice the beef. Sauté in butter in a pan over medium heat until lightly browned.

**2.** Toast the bread. Mince the olives. Thinly slice the ham and cheese.

**3.** Arrange the sandwich layers in this order: bread, beef, ham, olives, cheese, bread.

**4.** Wrap the sandwiches in foil and arrange on a trivet in the slow cooker. Pour water around the base of the trivet.

**5.** Cover and heat on a high setting for 1 to 2 hours.

# Baked Ham, Gruyere, and Roquefort Sandwich

*You can make these sandwiches on whole baguettes, then slice after assembly.*
*You can also use this trick to make lots of tiny sandwiches.*

**stats**

**SERVES 6**

Cooking time . . . . . . . 1–2 hours
Preparation time. . . . 30 minutes
Attention. . . . . . . . . . Minimal
Pot size . . . . . . . . . . . . 3–5 quarts

2 long French baguettes
½ pound Gruyère cheese
½ pound ham
½ pound Roquefort cheese
2 tablespoons mayonnaise
3 tablespoons dry white wine
3 tablespoons butter

**1.** Cut the baguettes to yield 6 pieces, each 6 to 8 inches in length. Slice each lengthwise to open, then toast the insides.

**2.** Thinly slice the Gruyère and ham. Mince the Roquefort and blend with the mayonnaise and white wine.

**3.** Arrange the sandwich layers in this order: bottom of baguette, butter, Gruyère, ham, Roquefort spread, top of baguette.

**4.** Wrap the sandwiches in foil and arrange on a trivet in the slow cooker. Pour water around the base of the trivet.

**5.** Cover and heat on a high setting for 1 to 2 hours.

# Saucisson en Croute

*Use a chewy roll, try lengths of French bread, or roll the sausages in pita bread.*

 *stats*

**SERVES 6**

Cooking time . . . . . . . 1–2 hours
Preparation time . . . . 30 minutes
Attention . . . . . . . . . . Minimal
Pot size . . . . . . . . . . . . 3–5 quarts

6 spicy Italian sausages

6 long sourdough rolls

2 tablespoons Dijon mustard

**1.** Sauté the sausages in a pan over medium heat until browned and cooked; drain.

**2.** Cut off the tips of the rolls. Use the handle of a wooden spoon to hollow out the center. Dip the sausages in the mustard and insert each into a roll. Wrap the sandwiches in foil and arrange on a trivet in the slow cooker. Pour water around the base. Cover and heat on a high setting for 1 to 2 hours.

# Sausage and Sauerkraut Sandwich

*Choose German or Hungarian sauerkraut, or make your own.*

*stats*

**SERVES 6**

Cooking time . . . . . . . 1–2 hours
Preparation time . . . . 30 minutes
Attention . . . . . . . . . . Minimal
Pot size . . . . . . . . . . . . 3–5 quarts

1½ pounds bulk pork sausage

1 cup spiced sauerkraut

¼ pound Gruyère cheese

6 poppy seed rolls

**1.** Form the sausage meat into six patties and sauté in a pan over medium heat until browned and thoroughly cooked; drain. Drain the sauerkraut and thinly slice the cheese; split and toast the rolls.

**2.** Arrange the sandwich layers in this order: bottom of roll, sausage, sauerkraut, cheese, top of roll.

**3.** Wrap the sandwiches in foil and arrange on a trivet in the slow cooker. Pour water around the base of the trivet. Cover and heat on a high setting for 1 to 2 hours.

# Sauerkraut and Bratwurst Roll

*These can be messy, but it's worth it. You can substitute caraway rye bread for pita—just split the bratwurst lengthwise.*

*stats*

**SERVES 6**

Cooking time . . . . . . . 1–2 hours
Preparation time. . . . 30 minutes
Attention. . . . . . . . . . Minimal
Pot size . . . . . . . . . . . . 3–5 quarts

1 apple

1½ pounds sauerkraut

1 tablespoon caraway seeds

2 tablespoons oil

6 bratwurst

1 tablespoon butter

½ cup white wine

2 tablespoons Dijon mustard

6 whole-wheat pita loaves

**1.** Core and chop the apple; drain the sauerkraut. Sauté the sauerkraut, apple, and caraway seeds in the oil in a pan over medium heat until the apple is soft and the liquids are reduced.

**2.** Sauté the bratwurst in butter in a pan over medium heat until browned on both sides; drain. Add the wine and continue to sauté over medium heat until the liquid has evaporated.

**3.** Roll each bratwurst, with sauerkraut and mustard, into a pita loaf.

**4.** Wrap the sandwiches in foil and arrange on a trivet in the slow cooker. Pour water around the base of the trivet.

**5.** Cover and heat on a high setting for 1 to 2 hours.

# Classic Sloppy Joes

*Make this sandwich filling at your convenience, then chill or freeze.*
*Reheat in your slow cooker just before serving.*

 **SERVES 8**

Cooking time . . . . . . . 3–4 hours
Preparation time . . . . 30 minutes
Attention . . . . . . . . . . Minimal
Pot size . . . . . . . . . . . . 3–5 quarts

2 onions

1 clove garlic

2 tablespoons oil

1 pound ground beef

1 pound ground pork

¼ cup molasses

½ cup cider vinegar

½ cup tomato paste

¼ teaspoon salt

½ teaspoon black pepper

**1.** Thinly slice the onions; crush and mince the garlic. Sauté the onion and garlic in oil in a pan over low heat until soft. Transfer to the slow cooker.

**2.** Brown the meat in the same pan over medium heat; drain. Add the meat, molasses, vinegar, tomato paste, salt, and pepper to the slow cooker.

**3.** Cover and heat on a low setting for 3 to 4 hours.

339

# Mexican Sloppy Joes

*Try replacing the pinto beans with black beans or garbanzos for a different texture and flavor. Serve with tortilla chips and salsa.*

**SERVES 8**

Cooking time ....... 3–4 hours
Preparation time.... 30 minutes
Attention.......... Minimal
Pot size ............ 3–5 quarts

1 onion

1 clove garlic

2 tablespoons oil

1 pound ground beef

1 pound ground pork

½ cup pitted black olives

¼ cup sliced jalapeño peppers

¼ cup sliced green chilies

¼ teaspoon chili pepper

¼ teaspoon salt

1 cup cooked pinto beans

½ cup red wine vinegar

½ cup tomato sauce

¼ pound Monterey Jack cheese

**1.** Thinly slice the onion; crush and mince the garlic. Sauté the onion and garlic in oil in a pan over low heat until the onion is soft. Transfer to the slow cooker.

**2.** Sauté the meat in a pan over medium heat until browned; drain. Add to the slow cooker.

**3.** Slice the olives. Add to the slow cooker, along with the jalapeño peppers, chilies, chili pepper, salt, beans, vinegar, and tomato sauce.

**4.** Cover and heat on a low setting for 3 to 4 hours.

**5.** Before serving, grate the cheese and stir in.

# Asian Sloppy Joes

*Serve this filling on sesame seed buns or in pita pockets. Provide thinly sliced pickled ginger root and some fresh green onion shoots for toppings.*

**stats**

**SERVES 8**

Cooking time . . . . . . . 2–3 hours
Preparation time . . . . 30 minutes
Attention . . . . . . . . . . Minimal
Pot size . . . . . . . . . . . . 3–5 quarts

1 onion
1 clove garlic
2 tablespoons sesame oil
1 pound ground beef
1 pound ground pork
¼ cup water chestnuts
3 green onions
1 teaspoon cornstarch
2 tablespoons water
½ cup rice vinegar
¼ cup soy sauce
¼ teaspoon salt

**1.** Thinly slice the onion; crush and mince the garlic. Sauté the onion and garlic in the sesame oil in a pan over low heat. Transfer, with oil, to the slow cooker.

**2.** Sauté the meat in a pan over medium heat until browned; drain. Add to the slow cooker.

**3.** Slice the water chestnuts and green onions. Dissolve the cornstarch in water; stir in the vinegar, soy sauce, and salt. Add the sliced vegetables and the starch mixture to the slow cooker.

**4.** Cover and heat on a low setting for 2 to 3 hours.

# Southern-Style Barbecued Pork Ribs

*These Southern treats will fall off the bone and make your mouth water.*

**SERVES 4**

Cooking time ....... 6–9 hours
Preparation time.... 20 minutes
Attention.......... Medium
Pot size............ 4–8 quarts

2 pounds pork ribs

1 medium-sized yellow onion

¼ cup fresh green pepper, chopped

1 cup brewed coffee

1 cup ketchup

½ cup sugar

½ cup Worcestershire sauce

¼ cup white vinegar

¼ teaspoon ground black pepper

¼ teaspoon garlic salt

1. Cut the ribs into pieces that will easily fit into the slow cooker. Cover and cook the ribs on low setting for 4 to 5 hours.

2. Cut the onion and green pepper into dime-sized pieces. Combine the coffee, ketchup, sugar, Worcestershire sauce, vinegar, black pepper, garlic salt, onion, and green pepper. Stir until all ingredients are well mixed; pour mixture over the ribs and continue to cook covered on low setting for another 2 to 4 hours.

# Sauerkraut-Stuffed Roast Duck

*Sounds tricky, but it's not! Even though this takes a lot of time, this recipe is worth the wait.*

*stats*
**SERVES 6**

Cooking time . . . . . . . over 2 days*
Preparation time. . . . 30 minutes
Attention. . . . . . . . . . Minimal
Pot size . . . . . . . . . . . . 6–8 quarts

*day 1, 6 hours; day 2, 8 hours

1 domestic duck

1 cup vinegar

¼ teaspoon salt

Dash of pepper

2 apples

1 medium yellow onion

1 quart (4 cups) sauerkraut

1 pound pork spareribs

**1.** Clean and wash the duck, then place it in a large kettle. Cover with water and add the vinegar. Soak for 3 hours. Remove the duck from liquid, dry it off, and season with salt and pepper, cover and place in the refrigerator overnight.

**2.** While the duck is being soaked, core and chop the apples and chop the onion into ½-inch chunks. Combine the apple, onion, sauerkraut, and spareribs in the slow cooker. Cook for 6 hours, or until the meat from the ribs falls from the bones. Discard the bones and refrigerate the slow-cooker mixture. The next day stuff the sparerib-sauerkraut mixture into the duck. Place the stuffed duck into the slow cooker and cook on medium for 8 hours, or until golden and tender.

# Ham Hocks and Beans

*Smoked ham hocks are quite salty,*
*so resist the urge to salt this dish before serving.*

**SERVES 4**

Cooking time . . . . . . . 6–8 hours
Preparation time . . . . 15 minutes
Attention . . . . . . . . . . Minimal
Pot size . . . . . . . . . . . . 3–6 quarts

2 cups dried pinto beans, rinsed

3 smoked ham hocks

4 cups water

1 bay leaf

½ teaspoon ground black pepper

**1.** Place all the ingredients in the slow cooker. Cover and cook on high setting for 6 to 8 hours. Remove the ham hocks and take the meat off the bones. Discard the bones and return the meat to the slow cooker; stir well. Remove the bay leaf before serving.

# Sweet and Saucy Beef Roast

*The name says it all! Sweet, saucy, scrumptious . . .*

*stats*

**SERVES 6**

Cooking time . . . . . . . 10–11 hours
Preparation time. . . . 30 minutes
Attention. . . . . . . . . . Minimal
Pot size . . . . . . . . . . . . 4–6 quarts

3-pound chuck roast

1 teaspoon vegetable oil

1 large white onion

1 (10¾-ounce) can cream of mushroom condensed soup

½ cup water

¼ cup sugar

¼ cup vinegar

2 teaspoons table salt

1 teaspoon prepared yellow mustard

1 teaspoon Worcestershire sauce

**1.** Place the beef roast and oil in a skillet on the stove and cook on medium-high heat until the roast is brown; flip the roast so it browns on both sides. Transfer the roast to the slow cooker.

**2.** Chop the onion into ¼-inch pieces. Combine the onions and the remaining ingredients in a medium-sized bowl, stirring so they are well mingled; pour mixture over the beef roast. Cover and cook on low setting for 10 to 11 hours.

# Beef Dumpling Soup

*Delicious dumplings and beef come together in this tasty treat.*

**SERVES 6**

| | |
|---|---|
| Cooking time | 8–9 hours |
| Preparation time | 15 minutes |
| Attention | Medium |
| Pot size | 3–6 quarts |

1 pound lean steak

1 package dry onion soup mix

6 cups hot water

2 carrots

1 celery rib

1 tomato

1 tablespoon fresh chopped parsley

1 cup packaged biscuit mix

6 tablespoons milk

**1.** Cut the steak into 1-inch pieces. Sprinkle with the dry onion soup mix. Place in the bottom of the slow cooker and add the hot water. Peel the carrots with a potato peeler, then shred the carrots using a vegetable grater. Chop the celery. Peel and chop the tomato into ¼-inch pieces. Add the vegetables to the slow cooker. Cover and cook on high setting for 8 to 9 hours.

**2.** Finely chop the parsley. In a small bowl, combine the biscuit mix with the parsley. Add the milk and stir until the biscuit mix is moistened. About 30 minutes before serving, drop the batter by heaping teaspoonfuls onto the top of the soup. Cover and cook on high for remaining 30 minutes.

# Barbecued Pork and Beans

*Serve with steamed broccoli and baked potatoes for a complete meal.*

**SERVES 4**

Cooking time ....... 4–6 hours
Preparation time.... 20 minutes
Attention.......... Minimal
Pot size ............ 3–6 quarts

*2 tablespoons yellow onion, chopped*

*1 pound canned or fresh baked beans*

*4 lean pork chops*

*½ cup prepared mustard*

*½ cup prepared ketchup*

*¼ cup lemon juice*

*¼ cup sugar*

**1.** Chop the onion with a medium-sized knife into pieces about the size of a dime. Mix with the beans and place in the bottom of the slow cooker.

**2.** Using a butter knife, spread the mustard and ketchup over both sides of the pork chops. Sprinkle both sides with lemon juice and sugar. Lay the pork chops on top of the beans. If possible, do not layer them. Cook on low heat for 4 to 6 hours.

# Sausage, Red Beans, and Rice

*This simple combination of ingredients makes a*
*mouth-watering meal you can reuse for lunch the next day.*

**stats**

**SERVES 8**

Cooking time . . . . . . . 6–8 hours
Preparation time. . . . 30 minutes
Attention. . . . . . . . . . Medium
Pot size . . . . . . . . . . . 3–6 quarts

1 pound dry red kidney beans

6 cups water

1 meaty ham bone

2 large yellow onions

1 green bell pepper

2 ribs celery

¼ cup chopped fresh parsley

2 cloves garlic

1 teaspoon table salt

½ teaspoon ground black pepper

¼ teaspoon sugar

1 bay leaf

2 pound smoked sausage, cut up

8 cups prepared long-grain
white rice

**1.** Soak the beans overnight in the water. Drain and rinse the beans. Trim the fat from the ham bone. Peel and chop the onions into ¼-inch pieces. Seed and chop the green bell pepper into ¼-inch pieces. Chop the celery into ¼-inch pieces. Chop the parsley into ¼-inch lengths. Peel and slice the garlic paper-thin with a sharp kitchen knife.

**2.** Put the beans, ham bone, onions, green pepper, celery, garlic, salt, pepper, sugar, and bay leaf in the slow cooker. Cook covered on low setting for 3 to 4 hours.

**3.** Slice the sausage into ½-inch pieces. Brown the sausage in a medium-sized skillet on medium-high heat on the stove; cook until the sausage is crisp. Drain off the grease and place the sausage pieces on paper towels to soak up remaining grease. Add the sausage to the slow cooker. Cook covered on low setting for 3 to 4 additional hours.

**4.** Just before serving, remove the bay leaf and add the parsley. Serve over rice.

# Easy Steak Stroganoff

*This is excellent served over wide egg noodles.*
*Sprinkle with parsley to serve; enjoy with a heavy red wine.*

*stats*

**SERVES 4**

Cooking time . . . . . . . 6 hours
Preparation time . . . . 20 minutes
Attention . . . . . . . . . . Medium
Pot size . . . . . . . . . . . . 3–6 quarts

2 pounds round steak

1 garlic clove

¼ cup flour

½ teaspoon ground black pepper

½ teaspoon table salt

1 small yellow onion

½ pound (1 cup) fresh
mushrooms, sliced

3 tablespoons butter

1 tablespoon soy sauce

½ cup whole milk

1 cup water

2 beef bouillon cubes

1 (8-ounce) package cream
cheese

**1.** Cut the steak into 1-inch cubes. Peel and mince the garlic using a sharp paring knife. Mix the steak with the flour, pepper, salt, and garlic. Peel and chop the onion into ¼-inch pieces. Clean the mushrooms by wiping with a damp cloth; slice paper-thin.

**2.** Add all ingredients except the cream cheese to the slow cooker. Cover and cook on low setting for 6 hours, stirring occasionally. Approximately a half-hour before serving, cut the cream cheese into 1-inch cubes and stir into the slow cooker. Continue stirring until melted.

# Hamburger Rice Skillet

*Serve with a vegetable medley of broccoli,*
*cauliflower, and carrots drizzled with honey.*

**SERVES 4**

Cooking time . . . . . . . 6–8 hours
Preparation time. . . . 30 minutes
Attention. . . . . . . . . . Minimal
Pot size . . . . . . . . . . . . 3–6 quarts

1 medium-sized yellow onion

1 medium-sized green bell pepper

1 clove garlic

4 medium-sized tomatoes

1 pound lean ground beef

1 cup medium-grain dry rice

1 (8-ounce) can tomato sauce

1 teaspoon Worcestershire sauce

½ teaspoon dry crushed basil

1½ cups water

1 teaspoon table salt

**1.** Peel and slice the onion into rings. Remove the stem and seeds from the green pepper and chop the pepper into ¼-inch pieces. Peel and the mince garlic using a sharp paring knife. Cut the tomatoes into quarters.

**2.** Combine the beef, onion, pepper, and garlic in a skillet on the stove. Cook on medium-high heat, stirring constantly, until the meat is browned. Drain off the grease and put the meat and vegetables into the slow cooker. Add the rice, tomatoes, tomato sauce, Worcestershire sauce, basil, water, and salt; stir well. Cover and cook on low setting 6 to 8 hours.

350

# Northwestern Baked Beans

*Baked beans are great on their own or with a pork or beef meal.*

**stats**

**SERVES 8**

Cooking time . . . . . . . 6–8 hours
Preparation time . . . . 20 minutes
Attention . . . . . . . . . . Minimal
Pot size . . . . . . . . . . . . 3–6 quarts

*1 pound ground beef*

*¾ pound bacon*

*1 large white onion*

*1 cup ketchup*

*¼ cup brown sugar*

*½ teaspoon ground black pepper*

*1 teaspoon hickory smoke flavoring*

*1 (16-ounce) can pork and beans*

*1 (16-ounce) can lima beans*

*1 (16-ounce) can butter beans*

*1 (16-ounce) can kidney beans*

**1.** Brown the ground beef in a medium-sized skillet on medium-high heat. Drain off the grease and place the meat in the slow cooker.

**2.** Fry the bacon in medium-sized skillet on medium-high heat. Drain off the grease and lay the bacon on paper towels to cool. Crumble the bacon and add it to the slow cooker.

**3.** Remove the skin from the onion and chop into ¼-inch pieces. Add the onion, ketchup, brown sugar, pepper, hickory flavoring, and all the beans, including their liquid, to the slow cooker; stir well. Cook covered on low setting for 6 to 8 hours.

# Aunt Mary's Easy Lasagna

*Serve with a fresh green salad and Italian dressing.*

**stats**

**SERVES 8**

Cooking time . . . . . . . 5 hours
Preparation time. . . . 20 minutes
Attention. . . . . . . . . . Minimal
Pot size . . . . . . . . . . . . 3–6 quarts

1 pound lean ground beef

1 teaspoon Italian seasoning

1 cup fresh mushrooms, sliced

1 tablespoon shortening, for greasing

8 lasagna noodles, uncooked

1 (28-ounce) jar spaghetti sauce

⅓ cup water

2 cups ricotta cheese

2 cups mozzarella cheese, shredded

**1.** Brown the ground beef in a medium-sized skillet on medium-high heat until no pink remains. Stir in the Italian seasoning. Drain off the grease. Wash the mushrooms by wiping with a damp cloth; slice ⅛-inch thick.

**2.** Grease the slow cooker by putting the shortening on a paper towel and rubbing it around the inside of the slow cooker. Break the noodles and place half of them in the bottom of the slow cooker. Spread half of the ground beef over the top. Laver half of the sauce, water, mushrooms, ricotta cheese, and mozzarella cheese over the beef. Repeat layers.

**3.** Cover and cook on low setting for 5 hours.

# Scrumptious Summer Meals

# Risotto with Fresh Summer Vegetables

*Serve with assorted gourmet crackers and cheeses.*

 *stats*

**SERVES 8**

Cooking time . . . . . . . 8–9 hours

Preparation time. . . . 20 minutes

Attention. . . . . . . . . . Medium

Pot size . . . . . . . . . . . . 3–6 quarts

1 tablespoon butter

1 large white onion

1 cup fresh zucchini, chopped

⅓ cup fresh parsley, chopped

1 cup uncooked white rice

4 cups chicken broth

1 cup fresh or frozen green beans

1 cup fresh or frozen snow peas

½ teaspoon table salt

¼ teaspoon ground black pepper

**1.** Melt the butter in small skillet on medium-high heat on the stove. Peel and chop the onions into ¼-inch pieces. Sauté the onions in the butter for 3 to 5 minutes, until the onions are translucent; drain.

**2.** Chop the zucchini into 1-inch pieces. Chop the parsley into ¼-inch lengths. Place the onions, zucchini, uncooked white rice, chicken broth, green beans, salt, and pepper in the slow cooker; mix well. Cook covered on low setting 7 to 8 hours, or until the rice is soft. Add the peas and cook 1 to 2 hours more.

**3.** Add the parsley; stir well. Cook uncovered 15 to 30 minutes.

# Brussels Sprouts à la Orange

*Healthy with a sweet taste, this meal is a great way to get kids to eat healthy.*

**SERVES 4**

Cooking time....... 2 hours
Preparation time.... 15 minutes
Attention.......... Medium
Pot size ............ 2–4 quarts

1¼ cup fresh-squeezed orange juice

4 cups fresh Brussels sprouts

½ teaspoon cornstarch

¼ teaspoon ground cinnamon

**1.** Squeeze 6 to 8 oranges to make 1¼ cup orange juice; ripe oranges produce the most juice. In the slow cooker, combine the Brussels sprouts, juice, cornstarch, and cinnamon. Cover and cook on low for 1 hour.

**2.** Uncover and cook on low for 1 additional hour until the sauce has thickened and the Brussels sprouts are tender.

# Green Beans in Lemon Honey

*Even vegetable haters will love this combination of sweet and tart flavors!*
*Use this recipe to complement a grilled steak or pork chops.*

*stats*

**SERVES 4–6**

| | |
|---|---|
| Cooking time | 1 hour |
| Preparation time | 25 minutes |
| Attention | Minimal |
| Pot size | 3–6 quarts |

*½ lemon*

*2 tablespoons butter*

*3 tablespoons honey*

*1 teaspoon cider vinegar*

*½ teaspoon salt*

*1 tart apple*

*1 teaspoon cornstarch*

*1 tablespoon water*

*3 cups fresh green beans*

*1 medium yellow onion*

**1.** Slice the lemon into wedges no thicker than ⅛ inch. Combine the butter, honey, vinegar, salt, and lemon slices. Bring to a boil, stirring constantly, for 5 minutes.

**2.** Core and dice the apple into pieces about ¼ inch square; do not remove the peel. Add to the lemon mixture and cook on medium heat for about 5 minutes.

**3.** Stir together the cornstarch and water until you have a light paste. Stir this into the apple-lemon mixture. Bring to a boil, then cook on low heat for about 3 minutes.

**4.** Snap the ends off the green beans and discard. Wash the green beans thoroughly in cold water. Peel and slice onion into ¼-inch rings. Place the green beans and onions in the slow cooker and pour the apple-lemon mixture over them. Cook on low heat for 1 hour.

# Czech Garlic and Bean Soup

*Garlicky and light, combine this soup with a light bread or small salad.*

**stats**

**SERVES 8**

Cooking time . . . . . . . 8–10 hours

Preparation time . . . . 10 minutes

Attention . . . . . . . . . . Minimal

Pot size . . . . . . . . . . . . 3–6 quarts

6 garlic cloves

4 tablespoons chopped fresh parsley

3 tablespoons olive oil

1 pound (2 cups) dry white beans

1 quart (4 cups) beef broth

1 quart (4 cups) water

2 teaspoons table salt

1 teaspoon ground white pepper

**1.** Remove the skins from the garlic and mince with a sharp paring knife. Finely chop the parsley. Sauté the garlic and parsley in olive oil in a medium-sized skillet on medium-high heat. The garlic should be slightly brown but not hard. Do not drain the oil.

**2.** Add all the ingredients to the slow cooker. Cover and cook on low setting for 8 to 10 hours.

# Lemony Chicken and Okra Soup

*Serve with spicy dill pickles and assorted cheeses.*

**SERVES 8**

| | |
|---|---|
| Cooking time | 7–9 hours |
| Preparation time | 30 minutes |
| Attention | Minimal |
| Pot size | 3–8 quarts |

6 chicken breasts

2 tablespoons lemon juice

1 large yellow onion

3 medium tomatoes

2 cups fresh okra, sliced

⅓ cup uncooked long-grain rice

6 cups chicken broth

½ cup (4 ounces) tomato paste

2 teaspoons table salt

¼ ground black pepper

½ teaspoon cayenne pepper

1 teaspoon ground turmeric

**1.** Remove the bones and skin from the chicken breasts. Rub the chicken with lemon juice, then cut into 1-inch cubes. Peel and chop the onion into ¼-inch pieces. Peel and chop the tomatoes into ½-inch pieces. Wash and slice the okra into ¼-inch rounds.

**2.** Put all the ingredients in the slow cooker. Cover and cook on low setting for 7 to 9 hours.

# Wild Rice–Stuffed Zucchini

*This is a wonderful complement to a grilled steak or pork chops.*

**SERVES 4**

Cooking time . . . . . . . 8–9 hours
Preparation time . . . . 20 minutes
Attention . . . . . . . . . . Minimal
Pot size . . . . . . . . . . . . 4–6 quarts

2 small zucchini

1 cup wild rice

1 small yellow onion

½ cup chopped fresh chives

½ teaspoon ground black pepper

½ teaspoon table salt

½ cup shelled, salted, and roasted sunflower seeds

**1.** Cut the zucchini in half lengthwise and scrape out the inside, leaving about ¾-inch around the sides; discard the insides.

**2.** Precook the wild rice according to the package directions. Peel and chop the onion into ¼-inch pieces. Chop the chives into ¼-inch lengths. Combine the wild rice, onion, black pepper, salt, and chives in a medium-sized mixing bowl. Use the mixture to stuff the zucchini boats. Sprinkle with sunflower seeds. Place the stuffed zucchini in the slow cooker. Cover and cook on low setting for 8 to 9 hours.

# Mushroom Vegetable Barley Soup

*This soup is scrumptious and satisfying any time of the year.*

**stats**

**SERVES 6**

Cooking time . . . . . . . 3–4 hours
Preparation time . . . . 45 minutes
Attention . . . . . . . . . . Minimal
Pot size . . . . . . . . . . . 3–6 quarts

1 pound (2 cups) fresh
mushrooms, sliced

4 celery stalks

5 medium carrots

1 cup fresh chopped broccoli

2 cups chopped yellow onion

1½ tablespoons minced garlic

3 tablespoons olive oil

½ teaspoon ground thyme

1 bay leaf

½ cup dry barley

8 cups chicken broth

1 teaspoon salt

½ teaspoon pepper

**1.** Clean the mushrooms by rubbing with a damp towel, then slice into quarters. Wash the celery, carrots, and broccoli thoroughly in cold water, then cut into ½-inch pieces. Peel the onions and chop into ¼-inch pieces. Peel and mince the garlic.

**2.** Place the olive oil in the slow cooker. Add the onions and cook on high for about 10 minutes. Add the garlic, thyme, bay leaf, and mushrooms. Cook for about 20 minutes on low heat, stirring occasionally.

**3.** Add the barley, celery, broccoli, carrots, and broth. Stir in the salt and pepper. Cook covered on low heat for 3 to 4 hours. Remove the bay leaf before serving.

# Harvest Vegetable Soup

*Perfect for springtime veggies, this soup makes the most of the season!*

**stats**

**SERVES 8**

| | |
|---|---|
| Cooking time | 6–8 hours |
| Preparation time | 20 minutes |
| Attention | Minimal |
| Pot size | 3–8 quarts |

3 cups fresh tomatoes, chopped

2 cups fresh carrots, sliced

2 cups fresh zucchini, sliced

2 cups fresh green beans

1 large onion

⅛ cup diced fresh red bell pepper

1 cup fresh, canned or frozen whole kernel corn

1 cup fresh or frozen peas

1 bay leaf

½ teaspoon thyme (optional)

½ teaspoon marjoram (optional)

½ teaspoon table salt

3 cups water

**1.** Cut the tomatoes, carrots, and zucchini into 1-inch pieces. Snap the ends off the green beans and discard; cut the green beans into 1-inch lengths. Peel the onion and chop into ¼-inch pieces. Remove the stem and seeds from the red pepper and chop into ¼-inch pieces.

**2.** Combine all the ingredients except the peas in the slow cooker. Stir with a wooden spoon until the ingredients are evenly distributed and covered with liquid. Cover and cook on low heat for 5 to 7 hours.

**3.** Add the peas and cook 1 to 2 hours more.

**4.** Remove cover 15 minutes before serving; stir well. Remove and discard the bay leaf.

# Pistachio-Buttered Vegetable Medley

*With a rich flavor, your kids will love this veggie medley.*

**SERVES 6**

Cooking time . . . . . . . 2–3 hours
Preparation time . . . . 30 minutes
Attention . . . . . . . . . . Minimal
Pot size . . . . . . . . . . . . 3–5 quarts

*1 cup fresh asparagus tips*

*3 medium-sized fresh carrots*

*1 cup fresh green beans*

*½ cup chopped pistachio nuts*

*½ cup butter (or margarine), melted*

*1 tablespoon fresh lemon juice*

*½ teaspoon dry marjoram*

**1.** Clean the vegetables and slice into ½-inch pieces. Shell and finely chop the pistachio nuts with a sharp paring knife. Mix the vegetables and nuts together and place in the slow cooker.

**2.** Add the butter, lemon juice, and marjoram. Cook covered for 2 to 3 hours on low setting. Place the mixture in a serving bowl and top with pistachio nuts if desired.

# Romanian Sauerkraut

*Serve with an assortment of fresh summer fruits.*

 **SERVES 6**

Cooking time ....... 4 hours
Preparation time.... 30 minutes
Attention.......... Minimal
Pot size ............ 3–5 quarts

6 cups sauerkraut

6 ripe tomatoes

1 large yellow onion

1 green bell pepper

2 garlic cloves

1½ pounds kielbasa

**1.** Drain and rinse the sauerkraut. Chop the tomatoes into ½-inch pieces. Peel the onion and chop into ¼-inch pieces. Remove the stem and seeds from the green pepper and chop into ¼-inch pieces. Peel the garlic and mince with a sharp kitchen knife. Chop the kielbasa into 1-inch pieces.

**2.** Mix all the ingredients in the slow cooker. Cook covered on low setting for 4 hours.

# German-Style Hot Potato Salad

*Use as a side dish when grilling steaks or pork chops.*

**SERVES 6**

Cooking time . . . . . . . 5–6 hours
Preparation time. . . . 30 minutes
Attention. . . . . . . . . . Minimal
Pot size . . . . . . . . . . . . 2–4 quarts

4 slices bacon

½ cup onion, chopped

½ cup celery, sliced

¼ cup diced green pepper

2 potatoes

¼ cup chopped fresh parsley

1 teaspoon sugar

½ teaspoon salt

½ teaspoon ground black pepper

¼ cup white vinegar

¼ cup vegetable oil

**1.** Fry the bacon in frying pan or cook in the microwave until crisp, then crumble by placing the bacon in a paper towel and wringing it with your hands. Peel and chop the onions into ¼-inch pieces. Chop the celery into ¼-inch pieces. Remove the stem and seeds from the green pepper and chop into ¼-inch pieces. Wash and scrub the potatoes thoroughly; do not peel. Slice about ¼-inch thick. Roughly chop the parsley.

**2.** Combine all the ingredients except the parsley and bacon; stir well. Cook covered on low setting 5 to 6 hours. Stir in the bacon and parsley before serving.

# Fresh Zucchini Casserole

*Simple, fresh, delicious—what more could you ask for?*

 **SERVES 8**

Cooking time . . . . . . . 6–7 hours
Preparation time . . . . 20 minutes
Attention . . . . . . . . . . Minimal
Pot size . . . . . . . . . . . . 3–6 quarts

2 cups zucchini, diced

2 cups yellow summer squash, diced

1 large yellow onion

2 cups fresh mushrooms, sliced

2 cups cubed Cheddar cheese

1 package onion soup mix

1 quart (4 cups) fresh or canned spaghetti sauce

**1.** Clean but do not peel the zucchini and summer squash; chop into bite-size pieces. Peel and chop the onion into ½-inch pieces. Clean the mushrooms by wiping with a damp cloth; slice paper-thin with a sharp paring knife. Cut the cheese into ½-inch cubes.

**2.** Combine all the ingredients in the slow cooker; mix well. Cook uncovered on low setting 5 to 6 hours. Remove the cover, stir well, and cook 1 hour uncovered on low setting.

# Lemony Chicken

*Serve over long-grain brown rice and complement*
*with a variety of pickled vegetables.*

*stats*

**SERVES 4**

Cooking time . . . . . . . 8 hours
Preparation time . . . . 30 minutes
Attention . . . . . . . . . . Minimal
Pot size . . . . . . . . . . . . 4–6 quarts

*4 chicken breasts*

*½ teaspoon table salt*

*¼ teaspoon ground black pepper*

*2 tablespoons butter*

*¼ cup sherry*

*4 cloves garlic, minced*

*1 teaspoon crumbled dry oregano*

*¼ cup lemon juice*

*1 teaspoon grated lemon peel*

**1.** Wash the chicken breasts; do not remove the bone or skin. Sprinkle the chicken with salt and pepper. Heat the butter in medium-sized skillet. Sauté the chicken until brown. Using a slotted spoon or tongs, transfer the chicken to the slow cooker.

**2.** Add the sherry to the skillet and stir to loosen the brown bits on the bottom of the skillet (deglaze). Pour the sherry mixture over the chicken. Sprinkle the chicken with the oregano and garlic. Cover and cook on low for 7 hours.

**3.** Cut the lemon peel into ⅛-inch squares. Add the lemon juice and bits of lemon peel. Cook covered on low for 1 additional hour.

# Pizza-Stuffed Potato Boats

*Serve with a fresh green salad and Italian dressing*
*for a completely balanced meal.*

**SERVES 8**

Cooking time . . . . . . . 5–6 hours

Preparation time. . . . 30 minutes

Attention. . . . . . . . . . Minimal

Pot size . . . . . . . . . . . 4–8 quarts

4 large potatoes

½ pound (1 cup) pepperoni,
diced

1 medium-sized yellow onion

1 cup shredded mozzarella
cheese

1 cup spaghetti sauce

¼ cup grated Parmesan cheese

**1.** Bake the potatoes in the microwave or conventional oven; slice in half lengthwise. Scoop out the insides (do not discard), leaving about ¾-inch of potato all around.

**2.** Cut the pepperoni into ¼-inch pieces. Peel the onion and chop into ¼-inch pieces. Shred the cheese with a vegetable grater. Mix the leftover potato insides, onion, pepperoni, cheese, and spaghetti sauce in a medium-sized mixing bowl. Put into the potato boats, stuffing firmly. Sprinkle with Parmesan cheese. Place potato boats in the slow cooker. You may have to stack them. Cover and cook on low setting for 5 to 6 hours.

# 19

# Potluck Possibilities

# Squishy, Squashy Succotash

*Fun to say and eat, serve with an assortment of pickled vegetables.*

**stats**

**SERVES 6**

| | |
|---|---|
| Cooking time | 8–10 hours |
| Preparation time | 30 minutes |
| Attention | Minimal |
| Pot size | 3–6 quarts |

*1½ pounds acorn squash*

*4 garlic cloves*

*2 medium-sized yellow onions*

*2 jalapeño peppers*

*1 medium-sized yellow bell pepper*

*¼ fresh minced cilantro*

*2 cups fresh corn kernels*

*1 tablespoon olive oil*

*1 teaspoon cumin seeds*

*1 teaspoon red pepper flakes*

*1 teaspoon table salt*

*1 cup water*

*2 tablespoons tomato paste*

*1 teaspoon table salt*

*2 cups precooked lima beans*

**1.** Peel the acorn squash and cut into 1-inch pieces. Peel the garlic cloves and mince with a sharp kitchen knife. Peel the onions and chop into ¼-inch pieces. Remove the stems from the jalapeño peppers and cut the peppers into ¼-inch pieces. Remove the stem and seeds from the yellow bell pepper and cut into ¼-inch pieces. Mince the cilantro with a sharp kitchen knife.

**2.** Add all the ingredients except the lima beans and cilantro to the slow cooker. Cover and cook on low setting for 7 to 9 hours. Add the cilantro and lima beans; stir gently. Cook uncovered on low setting for 1 additional hour.

# Almondy Rice Pilaf

*Great alone or with a meat dish, this pilaf is sure to please.*

 **SERVES 4**

Cooking time . . . . . . . 6–8 hours
Preparation time . . . . 15 minutes
Attention . . . . . . . . . . Minimal
Pot size . . . . . . . . . . . . 3–8 quarts

*1 medium-sized yellow onion*

*8 ounces (1 cup) fresh mushrooms*

*2 cups vegetable broth*

*1 cup raw converted rice*

*1 cup canned or frozen peas*

*2 tablespoons butter*

*½ cup almond slivers*

Peel the onion and mince. Clean the mushrooms by wiping with a damp cloth; slice paper-thin. Add all ingredients to the slow cooker. Cover and cook on low setting for 6 to 8 hours.

# Cook's Surprise Meatballs

*Serve the meatballs over fresh egg noodles and peas for a complete meal.*

**stats**

**SERVES 4**

Cooking time . . . . . . . 4 hours
Preparation time. . . . 45 minutes
Attention. . . . . . . . . . Medium
Pot size . . . . . . . . . . . . 4–6 quarts

1 large yellow onion
1 green bell pepper
1 red bell pepper
2 garlic cloves
½ cup crushed saltine crackers
1 egg
1 pound ground turkey
1 pound ground beef
1 pound ground pork
1 (6-ounce) can tomato paste
1 teaspoon oregano
½ teaspoon basil
1 teaspoon salt
1 teaspoon ground black pepper
2 tablespoons vegetable oil

**1.** Peel the onion and chop into ¼-inch pieces. Remove the stems and seeds from the bell peppers and chop the peppers into ¼-inch pieces. Crush the garlic by laying a large knife on its side over the top of each garlic clove; push down until the garlic clove "pops." Crush the crackers using a spoon in a small bowl. Beat the egg with a fork in a small bowl until the egg yolk and white are thoroughly mixed.

**2.** In a medium-sized bowl, use your hands to mix the meat, egg, tomato paste, onion, red pepper, green pepper, oregano, basil, garlic, salt, black pepper, and crushed crackers. Form into firm balls about the size of golf balls. Place the meatballs on a cookie sheet and bake in a 350°F conventional oven for about 10 minutes.

**3.** Put the vegetable oil in the slow cooker. Transfer all the meatballs to the slow cooker and cook covered on low setting for 4 hours.

# Hot Dog Lentil Soup

*Substitute Polish sausage or kielbasa for a more robust flavor.*

**stats**

**SERVES 8**

Cooking time....... 7–9 hours
Preparation time.... 30 minutes
Attention.......... Minimal
Pot size............ 3–8 quarts

*1 pound all-beef hot dogs*

*2 medium-sized yellow onions*

*3 garlic cloves*

*2 medium carrots*

*2 ribs celery*

*2 tablespoons olive oil*

*8 cups water*

*2 cups lentils, rinsed and drained*

*1 bay leaf*

*1 teaspoon salt*

*½ teaspoon ground black pepper*

*2 tablespoons cider vinegar*

**1.** Cut the hot dogs into 1-inch pieces. Peel and chop the onion into ¼-inch pieces. Peel and mince the garlic with a sharp kitchen knife. Peel the carrots, then chop carrots and celery into ¼-inch pieces.

**2.** Heat the olive oil in a medium-sized skillet on medium heat. Add the onions, garlic, carrots, and celery; sauté until the onions are limp and translucent. Drain off the grease and put the vegetables in the slow cooker. Add the water, lentils, bay leaf, salt, pepper, cider vinegar, and hot dog pieces. Cover and cook on low setting for 7 to 9 hours.

# Italian Beef Sandwiches

*Simple sandwiches are a great option for busy parents.*

**stats**

**SERVES 6**

Cooking time....... 8–10 hours
Preparation time.... 10 minutes
Attention.......... Minimal
Pot size............ 6 quarts

1 teaspoon salt

1 teaspoon pepper

1 teaspoon oregano

1 teaspoon onion salt

1 teaspoon garlic salt

1 teaspoon basil

1 cup Italian salad dressing

2 cups water

5-pound beef pot roast

**1.** Mix the spices with the salad dressing and water in the slow cooker. Place the beef roast in the slow cooker. Cover and cook on low setting for 8 to 10 hours. Thirty minutes before serving, remove the beef and shred it using 2 forks and pulling the meat apart. Return the meat to the broth and stir well. Cook covered on low setting for the remaining 30 minutes.

**2.** Cut loaves of French bread into 6-inch-long pieces, then cut each piece down the middle and ladle the meat inside. Add a slice of mozzarella cheese on top of the meat.

# Texas Barbecued Beef Sandwiches

*Potato chips and baked beans make this meal*
*an authentic American potluck event!*

*stats*
**SERVES 8**

Cooking time . . . . . . . 9 hours
Preparation time . . . . 15 minutes
Attention . . . . . . . . . . Minimal
Pot size . . . . . . . . . . . . 5–6 quarts

*4-pound chuck roast*

*½ cup water*

*2 cups ketchup*

*10 ounces cola*

*¼ cup Worcestershire sauce*

*2 tablespoons prepared mustard*

*2 tablespoons liquid smoke*

*¼ teaspoon Tabasco or other hot pepper sauce*

*8 hamburger buns*

**1.** Cover and cook the roast with the water in the slow cooker on high setting for 8 hours, or until tender.

**2.** Remove the roast. Shred the meat, trimming off the fat and discarding it in the process. Place the shredded meat in the slow cooker along with ketchup, cola, Worcestershire sauce, mustard, liquid smoke, and hot sauce. Cook covered on high setting for 1 hour. Ladle over buns to serve.

# Ham Barbecue

*So simple, so good—so long, stress!*

**SERVES 8**

Cooking time . . . . . . . 1–2 hours
Preparation time . . . . 15 minutes
Attention . . . . . . . . . . Minimal
Pot size . . . . . . . . . . . . 4–6 quarts

*2 pounds chopped ham*

*1 bottle chili sauce*

*½ cup ketchup*

*½ cup water*

*¼ cup white corn syrup*

*8 whole wheat bulky rolls*

**1.** Mix together all the ingredients in the slow cooker. Cook covered on low setting 1 to 2 hours, stirring occasionally.

**2.** Serve on whole wheat rolls.

# Cabbage Rolls

*Serve with a selection of pickled vegetables and hard cheeses.*

 **SERVES 12**

Cooking time . . . . . . . 8–9 hours

Preparation time. . . . 30 minutes

Attention. . . . . . . . . . Minimal

Pot size . . . . . . . . . . . . 3–6 quarts

12 large cabbage leaves

1 pound lean ground beef

½ cup cooked white rice

½ teaspoon salt

⅛ teaspoon ground black pepper

¼ teaspoon thyme

¼ teaspoon nutmeg

¼ teaspoon cinnamon

1 (6-ounce) can tomato paste

¾ cup water

1. Wash the cabbage leaves. Boil four cups of water in a saucepan on the stove. Turn off the heat and soak the leaves in the water for 5 minutes. Remove the leaves, drain, and cool.

2. Combine the ground beef, rice, salt, pepper, thyme, nutmeg, and cinnamon. Place 2 tablespoons of the meat mixture on each leaf and roll firmly. Stack the cabbage rolls in the slow cooker. Combine the tomato paste and water; pour over the stuffed cabbage rolls. Cook covered on low setting 8 to 9 hours.

# Award-Winning Tuna Noodle Casserole

*Try this new take on a family favorite—*
*you never know what they'll ask for tomorrow!*

**SERVES 8**

Cooking time . . . . . . . 6–8 hours
Preparation time . . . . 15 minutes
Attention . . . . . . . . . . Minimal
Pot size . . . . . . . . . . . . 3–6 quarts

2 cups (16 ounces) water-packed tuna

3 hardboiled eggs

2 celery ribs

1 medium-sized yellow onion

1 cup frozen mixed vegetables

2 cups cooked egg noodles

1½ cups crushed potato chips

1 (10¾-ounce) can cream of mushroom condensed soup

1 (10¾-ounce) can cream of celery condensed soup

**1.** Drain the tuna. Chop the hardboiled eggs into ¼-inch pieces. Chop the celery into ¼-inch pieces. Peel the onion and chop into ¼-inch pieces. Thaw the frozen vegetables overnight in the refrigerator, or thaw them in the microwave. Precook the egg noodles in boiling water. Crush the potato chips while still in the bag.

**2.** Combine all ingredients except ½ cup potato chips. Put mixture into the slow cooker. Cover with remaining potato chips. Cover and cook on low setting for 6 to 8 hours.

# Spinach Callaloo

*Wash the spinach well to remove any sand or grit.*
*A dash of vinegar in the rinse water will help get rid of insects, too.*

**SERVES 6**

Cooking time . . . . . . . 3–4 hours
Preparation time . . . . 30 minutes
Attention . . . . . . . . . . Minimal
Pot size . . . . . . . . . . . . 3–5 quarts

¼ pound salt pork

2 onions

½ pound pork

4 cups chicken broth

½ teaspoon salt

1 tablespoon ground thyme

½ teaspoon black pepper

⅛ teaspoon bottled pepper sauce

1½ pounds fresh spinach

**1.** Mince the salt pork. Heat the salt pork in a pan over medium heat until browned; drain off all except 2 tablespoons of fat.

**2.** Slice the onions and cube the pork. Add the onions and pork to the browned salt pork; heat in the pan over medium heat until the pork cubes are browned. Drain.

**3.** Add the onions, pork, broth, salt, spices, and pepper sauce to the slow cooker.

**4.** Cover and heat on a low setting for 3 to 4 hours.

**5.** Trim the spinach, finely chopping large stems and cutting leaves into 2-inch strips. An hour before serving, add the spinach to the slow cooker.

# Sweet and Sour Beans

*This multibean dish keeps well in the refrigerator,*
*and can be served hot or cold. It also goes well with sandwiches.*

 **stats**

**SERVES 8**

Cooking time ....... 3–4 hours
Preparation time.... 30 minutes
Attention.......... Minimal
Pot size ............ 3–5 quarts

4 slices bacon

1 onion

1 clove garlic

1 pound cooked lima beans

1 1-pound can baked beans

1 pound cooked kidney beans

¼ cup brown sugar

1 teaspoon prepared mustard

1 teaspoon salt

¼ cup vinegar

**1.** Sauté the bacon in a pan over medium heat until crisp. Set aside the bacon strips to drain. Transfer 2 tablespoons of the bacon drippings to the slow cooker.

**2.** Coarsely chop the onion and mince the garlic. Drain all three kinds of beans. Add the onion, garlic, and beans to the slow cooker.

**3.** Crumble the bacon. Add the bacon, sugar, mustard, salt, and vinegar to the slow cooker.

**4.** Cover and heat on a low setting for 3 to 4 hours.

# 20

# Holidays & Special Occasions

# Mardi Gras: Festival Jambalaya

*Serve this spicy dish with crusty French bread and beer.*
*And don't forget the zydeco music!*

**stats**

**SERVES 8–10**

Cooking time . . . . . . . 4–5 hours
Preparation time. . . . 60 minutes
Attention. . . . . . . . . . Minimal
Pot size . . . . . . . . . . . . 3–5 quarts

*4 slices bacon*

*1 onion*

*3 cloves garlic*

*2 green peppers*

*1 cup uncooked rice*

*1 pound tomatoes*

*1 pound smoked ham*

*3½ cups chicken broth*

*1 pound shrimp*

*¼ teaspoon salt*

*½ teaspoon black pepper*

*¼ teaspoon red pepper sauce*

**1.** Cut the bacon into 1-inch lengths. Dice the onion, crush and slice the garlic, and slice the green peppers.

**2.** Sauté the bacon in a pan over medium heat until transparent, then add the onion, garlic, and green peppers. Sauté until soft, then stir in the rice and heat for 5 minutes.

**3.** Chop the tomatoes and ham. Combine the rice mixture, tomatoes, ham, and broth in the slow cooker.

**4.** Cover and heat on a high setting for 1 hour, then on low for 3 to 4 hours.

**5.** Half an hour before serving, add the shrimp, salt, pepper, and red pepper sauce.

# Mardi Gras: Sherry Jambalaya

*Every jambalaya is different—this one has sherry and lots of mushrooms.*
*Use wild mushrooms, like morels, if available.*

*stats*
**SERVES 10–12**

Cooking time . . . . . . . 5–6 hours
Preparation time . . . . 60 minutes
Attention . . . . . . . . . . Minimal
Pot size . . . . . . . . . . . . 3–5 quarts

3 onions

3 tablespoons butter

2 tomatoes

¼ teaspoon salt

½ teaspoon black pepper

1 bay leaf

2 cups uncooked brown rice

1½ pounds smoked ham

1 pound spicy pork sausage

1 tablespoon butter

4 cups chicken broth

1½ pounds mushrooms

1 pound shrimp, peeled and
deveined

½ cup sherry

2 tablespoons butter

**1.** Finely slice the onions; sauté in butter in a pan over medium heat until browned. Chop the tomatoes. Add the tomatoes, salt, pepper, bay leaf, and rice to the onions and continue to heat for 5 minutes.

**2.** Slice the ham. Brown the ham and sausage in butter. Drain; slice the sausage into bite-size pieces. Cut the ham into strips.

**3.** Combine the meat, rice mixture, and broth in the slow cooker.

**4.** Cover and heat on a high setting for 1 hour, then on a low for 3 to 4 hours.

**5.** Slice the mushrooms. Braise the mushrooms and shrimp in the sherry and butter in a pan over medium heat. Half an hour before serving, pour the mushroom and shrimp mixture over the other ingredients. Do not stir.

# Mardi Gras: Parsley Crab Gumbo

*You can buy fish stock and supplement it with*
*clam juice to make the fish broth or make your own.*

*stats*

**SERVES 10–12**

Cooking time . . . . . . . 4–6 hours
Preparation time . . . . 45 minutes
Attention . . . . . . . . . . Minimal
Pot size . . . . . . . . . . . 3–5 quarts

*1 onion*

*1 green pepper*

*2 tablespoons butter*

*3 tomatoes*

*1 pound fresh okra*

*8 cups fish broth*

*½ cup uncooked rice*

*1 teaspoon Worcestershire sauce*

*1 bunch parsley*

*1 pound crabmeat*

*¼ teaspoon salt*

*¼ teaspoon white pepper*

**1.** Chop the onion and green pepper; sauté in butter in a pan over medium heat until the onion is soft.

**2.** Cube the tomatoes. Cut the okra into 1-inch pieces.

**3.** Combine the onion and green pepper with the tomatoes, okra, fish broth, rice, and Worcestershire sauce in the slow cooker.

**4.** Cover and heat on a low setting for 3 to 4 hours.

**5.** Chop the parsley and shred the crabmeat. Half an hour before serving, add the parsley, crab, salt, and pepper.

# Fourth of July: Roman Candle Short Ribs

*As a variation, try using fresh jalapeño instead of pickled,*
*but use only a small spoonful to start.*

**SERVES 10–12**

Cooking time . . . . . . . 7–9 hours
Preparation time . . . . 60 minutes
Attention . . . . . . . . . . Minimal
Pot size . . . . . . . . . . . . 3–5 quarts

5 pounds pork ribs

½ teaspoon white pepper

¼ teaspoon salt

2 tablespoons oil

¼ cup black olives

¼ teaspoon chili powder

4 cups barbecue sauce

1 bottle beer

¼ cup pickled jalapeño peppers

**1.** Cut the ribs into serving-size pieces. Boil the ribs in water with the white pepper and salt, then drain.

**2.** Sauté the ribs in oil in a pan over medium heat until browned.

**3.** Pit and slice the olives. Combine the ribs with the olives, chili powder, barbecue sauce, and beer in the slow cooker.

**4.** Cover and heat on a low setting for 6 to 8 hours.

**5.** Slice the jalapeño peppers. Half an hour before serving, stir in the jalapeño peppers.

# Fourth of July: Celebration Pudding

*You can substitute other small dried fruits in this recipe.*
*Try dried cherries, or dried cranberries for a tart twist.*

**YIELDS 3 LOAVES**

Cooking time ....... 2–3 hours
Preparation time.... 45 minutes
Attention.......... Minimal
Pot size............ 5 quarts

1 cup butter

1 cup sugar

8 eggs

2 cups milk

1 cup molasses

1 tablespoon baking powder

3 cups flour

2 lemons

¼ teaspoon mace

2 cups dried currants

**1.** Cream together the butter and sugar, then add the eggs, milk, and molasses. Sift the baking powder with the flour; add the flour mixture to the liquids.

**2.** Grate the lemon rinds. Stir the grated rind, mace, and currants into the batter.

**3.** Grease and flour 3 loaf pans or the equivalent. Fill the baking dishes one-half to three-quarters full; cover each dish with foil or a glass or ceramic lid. Arrange the dishes on a trivet or rack in the slow cooker, and pour water around the base of the trivet.

**4.** Cover and heat on a high setting for 2 to 3 hours.

# Fourth of July: Independence Dinners

*Start a revolution in your kitchen. Let the guests, including kids, put together their own Independence Dinners, which can cook while you watch fireworks.*

**SERVES 8**

Cooking time . . . . . . . 3–4 hours
Preparation time . . . . 45 minutes
Attention . . . . . . . . . . Minimal
Pot size . . . . . . . . . . . . 3–5 quarts

*1 onion*

*1 clove garlic*

*2 pounds hamburger*

*1 cup bread crumbs*

*1 tablespoon Worcestershire sauce*

*½ teaspoon salt*

*½ teaspoon black pepper*

*16 baby red potatoes*

*24 baby carrots*

*16 asparagus spears*

*2 yellow bell peppers*

*16 cherry tomatoes*

*½ teaspoon salt*

*½ teaspoon black pepper*

*Aluminum foil*

**1.** Mince the onion and garlic. Combine with hamburger, crumbs, Worcestershire sauce, ½ teaspoon salt, and ½ teaspoon pepper and mix well. Divide the mixture into 8 patties or 16 balls.

**2.** Clean and halve the potatoes and carrots. Clean and trim the asparagus and yellow peppers; cut into 4-inch lengths.

**3.** Cut 8 1-foot lengths of heavy-duty aluminum foil (or double thickness of standard aluminum foil). In the center of each foil square, put one portion: 1 patty (or 2 balls) of meat mixture, 2 potatoes, 3 carrots, some asparagus, some pepper slices, and 2 cherry tomatoes. Sprinkle with salt and pepper and fold edges to seal.

**4.** Arrange on a trivet or rack in the slow cooker. Pour water around the base of the trivet.

**5.** Cover and heat on a high setting for 3 to 4 hours.

# Fourth of July: Paul Revere Baked Beans

*A colonial classic—but now you don't have to keep
the woodstove burning all day to get the same tasty result.*

**stats**

**SERVES 10–12**

Cooking time . . . . . . . 8–10 hours
Preparation time. . . . 30 minutes
Attention. . . . . . . . . . Minimal
Pot size . . . . . . . . . . . . 5 quarts

3 cups dried white beans

4 slices bacon

½ clove garlic

1 cup water

½ cup molasses

1 tablespoon prepared mustard

¼ teaspoon salt

1. Soak the beans overnight in cold water; drain.

2. Cut the bacon into 1-inch lengths. Crush and mince the garlic. Combine the bacon and garlic with soaked beans, 1 cup water, molasses, mustard, and salt in the slow cooker.

3. Cover and heat on a low setting for 8 to 10 hours.

# Halloween: Jack-o-Lantern Bread

*This bread freezes well. Make it ahead, freeze,*
*and then thaw and bring it out in the morning.*

**YIELDS 2 LOAVES**

Cooking time . . . . . . . 2–3 hours
Preparation time . . . . 45 minutes
Attention . . . . . . . . . . Minimal
Pot size . . . . . . . . . . . . 3–5 quarts

3½ cups flour

2 teaspoons baking soda

1½ teaspoons salt

1 teaspoon cinnamon

1 teaspoon nutmeg

3 cups sugar

1 cup shortening

4 eggs

2 cups pumpkin

⅔ cup water

1 cup raisins

½ cup chopped nuts

**1.** Sift the flour, baking soda, salt, and spices to mix.

**2.** Blend the sugar with the shortening, then blend in the eggs. Add the pumpkin and water to the egg mixture. Add the liquid mixture to the flour mixture and stir well. Fold in the raisins and nuts.

**3.** Grease and flour 2 loaf pans or the equivalent. Fill the baking dishes three-quarters or less full; cover each dish with foil or a glass or ceramic lid. Arrange the dishes on a trivet or rack in the slow cooker, and pour water around the base of the trivet.

**4.** Cover and heat on a high setting for 2 to 3 hours.

# Halloween: Trick-or-Treat Caramel Corn

*You can substitute roasted and salted peanuts, walnuts, or even macadamia nuts for pecans in this recipe. Better yet: use all of the above.*

**SERVES 10–12**

Cooking time . . . . . . . 1–2 hours
Preparation time. . . . 45 minutes
Attention. . . . . . . . . . Moderate
Pot size . . . . . . . . . . . . 5 quarts

*½ cup butter*

*1 cup brown sugar*

*¼ cup white corn syrup*

*⅛ teaspoon cream of tartar*

*½ teaspoon salt*

*½ teaspoon baking soda*

*2 tablespoons butter*

*3 quarts popped corn*

*1 cup roasted, salted pecans*

**1.** Melt ½ cup butter in a saucepan over low heat; add the sugar and syrup. Increase to medium heat and let simmer 6 minutes while stirring.

**2.** Remove the saucepan from the heat and add the cream of tartar, salt, and baking soda, stirring well.

**3.** Butter the inside of the slow cooker with the remaining 2 tablespoons butter. Put the popped corn in the slow cooker. Pour the liquid caramel over the top while mixing.

**4.** Cover and heat on a low setting for 1 to 2 hours. Stir periodically.

**5.** After the popcorn and caramel are mixed, add the pecans and mix again.

# Halloween: Caramel Apples

*You would certainly eat an apple a day if you could prepare them like this.*
*For a fun twist, let your family dip their own.*

**stats**

**SERVES 8**

Cooking time . . . . . . . 1–2 hours

Preparation time . . . . 15 minutes

Attention . . . . . . . . . . Minimal

Pot size . . . . . . . . . . . 3–5 quarts

*2 pounds caramels*

*¼ cup water*

*8 apples*

**1.** Unwrap the caramels and put them in the slow cooker with the water.

**2.** Cover and heat on a high setting for 1 to 2 hours. Stir periodically. Add more water to thin the caramel, if needed.

**3.** Skewer the apples on sticks and dip them into the melted caramel. Place apples on buttered waxed paper to cool.

# Thanksgiving: Apricot Sweet Potatoes

*Try substituting dried peaches for apricots, or supplementing with dried cherries.*
*You can also use 2 tablespoons of molasses instead of the brown sugar.*

**SERVES 6–8**

Cooking time . . . . . . . 5–6 hours
Preparation time . . . . 30 minutes
Attention . . . . . . . . . . Minimal
Pot size . . . . . . . . . . . . 3–5 quarts

*1½ pounds sweet potatoes*

*1 pound dried apricots*

*⅓ cup raisins*

*1 tablespoon cornstarch*

*2 cups water*

*3 tablespoons brown sugar*

*¼ teaspoon salt*

*⅛ teaspoon cinnamon*

*3 tablespoons sherry*

*¼ orange*

**1.** Peel and slice the potatoes. Cut the apricots into quarters. Intermingle the potatoes, apricots, and raisins in the slow cooker.

**2.** Dissolve the cornstarch in ¼ cup of water in a mixing bowl, then add the remaining water, sugar, salt, cinnamon, and sherry. Grate the orange peel and add.

**3.** Add the liquid mixture to the slow cooker.

**4.** Cover and heat on a low setting for 5 to 6 hours.

# Thanksgiving: Prairie Corn Pudding

*This steaming corn dish is delicious in the morning with real maple syrup.*
*Serve a few sizzling sausages on the side.*

**SERVES 4**

Cooking time ....... 2–3 hours
Preparation time.... 30 minutes
Attention.......... Minimal
Pot size ............ 3–5 quarts

1 cup milk
5 tablespoons cornmeal
⅔ cup molasses
1 teaspoon ground ginger
½ teaspoon salt
2 tablespoons butter
½ cup milk

**1.** Scald 1 cup of milk in a saucepan over medium heat, stirring constantly. Add the cornmeal and simmer over low heat for 20 minutes.

**2.** Mix the molasses, ginger, salt, and butter. Add to the cornmeal mixture.

**3.** Pour into a baking dish, filling one-half to three-quarters full. Pour ½ cup of milk over top. Cover the dish with foil or a glass or ceramic lid and arrange on a trivet or rack in the slow cooker. Pour water around the base of the trivet.

**4.** Cover and heat on a high setting for 1 to 2 hours.

# Thanksgiving: Sweet Potatoes and Apples

*Try this recipe with your favorite baking apple.*
*This dish is delicious as a side with ham or turkey.*

**SERVES 12**

Cooking time....... 4–5 hours
Preparation time.... 30 minutes
Attention.......... Minimal
Pot size............ 3–5 quarts

6 sweet potatoes

2 apples

½ cup brown sugar

½ teaspoon salt

1 teaspoon mace

½ cup butter

**1.** Peel the potatoes and the apples. Thinly slice the potatoes; core and slice the apples. Mix the sugar, salt, and mace together.

**2.** Use half of the butter to grease the slow cooker, then assemble these layers: potatoes (at the bottom), apples, brown sugar mixture, dabs of butter. Repeat.

**3.** Cover and heat on a low setting for 4 to 5 hours.

# Index